CLIMBING THE LADDER, CHASING THE DREAM

Frontispiece: This photo of Homer G. Phillips Hospital highlights the design of the building, which had four clinical wings emerging from a central administrative core. Photo ca. 1937–1939. Courtesy of the Missouri Historical Society, St. Louis.

# CLIMBING THE LADDER, CHASING THE DREAM

The History of Homer G. Phillips Hospital

Candace O'Connor

With help from Will R. Ross, MD, MPH

Foreword by Eva L. Frazer, MD

IIIIII
UNIVERSITY OF MISSOURI PRESS
Columbia

Copyright © 2021 by Candace O'Connor

Published by the University of Missouri Press, Columbia, Missouri 65211

Printed and bound in the United States of America

All rights reserved. First printing, 2021.

Library of Congress Cataloging-in-Publication Data

Names: O'Connor, Candace, author.

Title: Climbing the ladder, chasing the dream : the history of Homer G.
    Phillips Hospital / Candace O'Connor.

Description: Columbia : University of Missouri Press, 2021. | Includes
    bibliographical references and index.

Identifiers: LCCN 2021026146 (print) | LCCN 2021026147 (ebook) | ISBN
    9780826222473 (hardcover) | ISBN 9780826274656 (ebook)

Subjects: LCSH: Homer G. Phillips Hospital--History. |
    Hospitals--History--St. Louis, Missouri--1937 -1979 |
    Minorities--Medical care. | African Americans--Medical care. |
    Discrimination in medical care.

Classification: LCC RA964 .O26 2021  (print) | LCC RA964  (ebook) | DDC
    362.1109778/66--dc23

LC record available at https://lccn.loc.gov/2021026146

LC ebook record available at https://lccn.loc.gov/2021026147

♾™ This paper meets the requirements of the
American National Standard for Permanence of Paper
for Printed Library Materials, Z39.48, 1984.

Typeface: Sabon

# CONTENTS

# Eva L. Frazer, MD

WHEN HOMER G. PHILLIPS HOSPITAL (HGPH) opened in 1937, legalized segregation meant, in virtually all instances, inferior treatment and fewer opportunities for Black patients and physicians. In response to these injustices, the vision of attorney Homer G. Phillips—and others who worked passionately with him—led to the establishment of a nationally renowned hospital dedicated to the care of Black patients and the training of Black healthcare professionals. The tale of HGPH is particularly inspiring when contrasted with the Dred Scott decision of 1857 and the East St. Louis, Illinois, race riots of 1917, two historic events that had set a negative tone for race relations in the St. Louis region. This new history of the hospital is an uplifting and riveting narrative that includes an unsolved murder; an accidental electrocution; romance and war; and, during a time known for racial strife, an example of Black and white healthcare and civic leaders working together. It has all the makings of a historic biopic, spanning the Great Migration of Blacks from the South to the North, World War II, the civil rights movement, and the Vietnam War. Ironically, it was the passage of the Civil Rights Act of 1964 that led to the decline and ultimate closure of this esteemed hospital.

Noteworthy American stories feature men and women of integrity who overcome obstacles through hard work and perseverance. The history of Homer G. Phillips Hospital, named for the Black attorney who lobbied for its founding, is an outstanding example of such a story that has never before been fully recounted. This book takes on that challenge, integrating personal narratives with extensive research, bringing to life the institution and the people fundamental to its success.

As the daughter of an HGPH-trained surgeon and family practitioner, I lived in an East St. Louis neighborhood that included the homes, families, and offices of other HGPH graduates. My father's closest friends and colleagues were all connected to what was then the mecca of training programs for Black physicians. My pediatrician, dentist, and every other doctor who treated me or my family was an HGPH graduate and family friend. My mother belonged to women's social groups primarily made up of the wives of these physicians.

These men and women had risen to the highest level attainable by the descendants of slaves in the social circles of the Black and white communities. My childhood was one of privilege, freedom, and infinite possibility, which, as I look back, was extremely rare for a Black girl growing up during the volatile period of transition from segregation to legally mandated integration. I was molded by witnessing the character, diligence, and integrity of these physicians, who were also civil rights activists, war veterans, and esteemed leaders in the communities they served. As an adult, I would follow in my father's footsteps, becoming a physician and, in 1984, completing my training at the Mayo Clinic in Rochester, Minnesota—a mere 20 years after the passage of the Civil Rights Act. But the significance of HGPH was not limited to me, my community, or even the St. Louis region. The extraordinary importance of HGPH would reverberate nationwide since, by 1960, HGPH had trained more Black physicians and nurses than any other institution worldwide. These graduates provided medical care in towns and cities across the country, taking the same high standard of medical care and civic leadership to the communities where they settled.

In 1937, when the doors to HGPH finally opened to great fanfare, few academic institutions in the United States offered training slots for Black medical graduates. HGPH gained notoriety not only for its newly built, state-of-the-art facilities but also for the wide array of subspecialty training opportunities that evolved from its collaboration with the acclaimed Washington University. The white faculty of Washington University would—in an unprecedented move—work with the Black physicians and administrative staff of HGPH as partners rather than superiors. Together, they would work to ensure that the HGPH trainees had capabilities equal to their white peers. In addition, training for nurses and allied health professionals at HGPH created a community of Black healthcare workers united toward a common goal: providing the best care available to Black patients. Prior to HGPH, African Americans in St. Louis were treated in hospital basements, back rooms, or substandard facilities and under conditions in one instance decried publicly as not being fit for zoo animals. The lasting impact of the people who worked, trained, and became leaders in their respective fields and communities makes the history of HGPH one of the greatest American tales of success, perseverance, and social justice. By the time of its forced closing in 1979, HGPH had become a tangible symbol of racial pride and a legacy in a community and nation that otherwise remained mired in racial inequities.

My father, Charles R. Frazer Jr., M.D., almost always dressed in a suit and tie with freshly polished leather shoes, and he liked to wear a fedora hat. He once built a swing set in our backyard dressed in what was for him casual clothes: a crisp, freshly starched, collared plaid shirt with tan belted pants and brightly polished shoes. He never broke a sweat in the hot summer sun. He was always cool, calm, and collected, and he had a special talent—he took care of people. "Doc," as his friends and patients called him, was the doctor whom other doctors came to for advice. He was a man of few words, each one precise and to the point. He worked long hours as a solo family practitioner and general surgeon in East St. Louis in the late 1940s until his death in 1994. In our home, next to his office, it was not unusual for people to come knocking on the door in the middle of the night for help after an accident, sudden illness, unexpected death, or trouble with the law. As a child, I watched my father stitch people up, and on occasion he would let me cut the sutures as he worked. Doc gave otherwise frightening and chaotic situations a sense of order and redress. He took charge when needed but had the wisdom and grace to know when to sit back calmly and listen, always giving what was needed at just the right moment. It was a skill I instinctively wanted to acquire, and over time I tied much of it to his being a doctor. That was what defined him; it was not what he did, it was who he *was*.

In the same way, it is impossible to separate the type of doctor he was from the training he received at HGPH. I began to recognize that these characteristics were the defining qualities of all his friends who had trained or worked at HGPH: the strict dress code; self-assured demeanor; easy camaraderie; conversations filled with wit, wisdom, and compassion; and commitment to community and service. Like him, most of his friends had moved from their hometowns across the United States to pursue advanced training in medicine, and now they were connected by their unique experience as HGPH trainees. The only other time I have seen such a bond was among those who served in the military. As a child growing up, eavesdropping on adult conversations, I often heard "Homer G." discussed—a difficult case, a hard-working nurse, a resident who would be working in my father's office. To my young mind, it seemed that everything connected in some way to "Homer G."

Years after my father's death, a curiosity about the institution and, more importantly for me, the men and women who forged the path that I would follow, began to grow. My curiosity led me to articles in the records of the Missouri Historical Society. There were disappointingly few to be found. One was about Homer G. Phillips himself, a Black attorney who, with the NAACP, represented victims of the 1917 East St. Louis Race Riots free of charge and later lobbied the St. Louis Board of Aldermen to build a separate hospital devoted to the care of Black patients and the training of Black doctors. The article had an old black-and-white photo of a young Phillips, solemn-faced with intelligent, dark eyes that seemed to bear a heavy weight. A second article, about the opening of HGPH, highlighted the dignitaries who were present; another reported on the closing of HGPH. This closing sparked angry protests by the Black community, which had a deep and abiding connection to the institution where many were born, received medical care, or were employed. There was something visceral about the public outcry,

which included a series of protests and years of political maneu-
vering. Homer G. Phillips Hospital was the embodiment of Black
pride and accomplishment; its closing was an affront, a great loss
to the Black community, which had found within its walls sanctity,
opportunity, and a clear-cut example of Black excellence and unity.
The paucity of information was disappointing. I could find nothing
that told the personal stories of the people whose lives and passions
were the foundation of the institution.

As someone whose life has been impacted by HGPH, I find this
book deeply meaningful, as it connects my memories to historical
details, giving them context. Anyone who has an interest in the
history of medicine, in the stories of those who were part of the
Great Migration, in an example of the collaboration of Black and
white leaders during the turbulent period of racial segregation,
or in a true story of people overcoming adversity will be equally
moved and captivated by this work. The chronicle of HGPH as
told by Candace O'Connor is the culmination of hundreds of hours
of personal interviews with nurses and physicians who trained at
HGPH, as well as interviews with Ville residents and community
leaders—all woven together by an understanding of the history
of the institution and its national importance. These personal accounts give texture and vibrancy to the story of Homer G. Phillips
Hospital. In no other place has this uplifting segment of American
history been so thoroughly recorded.

Eva L. Frazer, MD
Daughter of Charles R. Frazer Jr., MD. HGPH, 1945–1949
Stepdaughter of Luther Forrest, DDS, HGPH, 1946–1947
Goddaughter of James M. Whittico, MD, HGPH, 1940–1941 and 1946–1949
Saint Louis, Missouri
January 2020

# PREFACE

SEVERAL YEARS AGO, a retired nurse named Ethel Long called me. She said she was a long-ago graduate of the Homer G. Phillips Hospital School of Nursing and still a member of its active, devoted alumni association. For years, her group had been hoping to find someone to write a history of the hospital—she called it, affectionately, "Homer G."—and she had gotten my name from the Missouri History Museum. Would I consider the project?

The idea was instantly intriguing. Homer G. had played a role in several books I had written, and I had heard stories about it for years, especially from my elderly friend Velma Baker, who had been a private duty nurse there. An African American herself, she was fiercely proud that a Black hospital had flourished in St. Louis from 1937 to 1979.

I quickly realized that this book would require a daunting amount of work: reading more than 40 years of stories from Black and white newspapers; consulting stacks of scholarly books and articles; conducting dozens of interviews with former staff members and others. Yet, I only knew the half of it; I didn't realize that I would have to do this all quickly, since Homer G. veterans were passing away every month. Further, I would have to become a kind of Sherlock Holmes, trying to solve the mystery of attorney Homer G. Phillips' death.

Still, I told Mrs. Long I would do it—and that launched me into a world I hadn't inhabited before: African American St. Louis a half-century ago and more.

Soon I was attending meetings of the nurses' association and interviewing as many Homer G. nurses and physicians as I could find,
as well as community residents and politicians. I met the nurses in
various places: at Gretchen McCullum's home, still in the Ville; in
Mary Vincent Clarke's apartment in the new senior living center
that used to be Homer G.; in Pauline Payne's living room, piled high
with scrapbooks; in Zenobia Thompson's basement room, decorat-
ed with memorabilia from the 1979 struggle to save the hospital.

How interesting they were! One was Alice Okrafo-Smart, more
than 100 years old, who rode in a parade on the brilliant day of the
hospital's dedication. Or Mary Crawford Lane, who lived with five
brothers and five sisters in a four-bedroom house on North Market.
Her father—blonde with gray eyes—had only gotten through
third-grade before his "passing" for white came to light, and he left
school for good. But, she said, he "loved to read and he would read
our schoolbooks, and we would discuss them with him."

If these nurses were lucky, they were inspired by their parents to
go higher, do better. Lillian Haywood's busy mother married at 13
in rural Alabama, had her first child at 18 and her eighth at 44, but
still set a vivid example of helping others. Jobyna Moore Foster's
father took her to one travelogue after another so that she could
see the world. As an adult, she says, "I went. Every place I saw on
those films, I went."

But sometimes they had to learn from others. After their mother's
death, the eight children in Marian Burns Bradley's impoverished
family were scattered into foster care. But Mrs. Bradley, who later
spent 16 years as a social worker at Homer G., got lucky. Her foster parents, who lived on a modest farm at Olive Street Road and
Wood's Mill, were educated, had a home with indoor plumbing,
and gave her the love she needed. "You know the expression from
soup to nuts? We went from nuts to soup," she said.

Some of the nurses had intersected with history. In World War
II-era Alabama, Marybelle Barnes made excuses to go on walks
so she could glimpse the Tuskegee Airmen. As a child in Detroit,
Jobyna Foster was staying with her grandmother when the 1943
race riot broke out around them. "I can see it and hear it now, the

shooting and fighting and fires," she said. Richard W. White was a ninth-grader in Houston, Texas, when his father found a large cross burning in their front yard; they doused the flames and never called the police. In 1956, Lula Couch Hall graduated from a segregated high school in Little Rock and knew every one of the famous "Little Rock Nine" who integrated Central High School in 1957.

Today, one-time hospital trainees still speak reverentially about the impact it had on their lives. For years, they flocked to St. Louis each year for their lavish, well-attended reunions. And nurses still gather regularly in an upstairs room of the old hospital building for their Homer G. Phillips Nurses' Association meetings; they hold reunions and take trips together, proud of the bond they share. Another joy of this project was traveling with them, by bus, to Branson, Missouri. We talked about old times at Homer G., we watched Tyler Perry programs, and we took in a play about Moses, complete with live camels, in the vast amphitheater.

This book will explore the full history of Homer G. Phillips Hospital, beginning with its two predecessor institutions and continuing through the aftermath of its closing. It will show that the hospital reflected broader social movements, including the national movement to build Black hospitals and the Great Migration of African Americans from Southern states to new lives in the North. To tell this story, I have organized the book into two kinds of chapters: chronological chapters that cover an entire decade and thematic chapters dealing with such topics as the Ville neighborhood or the surgery program.

Perhaps most of all, the book will weave together a wealth of stories—one major story per chapter in italics and others within the narrative itself—of people like Dr. Whittico, who arrived from small-town America and were transformed by this remarkable place, which became a stepping-stone to professional achievement.

Just as importantly, "it was family," said nurse Lillian Elliott Haywood, class of 1971. "And we loved it. It was Homer G., you know, and it became part of your heart. There was nothing like it in the world."

# CLIMBING THE LADDER, CHASING THE DREAM

This Homer G. Phillips monument in the Missouri Historical Museum's Emerson Center features an etching of the hospital and a faux building façade. The monument was created by David Mason and Associates in 2000. Courtesy of the Missouri Historical Society, St. Louis.

# Climbing the Ladder, Chasing the Dream
## Homer G. Phillips Hospital

*"In 1940, I graduated from Meharry Medical School and was accepted as an intern at Homer G. Phillips Hospital. After going home to visit my parents in West Virginia, I carried on to St. Louis so I could begin my training on July 1. I crossed the bridge over the Mississippi and came up Easton Avenue; I turned right on Whittier, keeping my eye out for the hospital, since I didn't know what it looked like. Finally, I saw it—and I had to pull over. I was amazed; I had never seen anything like it. I had to park and turn off the engine and just look at this beautiful hospital. I said to myself, 'Oh, my God. Oh, my God!'"*

> —James M. Whittico Jr., MD (1915–2018), general surgeon

FOR AFRICAN AMERICAN physicians and nurses, long accustomed to shabby, second-rate facilities, the first sight of Homer G. Phillips Hospital was electrifying. The Art Deco-style building, dedicated in a gala 1937 ceremony, stood a soaring seven stories high; it was built of earth-toned brick with elegant terra cotta trim. Fanning outward from a core section were four majestic wings with different services on each floor, such as medicine or surgery, pediatrics or obstetrics. As newly hired nurse Mary Vincent Clarke recalled, "I arrived here in 1941 on the bus from Virginia, and it was still nighttime when I got in. The next morning, I decided to walk around and look at this place. Oh, my goodness, I was just blown away! It was one of the most beautiful buildings I had ever seen."

3

Its stylish architecture was only the first shock. Next came the stunning realization that this hospital, unlike any other in the country, was almost entirely staffed by Black professionals. In 1947, Dr. Frank Richards, later a noted St. Louis surgeon, arrived to start his internship. "When I drove up in the cab and saw this big institution, I couldn't believe it, and when I walked inside, everybody there—the nurses, the clerks, the lab technicians—were all Afro-Americans. They were *running* things. You just didn't see that."

The pride they felt in this extraordinary place led to a powerful sense of solidarity. In 1952, newly arrived intern Dr. LaSalle Leffall, later a distinguished surgeon at his alma mater, Howard University College of Medicine, began bumping into staff members who had also attended Howard. Dr. Richards, just finishing his own residency, greeted Dr. Leffall with kind reassurance: "You're going to get excellent training here." The whole atmosphere filled Dr. Leffall with a sense of eager anticipation. "I knew this was the place I should be," he said later. "It was a welcoming attitude—a *warm*, welcoming attitude."

For its clientele—the indigent Black population of St. Louis—this hospital seemed a kind of miracle. Its sleek, modern beauty far outshone the previous Black medical facility: the ramshackle City Hospital #2 on Lawton Avenue, with its antiquated, even dangerous, equipment. Now the poor had a spacious, up-to-date place to go, especially the hospital's emergency department, which quickly attracted a reputation as the best trauma center in the city. In 1934, even before the hospital opened, an editorial in the *Journal of the National Medical Association*, an African American counterpart to the American Medical Association (AMA), lauded its construction, saying: "A $3,000,000 City Hospital with 600 beds for Negro patients comes as a God-send to the long-neglected colored sick in St. Louis."[1]

*"For the 1930s and '40s, the hospital was well-equipped. It had the latest of everything, the latest equipment. For the first time, we as African Americans were given equal care. And there was no such thing as being slouchy for interns at Homer Phillips Hospital. We had to dress in our intern uniform: white*

*shirt and white pants. We were so proud of our status; being part of Homer Phillips Hospital was exciting and high-scale, like nothing you'd ever experienced before."*

—Dr. James Whittico

Fig. Int.1: This is an early aerial view of the Homer G. Phillips Hospital complex. Photo ca. 1936. Courtesy of the Missouri Historical Society, St. Louis.

The hospital—known first as Homer G. Phillips Hospital for the Colored—was located in the heart of the Ville, a thriving African American neighborhood bounded by Saint Louis Avenue to the north, N. Sarah Street to the east, Easton Avenue (later Dr. Martin Luther King Drive) to the south, and N. Taylor to the west. From the 1930s to the 1950s, its dense population—which included more than a third of the city's Black leadership—represented a rich social mix: schoolteachers and janitors; doctors and meat packers; lawyers and railroad men; hospital staff and domestics. Around the corner from tidy, modest homes were two-room, cold-water flats with outhouses in back. Some of the city's most prominent Black

churches—Antioch Baptist, St. James AME, Kennerly Temple, later
St. Philip's Lutheran—were nearby. "The Ville was a self-contained
community, with everything in walking distance," said educator
John Wright, who lived in one of the small flats as a child. "A
barbershop, bakery, shoe repair—whatever you wanted was
right there."

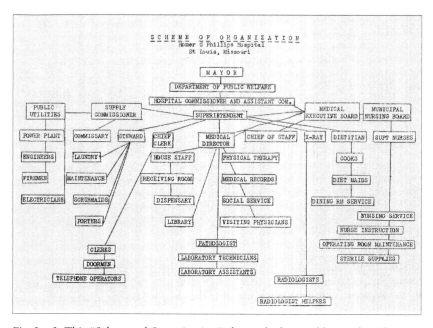

Fig. Int.2: This "Scheme of Organization" shows the hospital hierarchy. Photo
from *The History and Development of Homer G. Phillips Hospital*, by William
H. Sinkler, M.D., and Sadye Coleman, ca. 1944. Courtesy of the Missouri
Historical Society, St. Louis.

Already, the neighborhood was home to a number of cultural
icons, chiefly Poro College, a complex built in 1917 by entrepreneur
Annie Malone for her highly successful beauty product business
and cosmetology college. Although its founder left for Chicago in
1930, the Poro building remained, housing both a theater and the
Lincoln University law school for Black students. In 1908, celebrated Sumner High School, the first all-Black high school west of the
Mississippi River, moved to an elegant new building in the Ville,

where it educated future luminaries, among them tennis player Arthur Ashe, opera star Grace Bumbry, comedian Dick Gregory, rock-and-roll great Tina Turner, and attorney Margaret Bush Wilson, the first Black woman to head the national NAACP board.

But once the new hospital was built, it superseded Poro as the Ville's foremost point of pride. St. Louis newspapers joined in the chorus of praise when it opened; as a story in *The St. Louis Star and Times* noted, Homer G. Phillips was widely known as "the finest institution of its kind for Negroes in the world." While more affluent Black patients often sought care at People's, a private Black hospital on Locust Street, or the Saint Louis University-affiliated St. Mary's Infirmary on Papin Street, the poor were overjoyed to have this fine new facility. "I recall that we had patients coming in who would say, 'I'm so glad I live here, because we have Homer G. Phillips,'" said Dr. Leffall.

**Dr. James Malachi Whittico Jr.** *was born in the small town of Williamson, West Virginia, where racial lines were sharply drawn. His father, Dr. James Whittico Sr., was a physician—the only other doctor in town was white—and he treated Black residents there, along with a few hardscrabble white farmers and miners from the hills. Not everyone in those hills wished to consult a Black doctor, however. One day some boys—as the story goes, from the notorious Hatfield family—were unable to find the white doctor and ran in desperation to Dr. Whittico, begging him to hurry because their mother was having a baby. When he arrived, the boys' father, enraged that a Black man would be delivering his child, had to be tied up so the doctor could work. Another time, Dr. Whittico sat stone-faced on his front porch watching Ku Klux Klansmen march past to light a cross in the local schoolyard.*

As surely as Homer G. Phillips Hospital became a symbol of excellence for the Ville, both it and the neighborhood were visible symbols of the Jim Crow segregation that shackled African Americans. The diverse economic base of the Ville, which created a safe, congenial environment for its families, only existed because Black residents had so few housing choices. Many St. Louis streets were closed to them by racially restrictive covenants: private contractual agreements, signed by white property owners within a certain neighborhood, that prohibited the sale of houses to specific groups of people, usually African Americans. In 1948, a landmark case with roots in St. Louis—*Shelley v. Kraemer*—made its way through the courts to the U.S. Supreme Court, which ended the practice nationally. Thereafter, the higher-income Ville residents scattered to other neighborhoods that offered larger homes, leaving the Ville poorer for their loss. But until the housing covenants were outlawed, they left few housing options for Black buyers, even those with the money to move.

For many African Americans, the peaceful, accepting Ville was a kind of oasis. In the 1940s and into the 1950s, St. Louis remained a segregated city whose residents could display malignant racial attitudes. One 1955 nursing graduate, Minervia Williams, recalled

Fig. Int.3: Dr. James M. Whittico Jr. (1915–2018) graduated from Meharry Medical College, trained at Homer G. Phillips Hospital, and went on to become a prominent surgeon on its staff. Undated. Courtesy of the Bernard Becker Medical Library Archives, Washington University in St. Louis.

that her mother never let her enter Union Station until the moment they boarded their train back to Louisville, in order to shield her from disturbing signs. "They still had colored bathrooms and water fountains and only certain places where you could sit on the train," she said. Dr. Frank Richards, who had grown up in North Carolina and gone to college in Alabama, described the city's racial atmosphere as "terrible. You couldn't go to the movies. You couldn't go to the theaters or restaurants. The school system was segregated. St. Louis was a good old Southern town."

Still, doors to integrated medical care in St. Louis were creaking open, albeit slowly. Among the first to desegregate was Saint Louis University Hospital in the late 1940s or early 1950s.

In 1954, Jewish Hospital became the first private hospital to accept Black patients on the wards and a year later on the private service. The segregated wards at Barnes Hospital—especially the dim, poorly ventilated surgery ward, 0400—closed in 1964 after passage of the Civil Rights Act. But many older African Americans in St. Louis still remember the indignity of being shunted to a dreary basement ward for care.

> "I had first heard about Homer G. Phillips Hospital when I was a junior in medical school—about the construction and the grand opening in 1937—and I made up my mind. I said, 'Boy, I want to go to Homer Phillips Hospital to do my internship!' In those days, it was absolutely necessary to be an intern, but there were only two main places that trained Black doctors: Howard University in Washington, D.C., and Meharry, and each took only a few people. I learned about this new hospital and its big training program, so I applied and was accepted. Class members came from all over; two of them were Harry Riggs from Michigan and 'Jumpin' Joe' Wiggins, a football player from Fisk."
>
> —Dr. James Whittico

In 1905, the AMA's Council on Medical Education had recommended that all medical school graduates continue on to a one-year internship, and by 1914, some 80 percent of them were doing so.[2] But for Black graduates, anxiously scouring the country for slots, too few were available to meet the demand. Dr. M. O. Bousfield, director of the Negro Health Division of the Chicago-based Rosenwald Fund, lamented that, into the 1930s, "the shortage of approved internships worked a great hardship on colored graduates."[3]

The New Auction Block                                    By Bishop

Fig. Int.4: This cartoon, drawn by Daniel Bishop and printed in the *St. Louis Star-Times* in 1933, illustrates the despair felt by Black men and women who feared the treatment they would receive in poor medical facilities. Courtesy of the Missouri Historical Society, St. Louis.

The growth in the number of Black hospitals—a movement that gathered momentum in the 1920s, fueled by the need for training slots and by a flood of medical and surgical discoveries that made advanced training necessary—boosted the number of internship spots for Black medical graduates, but only by a little. In 1923, there were 202 Black hospitals across the country, though only six had internship programs and none offered residency training.[4]

Thus, the internship and residency spots at Homer G. Phillips, the largest number at any Black hospital in the country, came as a striking relief to Black medical graduates, starved for training. In 1939, there were 52 physicians on the house staff, and "the hospital accepted approximately 50 percent of the black graduates of United States medical schools annually," wrote Dr. Richards in his history of the hospital.[5] The large patient census—seen in wards filled to capacity and gurneys lining the hospital's hallways—was a huge benefit to these trainees. "It was one of the few hospitals that had a training program and a large enough patient population that we could get the kind of varied experience we needed," said Dr. George Simpson, who served an internship at Homer G. Phillips in 1950–51, along with his wife, Dr. Dazelle Simpson.

*"I remember my first patient, who was on 2 South, the female medicine ward. Oh, I'm ready to be a doctor, all right. I find my patient, and I pull up a chair and sit down. 'I'm Dr. Whittico. I'm here to take care of you, and I want to start by taking a history. Now, what's been bothering you?' She looked a little skeptical—I was real young at the time—but she said: 'Oh, doctor. I got the gas.' So, I was floored, first thing out of the box. I had no idea what she was talking about. 'I got the gas.' Oh, boy. That told me something right away: that I had to learn the language. Many times, the vernacular was way out from what I'd been used to in college and medical school. Be that as it may, this patient accepted me, I got some history on her, and she started me out in the right direction."*

—Dr. James Whittico

For Dr. Earle U. Robinson Jr., the training at Homer G. Phillips was exceptional. When he moved on to a job in Indiana as an attending physician in obstetrics and gynecology, he outshone other new staff members, bringing with him "far more advanced techniques. They were doing things 20 years behind what I was trained to do." Barbiturates for eclampsia? At Homer G. Phillips, they were using magnesium sulfate. "I thought I was still back in the 17th century!" he said.

In fact, the hospital's distinction and core purpose took some of the sting out of being excluded from trainee classes at white hospitals. Dr. Frank Richards declared that he would rather have been trained at Homer G. Phillips than at Barnes Hospital. "Barnes had a medical mission. We had a mission, too, and it was racial as well as medical: to take care of poor Black folks. And we did our best to do that."

Over many years, white physicians from area hospitals—Saint Louis University early on, followed by St. Louis Children's, Jewish, and especially Barnes—came to Homer G. Phillips to enrich the program: lecturing, teaching, engaging in research, and even heading various services. Washington University School of Medicine students sometimes did clinical rotations there, and later some Homer G. Phillips trainees, particularly in ophthalmology, spent time at the university. Gradually, private Black physicians and surgeons, like Drs. Richards and Whittico, gained admitting privileges at white hospitals or even joined their staffs.

Some of the Black medical staff at Homer G. Phillips were giants in their disciplines. The Nashes—Homer and Helen—were widely known brother-and-sister pediatricians. Dr. William Sinkler, head of surgery from 1956 and the hospital's medical director from 1941 until his death in 1960, was an outstanding surgeon; so was Dr. William Smiley, who came to the hospital in its first class of interns and later became director of obstetrics and gynecology. "Dr. Smiley was a great surgeon—a spectacular surgeon—one of the best I've ever seen," said Dr. Robinson.

*"Across the board, the hospital was a standard of perfection that was respected not only in the north side of St. Louis, but also in certain areas of the south side of St. Louis. It was respected by Washington University. It was respected by Saint Louis University. It was a highlight of medicine in this area."*
—Dr. James Whittico

The Black community felt great respect for Black physicians who had received the fine training this new hospital provided, said Dr. Eva Frazer, whose father was on staff there. In some cases, patients who had been seeing white doctors shifted over to Black physicians. "The reputation of the program grew to the point that Black patients preferred to be cared for by Black physicians who provided them not only with exceptional care but also with dignity and compassion not routinely given in other settings. This spread nationwide as trainees settled across the country."

In a quieter way, the physicians' wives were also heroines, managing households and rearing children so their husbands could move forward in medicine. This close-knit group of women served as "community advocates and leaders in their own right, becoming involved in youth organizations and civil rights matters," added Dr. Frazer.

The nurses at Homer G. Phillips—both the staff nurses and students from the affiliated nursing school—were also spectacular. Often, they had heard about the hospital by chance: from a family friend, a postcard, or a stray brochure. Somehow, they scraped together the modest tuition and embarked on their anxious journey to higher education. While some arrived from Ohio or Maryland, Indiana, or Illinois, many came north as part of the Great Migration that bled the rural South of Black residents from 1915 to 1970. Children of tenant farmers, sharecroppers, and laborers left impoverished lives for the promise of Northern cities, including St. Louis.

*"One thing I learned: the nurses knew more about these patients than I did. You got some book learning in school, but the nurses knew the treatment—they knew everything. They were also spic and span! There were no flies on them, you hear? They came to work to look like a nurse and act like a nurse. So what did Whittico do? He got close to the nurses. They were sweethearts, and they took care of me. Ain't no point in being punctilious, like: 'I'm Dr. So-and-so.' No, I'm here to learn. I'm here to learn."*

—Dr. James Whittico

Some Southern students had no choice but to travel north because there was little or no nursing education available in their home states. Johnnie Matthews Simmons, a 1968 nursing graduate, might have stayed closer to her hometown of Opelousas, she said, but "they weren't accepting Blacks into nursing school in Louisiana." Even when white nursing schools in Northern states did begin to accept Black students, there was often a strict quota. After Wanda Claxton Trotter graduated from a St. Louis high school in 1966, she applied to the nursing program at St. Luke's Hospital. "I got rejected, because they stated that they had their one Black person. Then I went to Barnes Hospital and made one of the highest grades on their entrance exam, but they rejected me as well, saying they *also* had their one Black person. So my mom said, 'Well, why don't you go to Homer Phillips?'"

Overall, wrote the Pulitzer Prize–winning journalist Isabel Wilkerson in her best-selling history of the exodus, "The Great Migration would become a turning point in history. It would transform urban America and recast the social and political order of every city it touched."[6] This effect also trickled down to individual lives. For Homer G. Phillips nursing students, their nursing school experience would dramatically influence their own futures, elevating their families and ensuring middle-class status for their descendants. Without the nursing school, said Georgia Anderson, a 1955 nursing graduate, she might have stayed on the old family farm in Moro, Arkansas:

> My grandfather Smith went through third grade, my mom finished eighth grade, and I was the first in the Smith family to go past high school. Now I am a nurse; I have a son who is a physician and a daughter who is a nurse. My granddaughter finished college last year and is expected to go to law school in September. So Homer G. Phillips has brought many, many, many, *many* people from here to there.

> *"Homer G. Phillips became a very highly respected place for the training of Black doctors. For patients, it was known for gunshot wounds, stab wounds, and trauma surgery. There was a saying going around, 'If I ever get shot, take me to Homer G.'"*
> —Dr. James Whittico

Homer G. Phillips Hospital was born at a time of virulent prejudice, but the Black community in St. Louis was growing and finding its voice. They had no interest in replacing the overcrowded City Hospital #2 with a segregated annex to City #1, as some proposed. During the 1920s, attorney Homer G. Phillips became an outspoken advocate for founding a new hospital, staffed by Black professionals and located in the Ville, the neighborhood most closely identified with Black St. Louis.

In 1923, Phillips also promoted the passage of an $87 million bond issue that would earmark $1 million for construction of a Black hospital. Thanks in part to the growing power of the Black electorate, the measure passed, and the Board of Aldermen found $200,000 to add to the project. Political wrangling over the hospital ensued, delaying construction for a decade. Tragically, Phillips himself was murdered in 1931 so he never saw the splendid new building. Yet the project went forward—and the new hospital acquired the dead attorney's name.

With all the struggles over equal treatment for Black physicians in the early twentieth century, it was ironic that the vast achievements of the civil rights movement eventually helped to undermine Homer G. Phillips Hospital and seal its fate. When patients could go anywhere for care, its census began to drop; when trainees could find internships and residencies at a range of hospitals, residency classes at Homer G. became harder to fill. When politicians realized that Black and white nurses could co-exist in nurses' training and save money in the process, the two public nursing schools in St. Louis merged in 1968.

In 1979, the storied Homer G. Phillips Hospital closed, leaving behind a trail of angry hospital partisans and years of political turmoil. For some, the wounds of that struggle are still fresh today, while others chalk up the closure to politics and changing times, tinged by racism. Most were thrilled when the long-vacant building reopened years later as a senior living center that still pays homage to its past with a portrait of attorney Homer G. Phillips, rooms named for staff doctors, and a bronze plaque in the front lobby listing all the nursing graduates. Hospital mementos are now in the collections of local museums—and some even made their way to the Smithsonian's National Museum of African American History and Culture.

Most of all, the hospital had a lifelong impact on the people who received top-notch training there. Throughout Dr. Whittico's long career—he only retired from medicine in 2015 at age 99—he was showered with honors. In 1968, he served as president of the National Medical Association (NMA). He won awards for mounting a nationally prominent campaign to build awareness of cancers that frequently affect Blacks. In St. Louis, he was only the fourth African American to be named a fellow of the American College of Surgeons.

Nursing graduates moved on to fine careers across the country. In many cases, they only had to mention that they were from Homer G. Phillips School of Nursing, and doors opened or jobs materialized. They had lives they could never have dreamed possible. "You can't climb up if there's not a ladder or some way to move yourself up," mused nurse Georgia Anderson. "In the areas where we came from, there were no opportunities." By the 1970s, the youth in rural areas had more access to college, but in earlier decades, they were often stranded and hopeless. "So Homer G. Phillips was the ladder for me—and I'm not sorry that I started climbing."

## CHAPTER ONE

# The Mysterious Life and Death of Homer Garland Phillips, 1878–1931

*"It was sad, very sad. Well, it was just a very sad day, that's what I remember. In 1931, when I was nine years old, Homer G. Phillips was shot down as he went to get on a streetcar to go to his office. It was just a very sad time in the Ville neighborhood, where I lived. It made people feel crushed, you know, like we didn't have anyone to speak for us. I also remember the anger that he had been killed when he was trying to speak out and be a leader."*

> —Mary Ellen Anderson, born in 1922 and childhood resident of the Ville, also widow of Dr. John Anderson, psychiatrist at Homer G. Phillips and Barnes hospitals

Fig. 1.1: Mary Ellen and John Anderson are shown on their wedding day, September 12, 1943. Courtesy of Dr. Dale Anderson.

THE OUTSPOKEN YOUNG attorney Homer Garland Phillips spent much of his time in the limelight: fighting for clients in well-publicized court cases, sparring with white politicians, and zealously promoting a new Black hospital. Local newspapers, white and Black, covered his progress; judges, politicians, and policemen knew him well. When he was brutally murdered in 1931, the bloody details of that day also became public fare. But behind this public persona was a man whose life and death remain in many ways mysterious.

Homer G. Phillips was not even his birth name. He was born Wesley Phillips in the tiny town of Smithton, Missouri, not far from Sedalia. His death certificate, based on information provided by his wife, says that his parents' names were unknown, along with their birthplaces. But, as Ida Perle Alexander Phillips surely heard from her husband, her father-in-law was Samuel M. Phillips, a free Black man born in 1834, who had served on the Union side in the Civil War. His unit was the 2nd Northeast Regiment of the pro-Union Missouri Home Guard under the command of Capt. Nicholas W. Murrow, and Phillips was discharged as a sergeant, after serving in a number of battles.

Following the war, he left Smithton briefly and returned to his native state of Tennessee to bring back a bride, Caroline Roberts, whom he married in 1867. Over the years, they had ten children, and the second-to-youngest was Wesley, born in 1878. Yet in many public records, including his death certificate and gravestone, his birthdate is listed incorrectly as April 1, 1880.

At the time of the 1870 census, and in all subsequent census records, Samuel Phillips was described as a farmer or more often a laborer, sometimes doing odd jobs. Early in Wesley's life, Caroline died, leaving her husband with a large family and, it's safe to assume, little money. There is some tradition that, at this point, Wesley was sent to live with an aunt, though the truth of that is unclear. Probably he received his elementary education at one of several "colored" grammar schools that existed near Smithton. In 1883, Samuel Phillips married again in a Methodist Episcopal ceremony to a woman named Sallie Shobe, and they took up residence in Sedalia.

That city, which called itself the "The Prairie Queen," was a Jim Crow town in mid-Missouri with separate but unequal schools, housing, newspapers, and neighborhoods. In the nineteenth century, its commercial base was railroad traffic, and that helped the town thrive. The roughneck workers passing through also fostered a booming business in prostitution, which the middle-class residents deplored. In 1891, the *Sedalia Weekly Bazoo* ran a front-page piece rebutting this image: "Sedalia has expended more in the erection of churches than any city of similar size in the west. . . . Whatever else Sedalia may be, it is no Sodom or Gomorrah." Around 1900, the city became infatuated with its hometown son, musician Scott Joplin, whom it nicknamed "The Ragtime King."

*"We looked up to our mother, Ruby Johnson—well, she was next to God—but she was very, very stern, and she had her rules. We did not go out of the gate in front of the house. We were not to play on the sidewalk; we were not to be street children. My mother did not let us go out and mix and mingle. She had a motto that she said almost every day: 'Get your education.' Almost every day, it was just drummed into your head: 'Get your education.'"*

—Mary Ellen Anderson

In 1893, the city celebrated an educational milestone: the construction of a new institution that would enrich the life of Wesley Phillips. The Freedmen's Aid and Southern Educational Society of the Methodist Episcopal Church was an organization aimed, it said, at educating "the colored race," five million of whom "in the south are unable to read their ballots or the gospel of Christ. Fettered and in darkness!"[1] By 1892, the society had founded 45 Southern schools, half for whites and half for Blacks, which enrolled some 70,000 students.

Then the society decided to build a college for Black students on the north side of Sedalia and name it for the late Gen. George R. Smith, Sedalia's founder, an ardent Unionist and a one-time slaveholder. Smith's two daughters donated 20 acres of land toward its construction. Progress on the $50,000 building was frustratingly

Fig. 1.2: In 1893, the Freedmen's Aid and Southern Educational
Society of the Methodist Episcopal Church founded a college on
the north side of Sedalia and named it for Gen. George R. Smith,
Sedalia's founder and an ardent Unionist. It was destroyed by fire in
1925. Courtesy of Pettis County Historical Society.

slow, and at one point the project stalled due to lack of funds. A report from the society that year exhorted its members to give gener-
ously to the cause. "Our prayers," it urged, "must be *gold-lined*."[2]

Finally, they accumulated enough to proceed with the new school,
which they called "the largest college in the West for the education
of colored people." After the cornerstone-laying on May 31, 1893,
the *Sedalia Democrat* gave the project an eloquent endorsement.
The day's events, said the editorial, "were memorable and of vast
importance to the state":

> It means for the country a pouring in of light; it means the
> refinement and elevation of a class of citizens whose future in
> the social economy of the country is one of the gravest prob-
> lems of the statesman and philosopher. . . . The only salvation
> is through the touchstone of education, directed and guided
> by strong, liberal minds, fully conscious of the future by the
> history of the past. Prejudices and superstitions are to be swept

away by mind culture, which more easily paves the way for heart culture.[3]

News of the college reached St. Louis, where wealthy brewer Adolphus Busch decided to donate a four-dial tower clock and a bell for the college's belfry—altogether, a $1,500 gift. As the school's new president, the Freedmen's Aid Society hired Rev. Dr. P.A. Cool, a white administrator with experience heading another of the society's colleges. At last, they announced that the doors of the magnificent brick-and-stone structure would be thrown open to male and female students in January 1894. For students who couldn't afford to pay tuition, a generous work-study option was available.

Sadly, this fine school was destroyed by fire in 1925, and with it all the student records. Still, it seems all but certain that one of the first students lining up for admission was a poor but ambitious fifteen-year-old, Wesley Phillips.

The new college got off to a solid start. By March 1894, 46 students had enrolled, and donations were coming in from far and wide; an Illinois minister died and left the college his valuable library. But in 1895, the school hit a scandalous snag, when two students accused the Rev. Cool of several serious charges: "inveterate usage of tobacco in the building"; "taking wine and other intoxicants to his room and drinking the same"; "coming from the girls' department at unseemly hours"; and allowing "Miss ___ and Miss ___ to visit his room." Supporting testimony came from nine student witnesses, including Wesley Phillips.[4]

A committee assigned to investigate the charges declared Cool innocent. Still, they quietly dismissed him and brought in a new head, Prof. E. A. Robertson. Once again, the school began to flourish and reported that, by 1896, it had 76 students. Religious faith may have been an important piece of college life, for one newspaper reported approvingly that nearly the entire student body of George R. Smith College had embraced religion.

Young Wesley Phillips had also embraced Republican politics, and he was just 18 when he served as one of the "colored" delegates to the county convention, where he supported the party platform and favored William McKinley for president. Under a Republican administration, said one speaker, "Confidence will then be restored, enterprise will be fostered . . . and our money kept as good as any in the world." By acclamation, the convention tried to appoint the beloved Sedalia lawyer, judge, and banker John Homer Bothwell as a Republican delegate, but he graciously refused and departed the hall amid a deafening ovation.[5]

College life continued, as George R. Smith grew and hosted attractions. "The marvelous musical prodigy, Blind Boone . . . will give one of his brilliant performances in the George R. Smith college chapel. . . . Do not miss this rare treat," announced *The Sedalia Democrat* in 1896. Wesley Phillips, then a college junior, sang with a group of students during the 1898 graduation ceremony.

By 1898–99, Phillips was a college senior. City directories list him as living off-campus in a flat on West Second Street; his father Samuel and older brother William, both laborers, lived in an apartment on nearby West Clay. Brother John, another laborer, was over on East Morgan.

Wesley must have been a top student, and he clearly had loftier dreams than any of his siblings. Somehow, he summoned the courage—and money—to travel east to Howard University, where he joined the law school class. Before that he took another momentous step: In March 1899, Wesley, then nearly 21, appeared before the Pettis County Circuit Court and changed his name legally to Homer Garland Phillips. The record of the case, neatly inscribed in the leather-bound Pettis County court ledger, gives no reason for the switch.

Why did he do it? The answer may lie in a vexing confusion that could have prodded him to action. In Sedalia, there were two other men (father and son) by the name of Wesley Phillips, and both of them were Black men, as well as laborers. While that was bewildering enough, the father had also served in Republican politics, church life, and civic affairs. Worst of all, Wesley Phillips Jr. was a bit of a troublemaker. In January 1899, just two months before the Howard-bound Wesley Phillips changed his name to Homer G.

Phillips, newspapers covered the arrest of Wesley Jr. on contempt charges for having attended an arson trial and loudly remarking, as he left the courtroom, "that if he was on the jury, he would send the defendant to the penitentiary."[6] Perhaps budding law student Wesley Phillips had had enough.

But why replace "Wesley" with "Homer Garland"? Any answer is pure speculation. Was he honoring the esteemed local Republican, John Homer Bothwell? George R. Smith College was a college-preparatory school, and it taught classical literature. Was he a classics scholar, struck by the beauty and heroism in Homer's poetry?

He left for Howard, where he joined a law class of 23 young Black men. Perhaps someone in Sedalia helped him get to Howard; he also had a year between college and law school to amass savings from janitorial work. At Howard, classes were held in the evening, so students could work during the daytime. One tradition says that he lived for a time in the home of poet Paul Laurence Dunbar, while another says that he worked briefly for the Department of Justice.

A leather-bound ledger at Howard recorded his progress: Homer Garland Phillips matriculated on October 1, 1900, moved to the middle class in 1901, and to the senior class in 1902. He graduated on May 25, 1903, with an LLB degree. At commencement, held in the First Congregational Church of Washington, D.C., he received

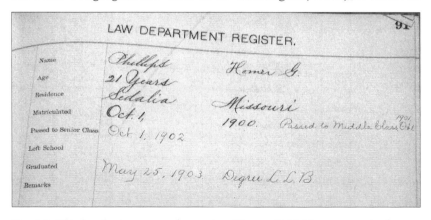

Fig. 1.3: This handwritten entry for student Homer G. Phillips appears in the leather-bound Law Department registry of Howard University. Courtesy of the Howard University School of Law Archives.

his diploma and had the signal honor of giving the graduate oration titled "The Supreme Law." A Washington newspaper, the *Evening Star*, described his talk:

> Mr. Phillips drifted into a discussion on reforms, and said that what constitutes a reform is the riddle of the hour; that reform is ambiguous, for the reason that conditions are continually changing. During the course of his remarks, he touched upon socialism, attributing its agitation to the tyranny of capital, which, he declared, is worse than the despotism of a monarch. In his summary, the speaker said that the destiny of the human race is glorious, and that fraternity, sympathy and love will ever grow wider and firmer.[7]

In 1904, Homer Garland Phillips returned to Sedalia with the same spirit of reform and progressive politics—but in a higher social stratum. The *Sedalia Weekly Conservator*, a Black newspaper associated with George R. Smith College, noted, "To say that he is heartily welcomed back would be putting it lightly, but coming as he does Attorney at Law, to practice his profession before the bar here, we feel safe in saying that the progressive element only can really heartily welcome him. . . . Mr. Phillips is very well known here, which will aid him greatly in establishing a law office. THE CONSERVATOR's staff, his old comrades, are loud in their voices of welcome."[8]

Despite his friends and fine reputation, it could not have been easy for Phillips to develop a new law practice. He took up residence in his old flat, though he also rented an office on Main Street. He became involved in the community, resuming his strong connection with the Republican Party and traveling to other states to give speeches. He joined the Grand Lodge of the Knights of Pythias and was named its "Grand Attorney" at a 1906 convention in Kansas City, where Booker T. Washington was the keynote speaker.

By 1907, his friends at the *Sedalia Weekly Conservator* reprinted a highly laudatory story about Phillips that had first appeared in the *National Mirror*, a Black newspaper published in Kansas City. "In the 4 years practice of his profession [he] has demonstrated his brilliancy therein," it said, adding that he had recently served as special counsel in a celebrated libel case, *State v. Washington*, "securing a conviction, thus vindicating his client. "Mr. Phillips has rare ability and much energy, and it is the opinion of the *National Mirror* that there is much good in store for him."[9]

Phillips must have been a persuasive, even mesmerizing, speaker, because he was soon turning up everywhere. In June 1908, he and Charlton H. Tandy, "the gifted colored orator of St. Louis," appeared together in Wood's Opera House in Sedalia to address the "colored" voters of Sedalia. A few weeks later, Phillips traveled to an Institute for the Teachers of Central Missouri and offered lectures on civics.

His legal career seemed to be going smoothly, but in 1910 Phillips suffered a humiliating public blow. A year earlier, he was a key founder of the new Central Missouri Forum Club, a "Negro club," said newspaper headlines, "organized for educational and social purposes."[10] He went before a circuit court judge that June to apply for its incorporation. Apparently, the club was successful; newspapers reported that not only was it popular with Black members, but some whites had joined as well. Yet the following February, the same judge ordered the club to forfeit its charter and close. The trial was long, with 110 witnesses subpoenaed to testify; prominent judges and lawyers represented both sides in the case. One defendant was Homer G. Phillips, described as the club's manager, who tried to rebut the prosecution's argument that the club featured "the sale of liquor and pool-playing . . . and the frequenting of the place by minors and other illegal practices."

That August, Samuel Phillips died, and Homer arranged for his burial in an unmarked grave along the outer edge of tiny Smithton Cemetery, where his descendants later placed a monument. In 1907, Homer's 35-year-old brother John, a plumber in Sedalia, had died of typhoid fever. Perhaps it was time for a broader horizon. In 1910 or 1911, Homer, then 33, soon struck out in a new direction, moving to St. Louis, a larger sphere for his considerable talents.

Once in St. Louis, Homer G. Phillips set up his new practice, running ads in the *Saint Louis Argus* that promoted him as a lawyer and a notary public. He must also have jumped quickly into the city's social life, because in June 1912 he married 28-year-old

Fig. 1.4: In 1984, Nesby Moore Jr. commissioned artist
Vernon Smith to paint this portrait of attorney Homer
Garland Phillips (1878–1931). Courtesy of the Missouri
Historical Society, St. Louis.

Ida Perle Alexander, born in Little Rock, Arkansas, and educated
at the French Convent of Notre Dame in Montreal. She was a sing-
er and budding actress, who appeared in local Black productions
and, after an unsuccessful first marriage, lived with her family at
4411 Labadie Avenue. True to Phillips's Methodist Episcopal roots,
Homer and Perle got married at St. Paul AME Church, the oldest
AME church west of the Mississippi, then located in the Black enclave of Mill Creek Valley.

Perle came from a solidly middle-class family. Her father, John,
was a respectable clerk for the government, who identified himself
as "mulatto" in the 1910 census; her mother Mary, born in Ohio,
was a dressmaker, described in census reports as "mulatto" or

"white." The family had several children, including Perle, Bertha, Clothilda, and an only son, Gustave Doré Alexander, fancifully named for the famed nineteenth-century artist.

Through the 19 years of their marriage, Homer and Perle lived at various addresses, including 4524 Cottage Avenue from 1917 to 1921, and finally 1121 Aubert Avenue. At times they shared a home with Perle's parents; later on, her mother lived with them. No children were born to the couple. In 1918, Phillips began purchasing real estate, perhaps for investment, including a nine-room brick house at 4040 West Belle Place.

Meanwhile, he missed serving in World War I. On his September 1918 registration card, he described himself as tall, slender, with brown eyes and black hair, and no physical disabilities; he also said he was 40 years old and born on April 1, 1879, not 1878—even though the math didn't add up. Still, he was older and married, and the war ended that November, so he was not drafted. Perle's brother Gustave, however, served in the 809th Pioneer Infantry and was discharged as a sergeant.

By 1915, St. Louis had an enormous African American population—more than 35,000 people—a number swollen by the arrival of newcomers from the South, part of the Great Migration. Restive white residents, appalled by this influx, determined to rein in the Black migrants and curb their influence. They called for a special election, a move that an Indiana newspaper called "the culmination of a feeling smoldering in St. Louis a long time," adding that, "Under the surface, St. Louis is a SOUTHERN city, with all that the term [im]plies."[11]

In 1916, by more than a three-to-one margin, voters passed two ordinances: one stipulating that people could not move onto a block occupied wholly by those of another race; and the second declaring that no one could move onto a block if more than 75 percent of the residents were of another race. Of the two ordinances, the second was the "more stringent," noted *The New York Times*, for it effectively mandated that "only about 150 blocks will be available for negro residences."[12] Thus, St. Louis had the dubious distinction of becoming the first American city to adopt such restrictive, and openly racist, housing ordinances in a public vote.

But the effect of these measures was short-lived. The next year, the U.S. Supreme Court decided in *Buchanan v. Warley* that such ordinances were illegal.[13] White St. Louisans responded by imposing racially restrictive covenants on neighborhoods, which had the same discriminatory effect.

Working on behalf of the young National Association for the Advancement of Colored People (NAACP), Homer G. Phillips passionately opposed the 1916 ordinances. He and fellow Black attorney George L. Vaughn worked closely together to file for an injunction to halt the special election—a fight, said a *New York Times* article, likely to "be carried to the United States supreme court." Phillips was particularly eloquent in his argument before the circuit court, added the *St. Louis Argus* gratefully in its August 2, 1918, edition. "The favorable impression he made in his argument before the Circuit Court . . . will long be remembered."

At this early date, Phillips and Vaughn were close allies—one article in the *St. Louis Argus* calling them "bosom friends"—and by the mid-1920s they were legal partners with offices at 2348 Olive. In 1915, they served together on a St. Paul AME committee to honor J. Milton Turner, one-time consul general to Liberia. The next year, at a caucus to choose delegates to the Republican National Convention, Phillips was a candidate; Vaughn, the floor leader, placed Phillips' name in nomination and made "a ringing speech in which he told of the Negro's loyalty to the party."[14] Ultimately, two white men won election as delegates, though one of them beat Phillips by only nine votes.

The plucky Phillips tried again in 1918, running as the Republican candidate for Justice of the Peace in the 4th District. In the primary, however, he claimed voter fraud—so instead filed as an independent. In the general election, he came in dead last, explained the *Argus*, because "it was necessary for a man, voting the Republican ticket, to scratch a candidate and write Phillips' name in. This was difficult to do."

Nevertheless, the tireless Phillips continued to make a name for himself in town. In 1912 and 1914, he won election as chairman of the Negro Auxiliary to the Republican State Committee. As a member of the Legal Committee of the NAACP, he recovered damages for some of the victims of the 1917 East St. Louis race riots, in which an unknown number of African Americans, probably several dozen, were killed by roaming mobs of whites. He also tried to bar a showing of the racist film *Birth of a Nation*.

In 1919, he, Vaughn, *St. Louis Argus* publisher Joseph E. Mitchell, and others banded together to found the Citizens Liberty League, an organization devoted to promoting and electing Black public officials. "He has always been a fighting Republican," said the *Argus*. "He permits nothing to stand in the way of his fighting the cause of his race at all times." As it turned out, Homer G. Phillips's biggest fight of all was yet to come.

During that same year, Phillips fought discrimination on many fronts. He stood up to Congressman L. C. Dyer, a white man representing a district that was 80 percent Black, when he failed to appoint a Black candidate to a state committee. Phillips publicly opposed a "back-to-Dixie" movement mounted by Southern white planters who wanted to lure Black workers back to the cottonfields. He favored the opening of a Black department store and proudly announced that some Market Street stores that depended on "Negro patronage, recently were induced to employ negro clerks, thus giving employment to 43 negroes."[15] By 1920, he had joined other Republicans in demanding representation for Blacks in police and fire departments, on juries, and even in Congress.

Personally, Phillips could be magnanimous. In 1921, St. Louisan Walthall M. Moore took office as Missouri's first Black member of the legislature and announced that he was studying to become a lawyer, aided by none other than Homer G. Phillips—who no doubt would have liked the legislative job himself. Phillips even wrote a cordial letter to a white newspaper commending the staff on their restraint in reporting on a recent murder. "That you did not yield to the inclination to fasten responsibility upon some colored man . . . was an exhibition of journalism that should commend itself to all believers in justice and fair play."[16]

*"It was a mean atmosphere. Homer G. Phillips was speaking out for a decent place where women of color could have their*

*children. He thought he had a right to speak in this country,*
*but we learned that you did not."*

—Mary Ellen Anderson


During these years, Phillips took on yet another new cause. In 1915, an acquaintance, Dr. Wallace Christian—later superintendent of Homer G. Phillips Hospital—asked him to join a Citizens' Committee that would back the efforts of St. Louis doctors to create better medical facilities for Blacks. In 1917, Phillips and other Black leaders visited St. Louis Mayor Henry Kiel, then up for re-election, to press for the creation of a hospital for Black patients. Soon City Hospital #2 opened in an old medical building; small and shabby, it quickly proved to be inadequate. In response, the indefatigable Phillips reconvened his group in support of an $87 million bond issue that Mayor Kiel had proposed for civic improvements—with the caveat that the measure include $1 million toward the creation of an entirely new Black hospital. While the bond issue passed easily in 1923, backpedaling soon began, as white politicians, eager to skim off some of the earmarked funds for their own pet projects, claimed that the measure required only the building of an *annex* to the white hospital, City Hospital #1. Phillips, who had earlier felt some ambivalence about segregated hospitals, changed his mind. He went to the Board of Aldermen, where the Welfare Committee and its Republican head, Louis Aloe, secured another $200,000 toward construction of a separate new hospital.

Phillips was widely known as an ardent Republican, and in the 1925 mayoral race, he supported Aloe. Aloe failed in his bid, but in the general election, the Republican candidate was Victor Miller, a man whom Phillips—along with a host of prominent Black Republicans, including Vaughn, *Argus* editor Mitchell, and Dr. A. N. Vaughn—regarded as racist, unbalanced, and incompetent. So Phillips and other Republicans bolted their party temporarily to support a Democrat for mayor, William L. Igoe—a defection that Miller never forgave.

As the fight over the location of the new hospital continued, Phillips made another bid for office, and likely made an enemy of George Vaughn in the process. In 1926, Phillips sought the Republican nomination for Congress from the 12th District on a platform that included greater opportunities for Blacks, equal accommodations on railroad trains, support of organized labor, and the use of "Negroes" as combat troops in the U.S. military. The problem was that Vaughn had already declared his candidacy for the same office and fully expected Phillips's support; thus, Phillips' announcement blindsided and angered him.

The campaign bumped messily along, as claims and counterclaims flew. The AME Ministers Alliance originally endorsed Phillips, believing that he was the only Black candidate in the running. But when they discovered that Vaughn was in the race, and that he had been the first to announce, they rescinded their endorsement of Phillips, a move that made headlines. One prominent minister, Rev. John Parker of Pleasant Green Baptist, wrote a letter to the *Argus* complaining that Phillips had used his name as an endorser without his consent. Others pointed out that Phillips didn't even live in the district he sought to represent. In a July 1926 editorial, the *Argus* pleaded with Phillips to drop out of the race, so that "the chances for the election of a Negro to Congress . . . [will be] almost assured."

Instead of withdrawing, Phillips came out fighting in a "desperate talk" at Tabernacle Baptist Church. "Candidate for Congress Uses Hour and Half In Abuse of Everybody Who Opposes Him," said *Argus* headlines. "Pictures Opponents as Liars, Thieves and Grafters; But Himself as a Spotless Lamb." As to George Vaughn, Phillips called him "a 'whining' candidate who had built up his strength on 'dirty work and lies.'" In the end, both Vaughn and Phillips ran—though Vaughn won the Black vote by 2,082 votes to Phillips's 1,835. The white incumbent, L. C. Dyer, won the day by a wide margin, more than the combined vote for Vaughn and Phillips.

Phillips did go on to win election to the executive committee and then in 1928 the presidency of the National Bar Association, which represented more than 400 Black lawyers across the country. In his private practice, he fought hard for his clients, safeguarding

a $100,000 bequest to Fisk University and exposing a bogus in-
surance claim by revealing that a coffin contained not a body, but
cement. In 1927, he represented a plaintiff suing Aaron Malone, recently divorced husband of Annie Malone, for damages in a shady
real estate deal; a year later, he became one of the original owners
of the *St. Louis American* newspaper after an earlier association
with the *St. Louis Argus*.

But by 1931, Phillips had made powerful enemies in four cases.
The first, just coming to trial in June 1931, involved a Black janitor,
William O. McMahon, suing his union for records after he was
ejected from his position as its secretary-treasurer. In a second matter, Phillips was representing John and Stella McFarland, a family
living in the Ville who wanted to recover $2,200 owed them from
the estate of her late father, George Fitzhugh, of Brooklyn, Illinois.
For his services, Phillips—who had hired other lawyers to assist
him and even travelled to Philadelphia on the McFarlands' behalf—
billed the couple $1,000 and put their check in a safety deposit box
at Laclede Trust Co. until they agreed to pay. John McFarland was
enraged at what he viewed as an outlandish fee and made public
threats against Phillips.

A third matter that had aroused passionate sentiment involved
the new Black hospital's location in the Ville, which Phillips had
ardently supported. During the Kiel administration, an ordinance
passed that allowed the city to begin condemning properties on the
site to make way for construction; after Victor Miller became may-
or in 1925, his administration tried to repeal that bill but failed. At
a hearing on the repeal, Phillips chided board members that a Black
hospital linked to the whites-only City Hospital #1 would amount
to "segregation with humiliation."[17] As a result, the forthcoming
hospital became a sore point for some city residents and especially
the city administration.

In the fourth case, Phillips was about to testify against his former
friend, attorney George Vaughn, who had been hired to represent
Walter Giles, the former athletic director at Sumner High School.
Giles was being sued for divorce by his wife Hazel; strengthening his
case was the testimony of two women, Hattie and Louise Robinson,

Fig. 1.5: George L. Vaughn, a St. Louis attorney, was a bitter rival of Homer G. Phillips. After Phillips' death, he was acquitted in a case of suborning perjury that could have disbarred him. *St. Louis Globe-Democrat*, August 18, 1949.

# George Vaughn Dies, Negro Bar Leader

George L. Vaughn, a Negro attorney, whose fight against real estate agreements segregating Negroes was upheld last year by the United States Supreme Court, died unexpectedly of heart disease yesterday.

Vaughn, 69, died at this home, 3744 Finney, as he was discussing a magazine article with his wife, Eva, his son, George L. Vaughn Jr., said.

As an alternate delegate to the Democratic National Convention at Philadelphia last year, Vaughn led the explosive fight to unseat the Mississippi delegation in the civil rights fight. His motion lost by a slim vote.

Vaughn, an assistant attorney general of Missouri, was a former Justice of the Peace for the Fourth District and in 1941 ran for Alderman in the old Nineteenth Ward but was defeated.

**GEORGE L. VAUGHN**, 69, Negro attorney, died of a heart disease yesterday.

who claimed to have seen Mrs. Giles with a young man in a notorious Pine Street rooming house. If true, this allegation would have lightened Giles's financial burden in the divorce settlement.

As the attorney representing Hazel Giles, Phillips obtained statements from the two women that they had been paid by Vaughn and his colleague James Hutt, a Black clerk in the assessor's office, to provide false affidavits concerning Mrs. Giles's behavior. In December 1930, before a specially called grand jury, the women admitted they had indeed given false testimony, and both Hutt and Vaughn were indicted. Hazel Giles was awarded her divorce, custody of her two children, and support in the amount of $80 a month.[18]

The trial of Vaughn and Hutt was due to take place on Monday, June 22, 1931, in St. Louis. For Vaughn, the stakes could not have been higher: His entire career was in jeopardy. In legal terms he was accused of "suborning perjury" which, if proven, would certainly have meant public disgrace and even disbarment.[19]

Just before 8 a.m. on June 18, 1931, Phillips—a model of punctuality—emerged from the door of his home at 1121 Aubert and walked to his usual streetcar stop, where he would catch a ride to his office at 23 North Jefferson. In front of the Rubicam

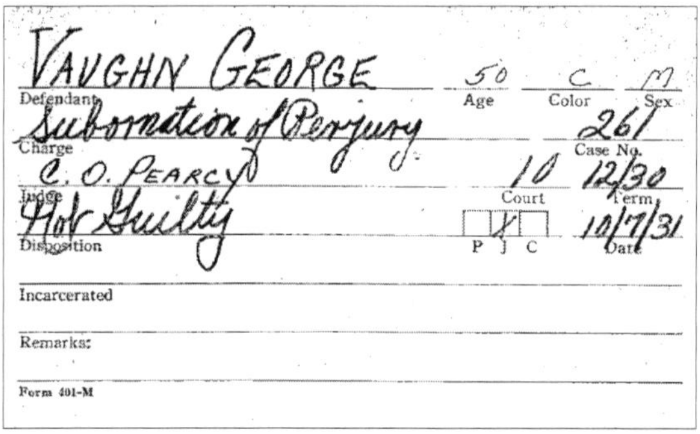

VAUGHN GEORGE — 50 — C — M
Defendant — Age — Color — Sex
Subornation of Perjury — 261
Charge — Case No.
C. O. PEARCY — 10 — 12/30
Judge — Court — Term
Not Guilty — P J C — 10/7/31
Disposition — Date
Incarcerated
Remarks:
Form 401-M

Fig. 1.6: With the key witness in the trial dead, George Vaughn was acquitted of suborning perjury in the Giles case. St. Louis County Court records.

Business School at 714 Aubert, near Delmar, he leaned against a ledge and began reading his paper. Suddenly, two young Black men approached him, one wearing a dirty gray cap. The older of the two, a heavyset youth, argued with Phillips briefly and punched him in the face, causing him to fall backwards. Next, he and his accomplice opened fire with 25-caliber pistols—six shots in all—hitting Phillips in the head and back. He died on the spot; his body was sent to City Hospital #2, where Dr. Henry Weathers pronounced him dead.

A thick police file and the medical examiner's report tell the whole story in chilling detail, recounting word for word the questions asked of witnesses, especially Abner Parker, a newspaper circulation agent living on nearby Fountain Avenue, who saw the whole thing from a distance of only ten feet. Horrified, Parker watched the teens run north through alleyways and streets, where other witnesses spotted them. Detectives arrived and gave chase, pursuing them all the way to the Ville, where they arrested 18-year-old Augustus Brooks in the yard of the McFarland family home at 4243 St. Ferdinand. They found the gray cap inside the house. Other officers picked up Brooks's cousin—19-year-old George McFarland, son of John—a little while later.

*"Why was he killed? I think there was a group of people—we called them gangs—that had people killed if they wanted to get rid of them. You heard these things from neighbors who had their ears to the ground, and they got the information.*

*But you'd better not speak about it or you'd lose somebody in your family."*

—Mary Ellen Anderson

Some of the city's finest white detectives investigated the murder, including Sgt. James Doherty, who testified at the June 19 inquest. Doherty reported briefly but emphatically on the search for McFarland and Brooks. There were clear indications of the boys' guilt: the police had several credible witnesses, he said, who positively identified the murderers; the boys bolted when they approached them; they had the clothing said to be worn by the youth; they even had motive, in the parents' estate matter. He and other officers who testified seemed almost bored, certain that their case was rock-solid.

Although police may have thought they had solved the case, complicating factors soon arose. A private detective, hired by the union janitor, got an anonymous phone call not long after the murder, at 11 a.m. A muffled voice said to him: "You heard what happened to Homer G. Phillips? That is what will happen to you." Was the murder somehow related to the janitor's case? Or could someone—perhaps George Vaughn, by now Phillips's bitter enemy—have been involved, even posing as the muffled voice?

There was another possible twist to the Vaughn connection. By the time of his murder, Homer Phillips was a bitter enemy of the pugnacious, unhinged mayor, Victor Miller, though George Vaughn was not. In fact, in 1928 Vaughn had served as a spokesman for

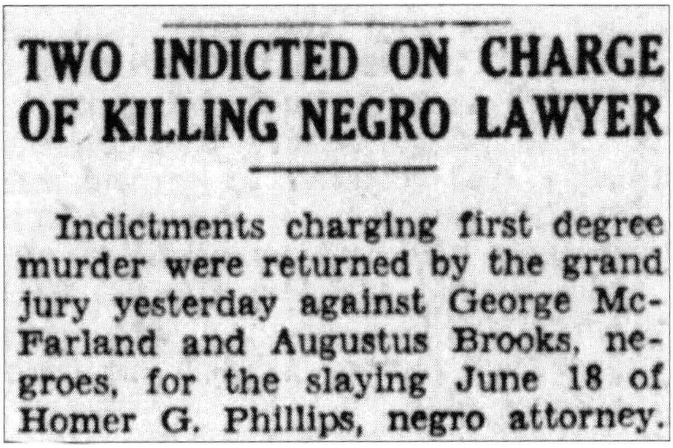

Fig. 1.7: On June 26, 1931, the *St. Louis Star and Times* newspaper reported on the indictment of two young men in the murder of Homer G. Phillips. However, they were never convicted. Courtesy of the Missouri Historical Society, St. Louis.

## TWO INDICTED ON CHARGE OF KILLING NEGRO LAWYER

Indictments charging first degree murder were returned by the grand jury yesterday against George McFarland and Augustus Brooks, negroes, for the slaying June 18 of Homer G. Phillips, negro attorney.

Miller during his re-election campaign. Could the two have colluded in some way to rid the city of Phillips, using the two boys—one of whom already had a grudge against Phillips—as paid killers?

Newspapers across the country reported the crime. In the *St. Louis Star*, the story made banner headlines, as the paper called the murder a likely "hired" killing. An editorial in *The St. Louis Argus* lauded Phillips, describing him as a "natural leader" and "a fighter for the rights of his people." In a probable reference to the 1926 controversy, the piece added that Phillips had made mistakes but that, in the end, "he was Homer Phillips, and his place will be hard to fill."[20]

As many as 10,000 mourners viewed Phillips's body lying in state at St. Paul AME Church, and several thousand, including white lawyers and judges, though not George Vaughn, attended the funeral. The Rev. Noah Williams, pastor at St. Paul, said in his funeral sermon: "Among the many great deeds Mr. Phillips has done for us was to get the negro City Hospital started. The hospital, or some other building, should be named in honor of him."[21] Four months later, the Board of Aldermen voted to name the new hospital, not yet under construction, for Phillips.

St. Louis waited breathlessly for the court appearances of the two young men, who were indicted by a grand jury and then tried separately. McFarland came first—but his legal team had an exculpatory bombshell in store: three witnesses who said they had seen him just at the time of the shooting in a grocery store on Goode Avenue, buying some cigarettes, and then at Kennerly Park. Both places were far from the crime scene. Oddly, at the time of his arrest, young McFarland had not mentioned this alibi to the detectives. By the time of Brooks's trial, most of the key witnesses, including Abner Parker, had disappeared from town, and one was said to have suffered a nervous breakdown. Both defendants were acquitted by all-white juries, and no one else was ever charged. Officially, the case remains unsolved.

In another strange and suspicious development, the court file on the Phillips murder disappeared decades ago from city court files, thus erasing part of the legal trail. The presiding circuit court judge was Clyde C. Beck, formerly a police court judge and a political appointee, as well as ally, of Mayor Miller. But who were the three witnesses testifying on McFarland's behalf? Could the witnesses have been suborned to commit perjury, as Vaughn was alleged to have done in the divorce case? After all, Phillips had once accused him of lies and dirty work. And could Vaughn, or someone else, have had access to the court file in order to steal or bury it?

Afterwards, life moved forward for everyone else involved in the Phillips' case. His widow, Perle Phillips, fell victim to a scam involving the Irish sweepstakes; she died in 1934 at Barnes Hospital of a lung abscess at age 49. The McFarlands went to court and induced the widow to settle for a $750 fee in the estate matter. George McFarland and Augustus Brooks who had, before the murder, served terms in the City Workhouse for larceny, continued on to lives of non-violent crime. McFarland was arrested 32 times before he died from tuberculosis in 1937, and "Brooks had 20 arrests before he disappeared in 1941 after serving a two-year prison term for burglary," said a St. Louis Globe-Democrat article.[22]

Vaughn and Hutt's legal case proceeded after Homer G. Phillips's death. But in June, Hutt decided to bail out, turning state's witness against Vaughn and accusing him of having asked him to round up false witnesses and pay them on his behalf. The trial of Vaughn was scheduled for the fall, but in the absence of Homer G. Phillips, the case against him fell apart. Hutt and the two women testified against Vaughn, but Vaughn's rebuttal that Hutt had never told him the women were lying convinced the jury, which deliberated for all of 40 minutes before acquitting him.

So, Vaughn's legal and political career was safe. Thus, it was Vaughn, along with political leader Jordan Chambers, who later had the glory of leading the Black exodus from the St. Louis Republican party to the Democrats. He would also be the attorney to garner fame from taking a racially restrictive covenant case to the U.S. Supreme Court—and in 1948 the court struck down such restrictions in the landmark Shelley v. Kraemer decision. Vaughn died of heart disease in 1949.

Who killed Homer G. Phillips or contracted for his murder? On the day of his death, Phillips's hometown newspaper, The Sedalia Democrat, explicitly made the link between Phillips's murder and

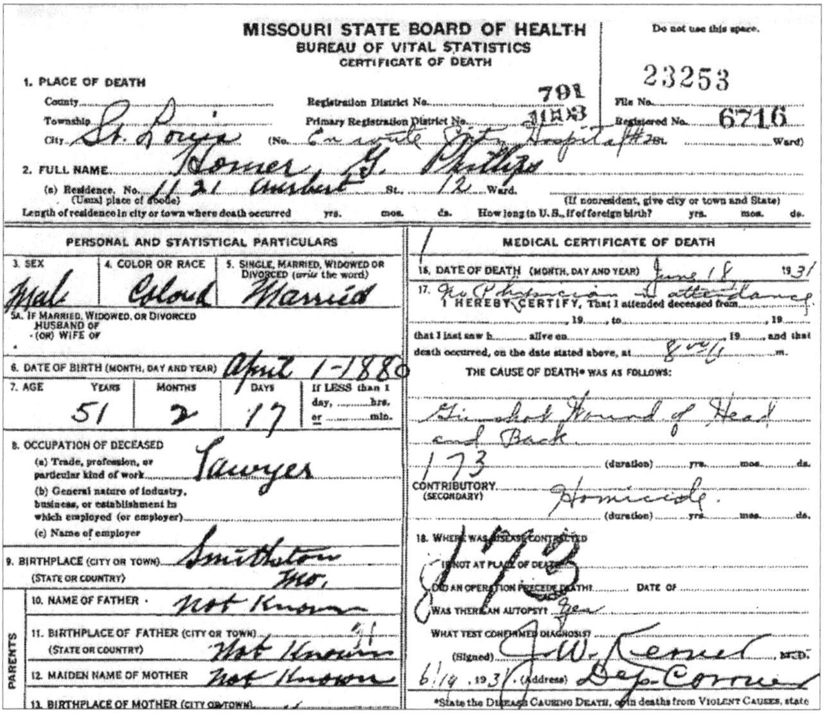

MISSOURI STATE BOARD OF HEALTH
BUREAU OF VITAL STATISTICS
CERTIFICATE OF DEATH

Do not use this space.

23253

1. PLACE OF DEATH
County ......... Registration District No. 791 File No. .........
Township ......... Primary Registration District No. 1103 Registered No. 6716
City St. Louis (No. En route City Hospital #2 St. ......... Ward)

2. FULL NAME Homer G. Phillips

(a) Residence. No. 1121 Aubert St. 12 Ward.
(Usual place of abode) (If nonresident, give city or town and State)
Length of residence in city or town where death occurred yrs. mos. ds. How long in U.S., if of foreign birth? yrs. mos. ds.

PERSONAL AND STATISTICAL PARTICULARS

3. SEX Male
4. COLOR OR RACE Colored
5. SINGLE, MARRIED, WIDOWED OR DIVORCED (write the word) Married
5A. IF MARRIED, WIDOWED, OR DIVORCED HUSBAND OF (OR) WIFE OF
6. DATE OF BIRTH (MONTH, DAY AND YEAR) April 1-1880
7. AGE Years 51 Months 2 Days 17 If LESS than 1 day, ... hrs. or ... min.
8. OCCUPATION OF DECEASED
(a) Trade, profession, or particular kind of work Lawyer
(b) General nature of industry, business, or establishment in which employed (or employer)
(c) Name of employer
9. BIRTHPLACE (CITY OR TOWN) Smithton (STATE OR COUNTRY) Mo.

PARENTS
10. NAME OF FATHER Not Known
11. BIRTHPLACE OF FATHER (CITY OR TOWN) (STATE OR COUNTRY) Not Known
12. MAIDEN NAME OF MOTHER Not Known
13. BIRTHPLACE OF MOTHER (CITY OR TOWN)

MEDICAL CERTIFICATE OF DEATH

16. DATE OF DEATH (MONTH, DAY AND YEAR) June 18 1931
17. No Physician in attendance
I HEREBY CERTIFY, That I attended deceased from ......... 19... to ......... 19...
that I last saw h... alive on ......... 19... and that death occurred, on the date stated above, at 8 ... m.
THE CAUSE OF DEATH* WAS AS FOLLOWS:
Gunshot Wound of Head and Back
173 (duration) ... yrs. ... mos. ... ds.
CONTRIBUTORY (SECONDARY) Homicide (duration) ... yrs. ... mos. ... ds.
18. Where was disease contracted if not at place of death?
Did an operation precede death? ... Date of ...
Was there an autopsy? Yes
What test confirmed diagnosis?
(Signed) J. W. Kenner M.D.
6/19, 1931 (Address) Dep. Coroner
*State the Disease Causing Death, or in deaths from Violent Causes, state

Fig. 1.8: This death certificate for Homer G. Phillips says that he died on June 18, 1931, en route to City Hospital #2. However, this information, likely dictated by his distraught widow, contains two errors: His birth year was 1878, not 1880; and his parents' names were not "unknown." Missouri Digital Heritage, Missouri Death Certificates, 1910–1970, Missouri State Archives.

Vaughn's court case. "Phillips, who bore a high reputation, was an important state witness in the trial of George Vaughn, Negro lawyer, and James Hutt, on charges of subordination [sic] of perjury which was set for next Monday."[23]

A writer for *Ebony Magazine*, Edward T. Clayton, came to St. Louis in 1951 and talked to many of Phillips' acquaintances before writing a thoughtful account of the case. "In St. Louis today, there are still whispered accusations, persistent rumors of a payoff to silence the feared and hated attorney, but no one has dared to point the finger of guilt. In all these years at least a half-dozen persons—some of them prominent in St. Louis and national affairs—have lived and died in the shadow of suspicion." At the end of his piece, he added: "Somewhere, someone knows. Someone knows who fired those fatal bullets. And some day the truth may be known."[24]

One final mystery remained: On his death certificate, Homer Garland Phillips was suddenly—and inexplicably—re-named "Homer Gilliam Phillips," the name that also appears on his tombstone in St. Peter's Cemetery.

## CHAPTER TWO

# "Old and Combustible and Altogether Unsafe"
## City Hospital #2, 1919–1937

*"When I started at City Hospital #2 School of Nursing, some of the girls were homesick, and they didn't know it was going to be so difficult. They began complaining: 'I'm going home. I'm not going to tolerate this. Aren't you going?' I said to them: 'No, somebody has already rolled over into my spot in bed back home. I've lost my spot; I've got to stay.' They were building Homer G. Phillips Hospital at that time, and we lived in its center section until the nursing school was finished. Everything was nice. I tell you I had a room to myself, brand-new, and a face basin with running water. My gosh, what more did you want?"*

> —Alice Augusta Burch Okrafo-Smart (1913–2019), a student in the City Hospital #2 nursing program and then a graduate of Homer G. Phillips School of Nursing in 1938. She later earned her B.S. degree from the University of Illinois School of Nursing in 1960 and her certification in physical therapy, and she worked for many years as a public health nurse.

WHEN HOMER G. Phillips moved to St. Louis in 1910 or 1911, he discovered that poor African Americans were receiving medical care—of a sort—in three segregated wards of the white City Hospital #1. White physicians, most from Washington University or Saint Louis University, provided all the treatment; Black physicians had no staff privileges at all. In 1910, the hospital's oversight committee considered hiring Black nurses for the segregated wards,

Fig. 2.1: Alice Augusta Burch Okrafo-Smart (1913–2019), born on Papin Street in St. Louis, studied nursing at City Hospital #2 and graduated from the Homer G. Phillips School of Nursing. Courtesy of Georgia Anderson.

but some physicians warned that "the white nurses will rebel." Some progressive voices argued that Black nurses were sorely needed. "[N]egro patients at the charity institutions do not get enough care," declared one newspaper article. Its headline referred frankly to racism: "Hospital Physicians Say the White Nurses Do Not Exert Selves for Black Patients."[1]

If the nurses *had* rebelled, it would hardly have been surprising. The rest of the staff at City Hospital #1, especially the interns, seemed to be griping or striking nearly all the time. In 1911, they told the *Star and Times* "they were treated like caged animals or kindergarten children, and that their intelligence is insulted" by the hospital rules. Later in 1911, 16 white interns quit, unhappy over an increase in paperwork, and grumbled that they had been promised comfortable quarters while they were actually sleeping three to a bed. In 1917, 46 of these unpaid interns staged a walkout, demanding $25 a month—but they settled for $10 a month, plus a $100-per-year bonus.

Certainly, the staff at City Hospital #1 must have been over-worked, because early in the twentieth century, St. Louis was buf-feted by waves of illness: typhoid fever; Spanish flu in 1918; and the continuing scourge of tuberculosis, especially among Blacks, who had around three times more deaths from this disease than whites.[2] The city population was also burgeoning—from 575,238 in 1900 to 772,897 only 20 years later—which meant increasing numbers of indigent patients. Thanks in part to the influx of poor migrants from the South, the Black population also soared during this period, from 35,516 to 69,854. In January 1915, the hospital admitted 829 white and Black patients, a new record, and some had to occupy beds in the hall.

Among them, the indigent Black patients received the most woe-fully inadequate care. In 1911, prominent Black physician Dr. W. P. Curtis reported on the appalling conditions to the Committee for Social Service Among Colored People. The three so-called colored wards, he said, were overcrowded; men occupied two basement wards near the engine room, while women had a spot next to the roof, the most "inferior, unsanitary and poorly ventilated parts of the Hospital." Patients with all kinds of diseases, including tuber-culosis, were jumbled together, and they had little nursing care.

The women fared worst of all, since they were relegated to a prison ward, located next to the "psychopathic ward, from which it is divided by an inner prison door of heavy wire netting. This ward is shared in common by social derelicts of the white race, who are irresponsible or ill on account of alcohol or narcotics, and colored women of all classes." Dr. Curtis went on to describe the shocking scene:

> In this ward, you hear the constant chattering of the insane from their cells, the mumbling of the drug-crazed fiends of the white race, mingled with the soft groans of the unfortunate negro women, seeking such relief as is offered to them by that high class of citizens known as the "Hospital Board." In this ward, there is no nurse stationed. The convalescent minister as best they can to the helpless.[3]

*"Altogether, Mamma had 13 children, but she had five still-births before she had one to live. Years ago, people had a lot of stillborns; they didn't have the care that we do now. Her first living baby was number six, Sammy Jr., then number seven was Laodicea—that was one of the seven churches that the apostle Paul wrote to—and I was number eight, Alice. I was born on November 29, 1913, at 2320 Papin Street in St. Louis. I am the only one of the children in our family who is left now."*

—Alice Okrafo-Smart

Some African American leaders, including Homer G. Phillips, had heard enough. They met at the Booker T. Washington Theater in midtown St. Louis and agreed that not only did Black patients need better care, but Black physicians and nurses also needed training. A petition they presented to city officials was unsuccessful, but they persisted, aided by persuasive voices from the local chapter of the NAACP. In 1918, Mayor Henry Kiel—keenly aware that Blacks formed a powerful voting bloc—agreed to establish a separate Black hospital, if he could find the money. Unexpectedly, a clerk in the city comptroller's office, Julius Weil, became an ally, turning up $165,000 in unused funds.

In 1918, Kiel and the Board of Aldermen decided to move forward with plans for the new hospital. For $62,000 they purchased the recently vacated Barnes Medical College at Garrison and Lawton, along with its associated Centenary Hospital, and lightly renovated them for $33,000.[4] This college was not, as some assume, the predecessor to Barnes Hospital on Kingshighway; rather, it was a proprietary school, founded by two white physicians, and named "Barnes" because they hoped to persuade the executors of the vast Robert Barnes estate to give his money to them. The ploy didn't work, and the school foundered; the nail in its coffin was the 1910 Abraham Flexner report on American medical schools, which blasted the shabby, poorly run place. By 1918, it was out of business.

The new City Hospital #2 was dedicated on November 16, 1919, at a ceremony attended by a large crowd, including Mayor Kiel. The six-floor facility, which could accommodate 200 patients, has "all

Fig. 2.2: In 1919, City Hospital #2, a shabby hospital for 200 Black patients, was established in the old Barnes Medical College building at 2945 Lawton Blvd. Its equipment was faulty and often dangerous. Courtesy of the Bernard Becker Medical Library Archives, Washington University in St. Louis.

the modern appointments," said one news story, cheerfully, "and an adequate staff has been engaged. Negro nurses for the institution have just completed a six-months' course at the city hospital." The first superintendent was Dr. Roscoe D. Haskell, a Sumner High School and Meharry Medical College graduate, who was also the "first Negro interne at the Kansas City Hospital six years ago"; his salary was "150 and keep."[5] All nurses, except head nurses, would be Black; a nurses' training school would accept young women with a high school education.

The situation for Black doctors remained galling. The attending staff at the hospital was divided into three services: physicians from Washington University School of Medicine, others from Saint Louis University, and some independent doctors. Not a single Black physician was on any of these services; those who wished to practice could apply for one of 24 associate staff member slots. Two white residents granted admitting privileges to these doctors, many years their senior, under the direction of the white visiting staff. Still, some well-known Black physicians—Drs. W. B. Christian, A. N. Vaughn, and E. T. Taylor among them—swallowed their pride and offered to serve as associate staff.

> *"Sammy Jr. died when he was 13. It was the Fourth of July and he was playing with those little cap guns, and one of them burned his hand. My father took him to see some doctor across the bridge, who gave my father a mason jar full of gray fluid and said to soak my brother's hand in it. But he died of tetanus. Grandma told us they had kept Sammy at the hospital. 'Where is he?' I asked. She said, 'He's in the morgue.' 'Well, what's a morgue?' 'It's like an icebox.' So, my prayer was that he was going to get cold and wake up and come home."*
>
> —Alice Okrafo-Smart

At long last, the new City Hospital #2 had a place for Black trainees, eleven in all: two residents, one each in surgery and internal medicine; a senior intern, who spent six months on surgery and six on internal medicine; and eight interns, who did six-week rotations throughout the hospital. The first four interns appointed were Drs. John Williams, Kelly Robinson, Henry Owens, and Charles Humbert, who later became assistant superintendent.[6] Despite the hospital's many shortcomings, these slots were highly coveted, because so few were available nationwide. An article in the *Argus* described their critical importance to trainees, who would soon be required by law to have advanced training:

Prior to 1919, there were only three or four standardized hospitals in the country whose doors were open to our men and accommodating only, at most, a total of 25 men yearly, while the schools were graduating a total of 70 to 75 men yearly. If the law now being adopted in several states had existed in every state, and it will be in the near future, it would mean that out of 75 graduates, only 25 or one-third a year would be eligible to practice medicine in this country. So you can readily see what an institution of this kind means to the medical profession of our race.[7]

The article added optimistically that these interns (then "internes") would have the chance to learn from "the highly trained, unbiased and unprejudiced physicians of the other race who have had years and years of experience." In fact, Black trainees at City Hospital #2 did take part in formal rounds, wrote Dr. Frank Richards, and they "did participate in surgical procedures; in fact, house officers were the principal surgeons in most cases," he said.[8] The surgical service at City Hospital #2 was an increasingly busy place. While 267 operations took place there in 1920, that number climbed to 802 ten years later.

Along with operating rooms, the remodeled hospital had other features, including a kitchen, small third-floor laboratory, social service program, and an X-ray room, with "all the most up-to-date outfit."[9] Each year, a Black trainee was appointed the "Radiologist Helper," and he learned to operate the X-ray machine. Over time, a number of prominent Black radiologists emerged from this program, notably Dr. William E. Allen Jr., a pioneer in the field, who served his internship at City Hospital #2 and then returned for his four-year residency after military service. His mentor was a white physician, Dr. Leroy Sante, the chief radiologist at City Hospital and then Saint Louis University. Coincidentally, both Drs. Sante and Allen would later receive gold medals from the American College of Radiology for their distinguished service to the field.

Newspaper accounts show that the hospital was busy right away. Some 150 patients were transferred there from the segregated wards at City Hospital #1, and new patients quickly began arriving. One group of Black workers was rushed to the hospital when a freight elevator gave way and plunged to the ground. Asians were also admitted. In 1921, a Chinese businessman, who was staying in a downtown neighborhood then known as "Hop Alley," was robbed and beaten, then taken to City Hospital #2 in critical condition with a possible skull fracture.

*"Why did I want to be a nurse? There were two things. Years ago, if you had an insurance policy, Metropolitan Life nurses would come to your house and help take care of the babies. I was fascinated by that. Mamma would clear off the kitchen table—everything was done in the kitchen, you know—so we could see it all. They wore those navy-blue uniforms with white cuffs, the navy-blue coats, and they had that black bag. I also remember when I had my tonsils taken out at Barnes Hospital. The nurses would say, 'Now, Alice, open your mouth. Say AHH!' I loved those starched dresses. Today, people don't use the sodium carbonate they cleaned the floors with then. Hospitals don't smell like that anymore, but they had a special odor, and I just loved those odors."*

—Alice Okrafo-Smart

After the hospital's nursing school opened in 1919 under the supervision of a strong-minded white administrator, Gertrude Martin, nursing students began arriving for the three-year program. It could accommodate 30 students from 20 to 35 years old, and the requirements for admission included a high school diploma, as well as a good moral character. The first five students, who graduated in 1922, were: Beatrice Hinch; Bessie Newsome [Cole], who later worked for the Visiting Nurses Association; Agnes Smith; Nellie E. Steele [Mischeaux], who was on the Homer G. Phillips Hospital staff; and Beatrice Wilkerson. One even passed the State Board Examination with the exceptional score of 90.5 percent.[10] While staff nurses received $50 a month, first-year student nurses got $9 a month, plus room and board.

A 1921 *Argus* story lavishly praised the qualities of nurses and predicted that the new City Hospital #2 nursing program would have an even greater impact on the nursing profession than the residency program did on medicine. "There have been very few approved training schools where 'Angels of Mercy' of our race could be trained . . ." it said. "Not only are there more and larger hospitals in existence which require a larger number of nurses, but the people themselves, rich and poor alike, have to come to realize

Fig. 2.3: This group portrait from 1919 shows the first entering class of nurses at the City Hospital #2 School of Nursing. Seated, left to right: Beatrice Hinch and Agnes Geneva Smith; standing, left to right: Nellie Steele (Mischeaux), Bessie Carolyn Newsome (Cole), and Beatrice Agnes Wilkerson (Walton). Courtesy of the Bernard Becker Medical Library Archives, Washington University in St. Louis.

that in a case of illness, the doctor needs the assistance of an intelligent, efficient and highly trained nurse to carry the patient thru to recovery and health."

Still, the early days of this hospital did not go smoothly. In May 1919, months before City Hospital #2 opened, the *Argus* reported that three "colored nurses," hired to study the methods at City Hospital #1 so they could join the City Hospital #2 staff, had already resigned in disgust. These able, experienced women—one a nursing graduate of Freedman's Hospital in Washington, D.C, another of Kansas City General Hospital, and a third of Provident (later People's) Hospital in St. Louis—charged "that the conditions under which they were compelled to work were unbearable and humiliating. They claim that no place was provided for them to spend their rest hours; that they had to eat in the diet kitchen, and that they were placed under the supervision of student nurses. One of the young ladies states she entered to be in the surgical department but had only been permitted to wash and make up beds and serve trays."[11] One nurse who did not quit was Ophelia Clark, later a well-known housemother and nursing staff member at Homer G. Phillips.

Another graduate was even more illustrious: Estelle Massey Riddle, a Texas-born teacher who decided to change professions and join the class of 1923 in the City Hospital #2 nursing school. After graduating, she was a head nurse at the hospital; then she became the first Black nurse to receive a scholarship from the Julius Rosenwald Fund, a philanthropic fund aimed at advancing the education of Black students. Later, she worked as a researcher for the Rosenwald Fund before returning to Homer G. Phillips as its first Black director of nursing.

> *"Papa was a messenger at Mercantile-Commerce Bank, Locust and 8th streets, but he died when I was about ten of double pneumonia. They didn't have antibiotics back then, you know. So Mamma started working as a housekeeper for a private family, the Roaches, around 58th and Clemens. They couldn't take in all eight of us. Mamma tried to get a housekeeper to come to our house, but the housekeeper was busier than Mamma was, so she sent the five smallest children out to Webster Groves, where my grandmother lived. Since my sister and I were ready for high school, she kept us in the city to go to Sumner, where she and Papa had gone. Mamma had Thursdays off and half day on Sundays, and she went out to Webster Groves then to see her children."*
>
> —Alice Okrafo-Smart

Whatever improvements the city had made when it acquired the old Barnes Medical College, they were not enough. Almost as soon as it opened, newspaper articles began describing City Hospital #2 as dingy and outmoded. It was also routinely overcrowded. In 1920, a survey conducted by the Health Department and Red Cross showed that City Hospital #2 was already caring for more patients than it could officially handle.[12] The next year, the hospital's lone elevator was out of service for five weeks, forcing staff members to carry surgical patients on stretchers from the basement X-ray department up a narrow staircase to the fifth-floor operating rooms.

Some city leaders publicly expressed their disgust at such conditions. Hospital Commissioner German A. Jordan called the building "old and combustible and altogether unsafe for use above the ground floor," adding that a fire could lead to "loss of life among aged and infirm negroes crowded in the basement and on the first floor."[13] A 1923 inquiry by the *Star and Times* echoed these charges:

> In City Hospital No. 2, five people to one room is the rule, and many of the rooms have no outside ventilation; dozens of patients sleep in the public corridors; the building is a ramshackle firetrap. The hospital is kept clean, but were it not for the constant work of the staff, conditions would be worse than in any county almshouse . . .[14]

To scholars of Black hospitals, none of this was surprising. What had happened at City Hospital #2—the reuse of a shabby building, discarded by whites, as a Black institution—was an old, familiar story, wrote Dr. W. Montague Cobb, Howard University medical professor, in a 1947 article. In denying "adequate hospital facilities to Negro patients and physicians," he said, "our segregated social system has achieved some of its most vicious effects." For white leaders, creating a "second-hand hospital" solves several pressing issues. "(1) It disposes of the real estate problem. (2) It provides Negroes with what appears to be better than they have. (3) It appeases the white conscience with the 'do-good' activity involved. (4) From the white point of view, although the problem is not settled . . . it is quieted for a while . . ."[15]

*"As children, we thought we were rich. We had plenty of food. Mamma made homemade bread every Saturday, four or five loaves to last the week. There was a butcher around Delmar and Hamilton who told Mamma that if she only traded with him, he would give her everything he couldn't carry over. We had wooden chip baskets with bale handles, and Mamma, Laodecia, and I each took two or three of them to get the food. I think my sister realized what we* didn't *have more than I did, because when we got on the streetcar, she would go to the back. She didn't want to be a part of us. In Webster Groves, my brothers would meet us down at the car line with their little wagons and carry up all the food."*

—Alice Okrafo-Smart

City Hospital #2 quickly became so congested that some patients were transferred to a private Black hospital, People's Hospital at 2221 Locust—though the city had to pay a daily charge for the service. Founded as "Provident Hospital" in 1894 and renamed in 1918, it was a far better institution than City Hospital #2 but not designed for a mass influx of the poor, since it was only three stories high with 75 beds. From the start, the staff was integrated, though mostly Black.[16]

Fig. 2.4: A private hospital at 2221 Locust that treated Black patients, People's Hospital was established as Provident Hospital in 1894. It was renamed in 1918 and closed in 1967. Photo by David Schultz, 1993. Courtesy of the Missouri Historical Society, St. Louis.

Soon, Homer G. Phillips and the 17-member committee that had once prodded the city into creating City Hospital #2 reconvened to get rid of it. Mayor Kiel, who had relied on electoral support from the Black community, agreed to include $1 million for a new Black hospital in his $87 million bond issue. Public support mounted to back the measure; Paul V. Bunn, general secretary of the Chamber of Commerce, dared anyone who doubted that City Hospital #2 and the city sanitarium needed replacing "to go visit the places. It is too easy to say, 'It's foolish,' vote the item down, kill a few hundred human beings who might be saved and then maybe contribute $10,000 spectacularly to some project that we could jolly well get along without," he wrote scaldingly.[17]

But the *Argus* was openly skeptical about other measures in this bond issue, worrying that some projects might hurt the Black community. What would happen to people whose modest apartments were taken for improvement efforts, especially in downtown St. Louis? Rents were already high, and housing was scarce. "Everything is not gold that glitters," warned an editorial. "The Negroes have more to lose if this Bond issue passes than any other group."[18]

Still, in 1923, 20 of the 21 items in the bond issue passed, including approval for the new hospital. Black voters supported the measure by a margin of more than four to one.[19] Banner headlines in the *St. Louis Post-Dispatch* announced the result: "$87,000,000 BOND ISSUE CARRIED BY BIG MAJORITIES: TRANSFORMATION OF THE CITY SOON TO BEGIN."

> *"Mamma lost her house, and she had to move to Grandma's house with all seven of her children. Grandma did not have central plumbing; we had two cisterns, as well as an outdoor toilet. We also used kerosene lamps. At that time, they could have afforded electricity, but Grandma was so afraid of fire that she wouldn't let them wire the house. So those lamps were part of our morning ritual; whoever did the morning dishes also had to clean the soot out of the kerosene lamps."*
>
> —Alice Okrafo-Smart

Supporters of the new Black hospital must have felt their excitement ebb as months passed by with no progress. Some city officials, regretting their earlier largesse, wanted to chip away at the bond issue money for their pet projects. So, the cramped, underfunded work of City Hospital #2 continued as Black leaders, especially attorney Homer G. Phillips, fought to preserve the hospital nest egg. Still, the total funds available did grow by $200,000 thanks to an appropriation from the Board of Aldermen, urged on by board president Louis P. Aloe, who was hoping to become mayor.

Around the country, other Black leaders engaged in similar fights, as a national movement to build Black hospitals gained momentum. Among the earliest were Provident Hospital in Chicago (1891) and Tuskegee Hospital in Alabama (1892), both with affiliated nurses' training programs. Through the first few decades of the twentieth century, the number of Black hospitals continued to climb as Black communities found their political voice: confronting racism, providing for their members, creating a place where talented Black physicians could become fully trained in the extraordinary medical advances then taking place, and providing excellent programs in which Black students could become nurses.[20]

In August 1923, the National Medical Association (NMA)—an organization of Black physicians, surgeons, dentists, and pharmacists founded in 1895—decided to create its own monitoring group to ensure that the quality of these new Black hospitals was high enough to impress white-run accrediting boards. During a "large and enthusiastic" meeting held in St. Louis at the YMCA auditorium on Pine Street, the NMA voted to form the National Hospital Association (NHA) as an affiliate group, and immediately 35 Black hospitals across the country signed up for its advice. Prominent Black St. Louis physicians Dr. A. N. Vaughn and Dr. W. P. Curtis— who had written the damning indictment of City Hospital #1's Black wards—gave addresses at the meeting as did Max Starkloff, the white health commissioner.[21]

*"I graduated from high school in 1931, but I did not go to nursing school until 1935. Until then, I did housework, and each payday I gave Mamma half of what I made. I got five dollars a week, so I gave Mamma two dollars and a half. A hairdo was fifty cents, and I'd get my hair done every other week. With another fifty cents, I would treat the family to hamburgers, and I also had to pay my tithe at church. I tried to buy some stockings and underwear to last me for the three years in training, because I knew there would be no money. You know, I never could save up the whole $75 I needed for*

*nursing school. To get to my job, I would pass by the Red Cross Office, and I decided to see whether they could help me out with a loan. They didn't tell me yes, but they didn't tell me no. I just kept going back and worrying them—but you know, they paid the $75, and they didn't charge me any interest. I paid them back the $75 after I started working."*
—Alice Okrafo-Smart

Where to locate this new hospital? The bond issue had included frustratingly vague language, calling only for "construction of additions to and extensions" to the existing hospitals. But did this mean a new building next door to City Hospital #1? That would allow some economies of scale, since the hospitals could share supplies. Harry Salisbury, the city's public welfare director, pointed out that this location could also give the new hospital "the use of extensive laboratory equipment at the City Hospital, especially the new radiology department, as well as cut down expenses by use of the same heating, laundry, and similar necessities."[22]

But others, especially a highly suspicious Homer G. Phillips, declared that this proximity might be disastrous for Black staff members: perpetuating the current staff arrangement and once again relegating them to second-class status. He took the bond issue wording to mean a Black hospital, staffed by Black professionals, located at a distance from City Hospital #1. Murmurs circulated briefly about one spot at Grand and Laclede, site of a ballpark, and then—more strongly—about another in the very heart of the Ville.

White and Blacks lined up on both sides of this question. As early as 1921, a group of white physicians, headed by St. Louis Children's Hospital pediatrician Borden Veeder, surveyed the local hospital scene and reported that a separate Black hospital would be "a waste of the hospital fund." Instead, wrote Veeder, "if it had been necessary to obtain more wards for negroes, this should have been done by adding to the present city hospital and not by duplicating administrative and operative expense."

Whites were not the only ones who harbored reservations about this proposal. Early in 1925, 50 angry Black residents who lived in the Ville near the planned site of the hospital paid a visit to the mayor. They told him that they feared losing their homes to the project, just at a time when their young children needed to live near good schools. Further, "many of the residents were getting old and had settled down in their little homes, and . . . it would work a great hardship upon them if they must break up and be forced to buy in some other neighborhood."

But in March, the Board of Aldermen overrode these objections and fixed the site of the hospital in a block bounded by Whittier and Goode, Kennerly and St. Ferdinand. Just below this announcement was another: that two trainees at City Hospital #2 had resigned, desperately upset with the hospital's management. "Threats are being made by some to expose the whole thing unless conditions are changed at this hospital."[23]

> *"City Hospital #2 was very old, with wooden floors and all, so they started you out in housekeeping. Cleanliness was part of your training. You had to learn how to clean the linen shelves and the bedpans and all. You did that before you could touch a patient, you know. You were also going to classes like anatomy, sciences, medications, and the action of the medications. Another step was you went to the diet kitchen, learned how to cook the foods and make foods for the baby wards, make special diets for people with heart trouble or something of that sort. As students, we got very little training in the emergency room. You've got to be top notch for that, and you've really got to move."*
>
> —Alice Okrafo-Smart

Weary St. Louisans might have hoped that, after the aldermanic ruling, the hospital issue was at last settled. But in 1925, a new mayor entered the picture, and he was not only a staunch enemy of attorney Homer G. Phillips but also a bitter opponent of building a northside hospital. The Republican Victor Miller was "possessed of a pungent and often unbridled tongue, which made him a colorful and controversial political figure," said a 1955 obituary[24]; he was also accused of having connections to the Ku Klux Klan. A *St. Louis Argus* headline reported a stunning scene in downtown St.

Louis shortly after midnight on the day of Miller's election: "Burns Fiery Cross After Miller Wins: Emblem of the Ku Klux Klan Flares on City Hall Lawn Celebrating Miller's Victory, It is Said. A Crowd Tears It Down, Smashing It to Pieces."[25]

With Miller as mayor, the whole issue of a new Black hospital came roaring back to life, and the next four years turned into a cat-and-mouse game as Miller's team tried to derail plans for it, even as Phillips and his Citizens Committee worked to push them forward. Alarmingly, the administration presented a new ordinance to the aldermen that would repeal the previous ordinance and begin condemning property near City Hospital #1. In November, 50 Black leaders formed a committee to oppose such a move and, noted the *Argus*, "happily, the colored people themselves are almost unanimously opposed to the proposed change." The paper further condemned the mayor's move as "an act of bad faith," and hinted that he had "a sinister motive."[26]

In the very next month, Mayor Miller gave a rambling, evasive speech to the Baptist Ministers' Alliance in which he claimed to be a great friend to Blacks, though he added that "there has always been, there is now, and possibly forever will be a barrier between the white race and the Negro." He also claimed not to care where the hospital was placed but then talked at length about the savings that would result if it were located at City Hospital #1. Sneered the *Argus* headline: "Tells His Auditors They Are Poor and Helpless and Must Take What Is Given Them."[27]

That December, alderman August Niederluecke announced that his Public Welfare Committee was opposed to the administration's proposal to return to the City Hospital #1 site—and, in fact, the board voted 26 to 6 against it. But the matter continued to percolate. By the following March, the *Argus* was proposing a compromise site—the old Deaconess Hospital location at West Belle and Sarah—though Phillips scoffed at this proposal as an attempt by white real estate agents to unload yet another ramshackle facility on the Black community.

*"Each year in training, you'd gain more responsibilities, you know—say, the special surgeries, and that sort of thing. What*

*I really wanted was to be a public health nurse, because you
have to delve into all of it. I remember one lady whose leg
had been amputated halfway. I was supposed to help her with
her exercises and the like, to get her ready for her prosthesis.
I said, 'What are you interested in?' She said, 'I want to go
down to the basement because I have a kitchen there.' So, I
said, 'All right, we'll go down in the basement.' I taught her
how to go down on her fanny, and she was tickled to death."*
                                        —Alice Okrafo-Smart

In 1926, Phillips and his group suffered what seemed a fatal
blow. Julius T. Muench, city attorney, announced that no separate
Black hospital could be built given the language of the bond issue.
"Only an actual extension or addition may be erected with bond
funds," said one newspaper account of Muench's position.[28] But
the fight was not yet over. Harry Salisbury of the Public Welfare
Committee, urged on by Phillips and other Black leaders, decided
to consult a higher authority—Ben Charles, legal adviser to the
Bond Issue Committee—for an interpretation of the wording in
the bond issue.

At that point, they must have held their collective breath. In
August 1926, Charles and his committee came back with a stunning
reversal, backing Phillips and his group. The hospital could be built
in the Ville after all. The Public Welfare Committee concurred, and
the stubborn opposition of the administration seemed to melt away.
Salisbury and the Public Welfare staff ordered the legal department
to begin compiling the necessary paperwork for the move.

St. Louisans, Black and white, wondered whether the political
shillyshallying was finally over. But in 1927, Miller struck again,
asking the aldermen to resurrect the idea of an addition to City
Hospital #1. This time, the Public Welfare Committee invited an array of distinguished speakers, all favorable to a new Black hospital,
including former mayor Henry Kiel, who had included the hospital
funding in his 1923 bond issue; former aldermanic president Louis
Aloe, who had added $200,000 to the fund; and finally Homer G.
Phillips, who had not wavered in his insistence on an independent
hospital. The *Argus* reported acidly on Mayor Miller's persistent

wish to shortchange Blacks. "The Mayor has said in so many words, 'let them die' (speaking of the patients at City Hospital #2)." [29]

Again in 1928, Miller resurfaced, this time with a report by the Bureau of Municipal Research contending that the City Hospital #1 site would save around $250,000. But the *Argus* was having none of this "back to No. 1" or "two-in-one hospital" movement, as they called it. "The eternal question of COST is a pretty handy argument when the welfare of the Negroes of the city is involved," they sniffed, adding that the real underpinning of the city's position was a belief that "the Negro doctors and nurses were not competent . . . . Get busy, Mr. Director of Public Welfare, and build the Hospital No. 2 where the law prescribes." [30]

Still Miller stonewalled, refusing to release the bond-issue funds. "Probably he does not realize that life is dear even to Negroes . . ." raged the *Argus*, "and the lives of our dear ones, though they may be poor, are dear to us." [31] Sure, this new hospital will be segregated, the paper admitted. But whether it is "to be down at No. 1 or whether it is to be elsewhere, it will be a segregated affair. That being the case, it will be far better . . . to have the segregated away from the segregator because the very environment is hostile, dangerous and is likely to explode at any time."

> *"When the Depression began, we were all having a terrible time. We had sewing rooms, where the Civil Rights Administration workers and young people working for the National Youth made the gowns and all for the hospital. Some of the workers also assisted us in nursing care and in practical nursing. But they weren't sure how long the funding for the program might last. So, we had a laughing joke that one lady was giving a patient a bath, and she had his arm up like this when she got the notice and left the patient there, with his arm up."*
>
> —Alice Okrafo-Smart

Late in 1928, the mayor struck again with a plan to add a "colored unit" to the white hospital, but it was once more struck down by the aldermen, this time on a technicality. Then early in 1929, with a new mayoral election on the horizon, the *Argus* ran banner headlines: "CITIZENS WIN HOSPITAL LOCATION FIGHT: COMMITTEE VICTORIOUS." Miller, eager for the Black vote to help in his re-election, had apparently capitulated. Attorney George Vaughn, speaking on the mayor's behalf, assured the crowd that the necessary paperwork for the Ville site had already begun. But the doubtful crowd, fearing some kind of treachery, called for Homer G. Phillips to appear and give his opinion. When Phillips did so, he was guarded, saying that he "had no faith in death bed repentance."

Miller won re-election, but still nothing happened. The Citizens Committee briefly considered the old Poro College block as the hospital site, since they were concerned about legal trouble from the 100 or so homeowners whose homes would have to be demolished for the St. Ferdinand Street location. Meanwhile, the Great Depression began in 1929, draining life and work from weary St. Louisans, especially Black ones, and funding from civic projects.

At least one obstacle was removed in 1930 when the Chouteau-Lindell Improvement Association—a group of white residents living in an area next to the hospital's proposed Ville site—lost their suit to oppose its construction, though they vowed to appeal. The *Argus* noted caustically: "To make an appeal to the State Supreme Court means anywhere from one to three years delay with the hospital. It may be, however, that the members of the Chouteau-Lindell Improvement Association will get some satisfaction out of the hope that many of the Negro patients will die while the matter is being held up in the courts."[32]

*"We had plenty of patients, and it was important to give them an admission bath. That bath was not only to clean them up, but it was a chance for us to inspect their bodies: to see what had happened surgical-wise and that sort of thing. In those days, people had coal furnaces, so we often had to clean up their feet, and they were sometimes so dirty and corroded that we used special soap or even wrapped them up in a soap pack. One time, I forgot and left my patient in the soap pack all night. He had some nice clean feet in the morning!"*

—Alice Okrafo-Smart

Over at City Hospital #2, the situation was descending into chaos. Dr. Roscoe Haskell, the original superintendent, was dismissed in 1925 so his post could go to Dr. O. F. Perdue, a supporter of Mayor Miller. However, the *Argus* noted that Haskell may have deserved his firing. He was dominated by the officious white head nurse, Gertrude Martin, they said, and had summarily dismissed an intern who then filed suit against him, charging that Dr. Haskell was partial to interns from certain parts of the country.

Worse still, a series of investigations strongly condemned the ramshackle hospital building as a firetrap. "The present hospital is being operated with a capacity of 348 beds, although the space in a well-conducted institution would not care for half that number. So crowded is it that one great ward has been moved into the west section, a portion of the building which the city has already condemned," said the *Argus*.[33] The St. Louis Colored Undertakers Association complained bitterly about deplorable conditions in the hospital morgue.

Other articles described the shocking proximity of patients who should have been isolated from one another. The tubercular ward was adjacent to the maternity ward, filled with 30 expectant mothers; on the other side was a pediatric room with "little sick children, all of them exposed to the horrors of the white plague through inefficient ventilation." Since the elevator was so often out of order, staff members had to carry the dead down winding staircases in plain view of other patients. "The time has come when something must be done to relieve the terrible conditions with which the patients of this hospital are surrounded," thundered Homer G. Phillips.[34]

The staff also suffered, and one young Black intern even lost his life to defective, outdated equipment. Dr. Bernise A. Yancey, brother of Dr. Asa Yancey, later the medical director of Grady Memorial Hospital in Atlanta, came from a distinguished medical family. He had a superb education himself, with a medical degree from the University of Michigan. In August 1930, only two months into his internship, he was helping another intern perform an X-ray examination of a patient's chest when he touched an exposed high-tension wire overhead and died instantly. The coroner ruled it an accidental death.

By February 1931, condemnation of property on the 6.3-acre site at Whittier and Goode, St. Ferdinand and Cottage, had already begun. As a little girl, Mary Ellen Anderson learned that she would be leaving her home. "My mother, my father—Clarence Epstein Johnson—my two sisters, one brother, and I lived in the Ville at 4209 Cottage Avenue. It was the Depression, and my father was doing everything he could to keep working: he dabbled in real estate, sold newspapers, worked as a clerk in the state grain department, whatever. Then we had a notice, and I remember my mother reading it, that we had to move because they were going to take land around there for the hospital. It said 'as soon as possible' because they had to clear the land. Pretty soon, only one tree was left that we saw. But it was good to move because we had experienced no running water coming into our old house, and we didn't have toilet facilities."

That June, attorney Homer G. Phillips was murdered, and in November, the Board of Aldermen unanimously passed a bill giving his name to the new hospital, officially known as the "Homer G. Phillips Hospital for the Colored." Finally, work began to creep forward as construction began in August 1932, and the official groundbreaking took place in September with 200 people watching. Ironically, Mayor Miller turned over the first spade full of dirt.

In December 1933 came the cornerstone-laying, attended by 4,000 people. Dr. Oral McClellan, the latest superintendent of City Hospital #2, introduced the main speaker: Dr. Numa P. G. Adams, dean of the Howard University School of Medicine, who talked about the significance of the new hospital nationally. "I know the tragedies and disasters that must at times result from inadequate equipment, insufficient personnel, inaccessibility to necessary laboratory aids, and the lack of a medical library. . . . I wonder how many in this audience can appreciate what a blessing this hospital will be, and in how many important ways it will serve not only this community but also the whole country."

A newly elected, more sympathetic mayor, Bernard Dickmann, wielded a silver trowel to lay the cornerstone. And finally, a lone woman—Ida Perle Phillips, the widow of Homer G. Phillips—"was introduced to the audience and expressed her joy over the progress of the new hospital."[35]

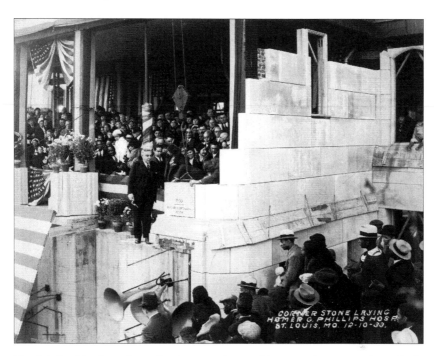

Fig. 2.5: In this photo from the *St. Louis Star and Times*, a large crowd watched as the cornerstone for the new Homer G. Phillips Hospital was laid on December 10, 1933. Photo by Richard Moore. Courtesy of the Missouri Historical Society, St. Louis.

## CHAPTER THREE

# "A Notable Advance in Negro Hospitalization"
## Homer G. Phillips Hospital, 1937–1940

*"The unselfishness, vision and dedication of that first small group of physicians and nurses at Homer G. Phillips Hospital made it possible for all the rest of us who followed. I don't think too much can be said about that, and to me that is the core of the Homer G. Phillips experience."*

—William L. Smiley, MD (1912–2005), trainee, staff member at Homer G. Phillips Hospital, head of obstetrics/gynecology, and one of the first two Black physicians to join the Washington University School of Medicine faculty. He did research studies at Homer G. Phillips, centering on female cancers.

ON THE BRISK morning of February 22, 1937, a parade of some 2,000 jubilant people—marching bands on foot and a 180-car motorcade—wound its way through the Ville to the front lawn of a majestic new building, the Homer G. Phillips Hospital for the Colored. On a platform festooned with flags and bunting sat a row of dignitaries invited to speak at the hospital's dedication ceremony. Alice Okrafo-Smart, then a nursing student, recalls dressing up for the gala. "We were in that parade, riding in ambulances," she said. "We had our uniforms on, and our capes and caps. The dress was blue-and-white-striped, with a white bib and apron. We were *something*."

As many as 10,000 people stopped by to take part in the festivities. They heard speeches by the governor, city officials, local ministers, medical deans from Washington and Saint Louis universities,

Fig. 3.1: A brilliant surgeon, Dr. William L. Smiley (1912–2005) trained at Homer G. Phillips Hospital and became head of obstetrics and gynecology there. He had the extraordinary ability to hold several instruments in readiness on his fingers. Photo ca. 1960s. Courtesy of Nina Smiley Wilkins.

and even a prominent Ville resident who had moved to Chicago in 1930: Annie Turnbo Malone, member of the planning committee for the event. Others on that committee came from the local Black elite, including politician Jordan Chambers, physicians A. N. Vaughn and W. P. Curtis, and attorney David Grant—along with another attorney, George Vaughn, bitter enemy of the hospital's murdered namesake, Homer G. Phillips.

Two eminent speakers, Edwin Embree and Dr. Midian O. Bousfield, who also had come from Chicago to attend, represented the remarkable Rosenwald Fund, a foundation established in 1917 by Sears president Julius Rosenwald to focus on the educational and health needs of Blacks. Soon, the fund would offer support to five Homer G. Phillips staff members: talented nursing graduate Estelle Massey Riddle, who had received a scholarship herself; and four promising physician trainees—ophthalmologist H. Phillip Venable, internist Jarone Johnson, psychiatrist H. J. Erwin, and surgeon William Smiley—being groomed to take over the leadership of their respective departments.

But more than all the others, it was a nationally prominent guest who captivated the audience. Harold L. Ickes, blunt-spoken Secretary of the Interior under President Franklin D. Roosevelt, a Democrat, praised the hospital as a necessity for patients. As census figures showed, Ickes said, among every 100,000 male Black newborns, some 4,000 fewer would survive their first year of life than their white counterparts. Furthermore, the hospital could help alleviate the shortage of Black doctors and nurses by providing many more opportunities for training than had previously existed. All in all, he said, this new institution would mark "a notable advance in Negro hospitalization—a field which has been sadly neglected in many sections of our country."

These views represented a historic shift in the political landscape that must have left some in the audience gasping. Dr. Bousfield, a noted Black physician devoted to eliminating health disparities in the Black community, said he was stunned by the recent work of Democrats on behalf of racial justice. "One of the 'impossible' things about this hospital is that the Democrats did it for us," he said, adding that Secretary Ickes "was one of the best friends of the Negro." This same party shift was also happening in St. Louis politics, where David Grant and George Vaughn had begun to lead a revolution, urging the solidly Republican Black electorate to change sides and vote Democratic.

Among the crowd at the dedication was a nine-year-old girl, Marion Meaux Smith (later Robinson), who had come with her grandfather—Fred Meaux, a postal carrier who lived on West Belle Place—to take part in the historic event. She still recalls the excitement of that day. "It was cold as anything," she said. "I remember that it had been muddy, and the ground had frozen, so it was lumpy. There was a parade, and I found out later that Jerome Williams, who became a physician at the hospital, had marched in it when he was 11 years old."

When the long speeches were over, said Mrs. Robinson, who later married an intern and resident at Homer G. Phillips, "we all went into the hospital to look it over, and we tracked in so much dirt that the newspapers said it cost $1,000 to clean it all up. To me, the hospital was big, just BIG. I really didn't understand much about it, but we walked around. Everyone was thrilled with the place."

*"My father was immensely proud of his affiliation with Homer G. Phillips Hospital, which was innovative, dynamic, and one of the best hospitals nationally for giving care to Black patients. His association with the hospital started when he was on his way to an internship at a Kansas City Hospital. He and a friend stopped off in St. Louis to see Homer G. Phillips, and he was so impressed that he decided to stay."*
—Nina Smiley Wilkins, daughter of Dr. William Smiley

In 1935, Victor Roberts and his parents had moved to a home at the corner of Whittier and Cote Brilliante just as demolition for the new hospital was taking place nearby. As many as 100 tidy homes quickly disappeared, "and some had been built recently. People didn't want to give them up, but they used a legal procedure to move them out," he said. Along with other neighborhood children, Roberts sneaked onto the construction site after hours. "They had all kinds of equipment, supplies and things, and we would play in the building as they developed it. We had fun over there. There were no lights, and we could play as much as we wanted."

The Art Deco-style hospital was designed by Albert A. Osburg, then chief architect for the city's Public Improvement Board. He was the genius behind a raft of elegant city buildings: five police stations, including the Third District station in Soulard; three community centers, among them the Tandy Community Center near the hospital; two market halls, Soulard and Biddle; hangars at Lambert Field; additions to several other hospitals; and the Missouri National Guard Armory on Market Street.

While it was certainly stylish, his design for this new hospital was also unusually sensitive to its residential context, noted the successful 1982 application to name Homer G. Phillips Hospital a national landmark. For one thing, the building was modest in height, which helped it blend in with its smaller neighbors. It was also created out of handsome earth-tone bricks and ornamented with intricate yellow terra cotta bands. At the top of the central section were ropes of terra cotta outlining the arched windows, and it was capped off by a fine red-tile roof.

Ideas for its interior layout came from a blue-ribbon committee of local experts working in concert with Dr. Oral S. McClellan, City Hospital #2 superintendent, as well as Dr. Henry Hampton, its medical director, and city health officials. The superintendents of Barnes, St. Luke's, Jewish, Missouri Baptist, and Shriner's hospitals—nearly all the major St. Louis hospitals—took part, as did the medical director of the Saint Louis University group of hospitals.

Fig. 3.2: This undated photo shows early trainees and staff in front of Homer G. Phillips Hospital. Courtesy of the Bernard Becker Medical Library Archives, Washington University in St. Louis.

"We would go down there after it had opened," recalled Roberts, "and walk around it, because some of the doctors there knew my dad, who was also a physician. So I had a chance to look through it. Everything was completely new, and it was really, really very nice. They did a great job with the architecture, and they had these wings—four different wings—with different types of services in each one."

*"As a nurse I had worked with Dr. Smiley many times, so he knew my capabilities. Then one day he asked: 'Would you come and scrub with me? Let's do this case.' So, I sat across the OR table from him during a hysterectomy, and instead of another doctor, there was me. I learned how to perfect my suturing, which nurses didn't do at that time. Dr. Smiley worked fast and was all business; he was also a one-man band, and he put most of his instruments—like scissors and a retractor—on his fingers. During surgery, he would sing to relax; we didn't do much talking. Afterwards, he said: 'Anytime you want a case done, Mrs. Thornton can do it.'"*

—Dorothy Payne Thornton, surgical nurse

The hospital was actually a five-building campus. One piece was the service building, containing the power plant, paint and carpentry shops, laundry, sewing room, and hospital cafeteria. A second was the administration building, with offices, laboratories, operating rooms, and an X-ray facility outfitted with equipment worth $35,000. A third was the five-story nurses' home at 2516 Goode Avenue, connected to the hospital by a tunnel, with dormitory space for 147 nurses plus 14 faculty; in an adjoining annex were quarters for 24 interns and residents plus apartments for the supervisor and medical director. The final two pieces, to the north and south of the administrative core, were the four wings of the hospital—685 rooms in all—where much of the work with patients took place.

But the construction of this splendid building had very nearly not happened at all, as Republican mayor Victor Miller did all he could to derail or diminish it. In the end, it was Mayor Bernard

F. Dickmann, a Democrat elected in 1933 with the help of Black voters, whose energetic support at last brought it to fruition. It was vastly overbudget, costing $3.16 million, almost triple the $1.2 million originally planned. A $625,000 federal grant—a reward from Ickes and Roosevelt for the city's Democratic shift—had helped to make up the difference. So had $845,000 no longer needed for a piece of the Municipal Bridge project and released through a special 1933 referendum, plus another $180,000 from a second bond issue in 1934.

During construction, a number of problems arose, including a protest over the lack of Black construction workers on the project. In 1933, government figures showed that 80 percent of Blacks in St. Louis were unemployed or underemployed and sorely needed work. Still, when skilled Black workers, some of them bearing union cards—20 plasterers, 31 carpenters, 35 electricians, and 44 painters—applied to take part in the Homer G. Phillips construction, the city refused to hire them.[1]

Thus, it had been a hard-fought battle, but by the end Dickmann felt triumphant; in fact, he called the hospital's dedication "one of the happiest moments of my administration." Others agreed. Homer G. Phillips was the "World's Finest Negro Hospital," boasted a *St. Louis Star-Times* headline. An *Argus* editorial added that it would "mean the preservation of life—sweet life, for the group of citizens who have suffered, lo, these many years, because of the lack of proper hospitalization." Staff and patients believed that all the accolades were well deserved. "It was an iconic building designed by a prominent architect," said Dr. Earle U. Robinson Jr., "and such a spectacular building sitting in the middle of a Black oasis."

*"My father and Dr. Smiley were in the first class of interns at Homer G. Phillips Hospital, and when I was a resident, Dr. Smiley was director of OB-GYN. He was very tough, but he was a spectacular surgeon, one of the best I've ever seen. Number one, he was very decisive. He never made purposeless movements. He used instruments like he was in an orchestra. What Dr. Smiley told interns was, 'There's no way you can learn OB by being on call every third or fourth night. If you're*

*on call every night, you'll get a chance to be exposed to maybe*
*200 or 300 deliveries a week.' So that was his concept. He*
*said, 'We will give you a half day off a week to take care of*
*personal things and get a haircut.'"*

—Dr. Earle U. Robinson Jr., MD, an intern and then a
surgeon, son of early intern Dr. Earle U. Robinson Sr.

Patients packed into the old City Hospital #2 must have been
eager to transfer to the new building, since their crumbling, 200-
bed hospital was admitting some 320 patients a day. Two days
before the Homer G. Phillips Hospital dedication, City Hospital #2
was damaged in a windstorm, said one newspaper, "which caused
Mayor Dickmann to remark significantly. . . . 'It looks like moving
day.'"[2] Still, the transfer of patients could not begin until all was in
readiness.

Meanwhile, City Hospital #2 had been shifting some of its overflow to People's Hospital and a newer private Black hospital: St.
Mary's Infirmary on Papin Street, which had opened in 1933 under
the Sisters of St. Mary's Benevolent Order. St. Mary's, affiliated
with Saint Louis University, was also a groundbreaking institution,
one "devoted to the care of the Negroes, in charge of Negro physicians and under the auspices of a white Sisterhood," read a story
in the *St. Louis Globe-Democrat*.[3] In another article, City Hospital
#2 superintendent McClellan said the city was paying a breathtak-
ing $98,500 a year to care for surplus patients at St. Mary's and
People's hospitals.[4]

At Homer G. Phillips, the staff was busy setting up the needed
equipment, floor by floor. In the basement was the morgue and
a laundry room, and on the first floor (1 North) was male medicine. Female medicine was on 2 North and psychiatry on 2 South;
gynecology on 3 South and male surgery on 3 North; obstetrics,
including labor/delivery and newborns, was on 4 South, and female
surgery on 4 North. Pediatrics was on 5 South, while ear, nose and
throat (ENT) plus orthopedics was on 5 North. The sixth floor
served as overflow space for medical trainees, and it had amenities
for their off hours, such as a large pool table.

Taking their cue from the hectic emergency department at City Hospital #2, the planners of the new hospital allotted ample space for the Emergency Department or Receiving Room, which occupied most of the Administration Building's basement. In it were two well-equipped emergency suites, plus a room for contagious diseases and poisonings; male and female diagnostic rooms; and tub rooms in which patients could take a pre-admission bath. Four doctors, assisted by interns and nurses, would be there around the clock on different shifts.

Finally, on June 1, 302 Black patients left the overcrowded firetrap they had tolerated for so long—the most seriously ill in ambulances, the less sick in buses, private cars, or patrol wagons—and entered the gleaming, spotlessly clean Homer G. Phillips Hospital. Later in the week, 30 others came from People's and 75 from St. Mary's.[5] Like a proud father, Mayor Dickmann stood by, overseeing the move. In years to come, the old City Hospital #2 building would become a bedraggled hotel for Black transients and then a warehouse. It was finally razed in 1948.

*"Dr. Smiley had hands like Michelangelo, you know. Great hands. I personally saw him operate with his right and left hand. Matter of fact, there's a procedure, where the baby is in the transverse position, and you got to turn that baby around to deliver it. Now they do C-sections automatically, but the obstetrician then would put on long gloves, put his hand into the uterus, and turn that baby around. I tell you that Dr. Smiley was one of the few people who was able to do it successfully. So, he's known for that, and for just being a tremendous clinician."*

—Dr. Lee Blount, surgeon

The public wasted no time filling the iron beds, made up with sheets that had tightly mitered corners. Newspaper accounts describe the early Black patients: a young man, shot in the elbow by detectives after stealing car radios; cases of encephalitis from the recent epidemic; a woman who fell off a truck while celebrating

Joe Louis's boxing victory; a man stabbed in a bar fight; an abusive father hit in the head with a baseball bat by his teenage son; a laborer shot in the neck during a scuffle; a telephone operator who swallowed acid in a suicide attempt.

But they quickly discovered that the city had neglected to let one contract: for much-needed window screens on the hospital's 2,200 windows. So, in the brutal heat of a St. Louis summer, patients and staff in this brand-new hospital—which had no air-conditioning—had to suffer the assault of insects. Kitchen staff tacked gauze over their window openings, but on the wards, said one account, "patients complained of being annoyed by flies."

Dr. Henry Hampton, who was appointed City Hospital #2's first medical director in 1937 and continued in the same job at the new hospital, worked to secure its accreditation. A successful surgeon in his own right, Dr. Hampton "had gentlemanliness written all over him," recalled Dr. James Whittico, "yet even though he was soft-spoken, he was very definite. I respected him greatly." His efforts ended successfully in October when the American Council of Medical Education and the American College of Surgeons named Homer G. Phillips a "Class A" hospital. "This is the first time . . . that full, unconditional approval has been given," announced an elated Dr. Hampton.

From the start, money was tight. "In the early history of the institution, the budget was very limited; however, the hospital was run fairly well despite this handicap, and the patients received good care," wrote Dr. William Sinkler, a surgeon.[6] At the time of the dedication, the hospital employed 500 people with a budgeted salary total of only $367,000. A welcome money-saver during the waning years of the Great Depression was the presence of federally supported Works Progress Administration and National Youth Administration staff members to help as clerks, occupational therapists, attendants, porters, dietary workers, and laundry workers.

*"Dr. Smiley became the head of the OB-GYN department at Homer G. Phillips Hospital, and he was also the first Black physician on the staff of Maternity Hospital here. He was a wizard. He held two instruments in one hand at the same time, so he*

*would have a second one ready for use. If he had a bleeder, for example, he would set down his scissors or scalpel and flip up his clamp to use it. That shows what an able and agile surgeon he was. All of us who saw him said, 'Wow, isn't that slick!'"*
                    —Dr. Jerry Middleton, Obstetrician/Gynecologist

Right away, the energetic staff began conjuring up enhancements to the program. Dr. Hampton advanced community education by hosting a series of medical lectures. He himself gave the first one: "a brilliant discussion of Cancer and Tumors," said the *Argus*, ". . . simple and informative and addressed to a widely variant audience."[7] Dr. James Nofles, though a resident physician, discussed ear, nose, and throat diseases "with all the dignity and poise of a seasoned specialist," while pathologist Dr. J. Owen Blache talked about venereal disease.

Dr. Blache, a resident in pathology at City Hospital #2 in 1934 who became chief of pathology at Homer G. Phillips in 1937, also decided to launch a new program: a School of Laboratory Technology, affiliated with Xavier University in New Orleans and Tougaloo College in Mississippi. Eventually, more than 60 students completed the program. Personally, he also made another kind of affiliation. Like other physicians who wed nurses at the hospital, he married a City Hospital #2 nursing graduate from the class of 1938.

Within two years of its opening, the hospital hosted two prominent conferences: the inaugural meeting of the Medical Institute for Physicians, a much-heralded event that included more than 100 Black physicians from across the country; and a national conference of hospital administrators that featured several of the hospital's old friends: Dr. Numa Adams, Dr. M. O. Bousfield, and Estelle Massey Riddle, now president of the National Association of Colored Graduate Nurses.

In 1939, Dr. Hampton opened a blood bank in refrigerators only 30 steps from the operating rooms, said an article, which called this addition "the latest of the ultramodern facilities added to the equipment of the new city hospital for Negroes."[8] With an eye to economy, Dr. Hampton cleverly reused glass jars and pumps from blood pressure devices, so that the cost of the new bank—the only one in the St. Louis area—was just $50. Within the first three months of its existence, the bank supplied blood for 110 transfusions.

Recognizing that cancer was an increasing problem, the hospital staff set up a Tumor Service in 1938 so that various specialties, along with radiology and pathology, could collaborate on diagnosis and treatment. Six years later, the service reported that, in one year's time, it had given nearly 1,200 X-ray treatments. That same year, it developed a department of physiotherapy for patients who had undergone orthopedic surgery.

In 1937, they also added a popular dental department, with a staff that included WPA dentists. "With such rapid growth manifested in the department," said one history, "in 1942 the Medical Director began plans to set up the department for the training of dental internes . . . and in July, the Dental Service accepted its first intern, Dr. G. R. Lewis of Meharry Dental School."

*"I was the charge nurse on labor and delivery one day when a pregnant woman in her 30s came in, semi-conscious. We put her in a small room and began monitoring her vital signs. But I didn't get any blood pressure, and then I used a stethoscope to check her heart. I turned to Dr. Smiley and said there was no heartbeat. At Homer G. Phillips, we were trained to be level-headed in a crisis, and Dr. Smiley was phenomenal—he didn't hesitate at all. He said, 'Get me a knife,' so somebody ran for a surgery kit and took a knife out of it. Right away, he cut a live baby out. Then he put the woman, who had died from a brain aneurysm, on life support for a couple of hours to give the family a little time to adjust. He said, 'They are not quite ready yet.'"*

—Zenobia Thompson, 1965 Homer G. Phillips nursing graduate

Mayor Dickmann had promised that the hospital's medical practice would be dominated by Black staff members, who would provide teaching without charge.[9] Experienced Black physicians and surgeons stepped in to do just that. Nearly all of them were also members of the active Mound City Medical Forum, a group founded in 1920 to advance the learning of Black physicians. The forum often invited specialists from Homer G. Phillips to speak at its meetings.

"We had a slew of outstanding Black physicians and surgeons at Homer Phillips," said Dr. Frank Richards, "including Dr. William Sinkler, probably the biggest influence during my training; Dr. A. N. Vaughn; Dr. J. J. Thomas; and Dr. Hampton." Among the earliest group, Dr. Vaughn often made the newspapers as a trailblazer: chief of staff for St. Mary's Infirmary in 1936; the first Black man appointed to the board of the St. Louis Community Chest; president in 1941 of the National Medical Association; board member of the Urban League of St. Louis; and a new member of the Saint Louis University medical faculty in 1946.

Thus, the hospital had a solid core of attending staff, but how to administer the various departments? Father Alphonse Schwittala, dean of the Saint Louis University School of Medicine, began working on a plan with the Mound City Medical Forum. They wanted to train Black physicians to take leadership positions in the various specialties, but until that training was complete, staff members from Saint Louis and Washington universities would serve as department chiefs. His own faculty, under surgeon Dr. John W. Stewart, chief of staff, would take the first two-year period; in June 1939, they planned to develop a new arrangement, probably with Washington University taking the lead.

Both Black and white physicians presided over a rigorous program to train the next generation of Black doctors. Incoming trainees, fresh out of medical school, would become junior interns and rotate through the medical services—medicine, pediatrics, surgery, obstetrics, anesthesia, neurology, and others—examining all patients admitted to the wards. After a year, some became senior interns and again rotated through the services to decide on an area of specialty. In the following year, some senior interns would be promoted to assistant residents, and in another year, selected assistant residents would become residents themselves.

This program was different from others, recall some trainees. "It was one of the few hospitals that had a training program and a large enough patient population so that we could get the kind of varied experience we needed," said Dr. George Simpson, then an intern. At Meharry, where he had been a medical student, the training was "like going to medical school twice because you got exposure again to histology, embryology, pathology, and physiology. In the program at Homer G. Phillips, you didn't get that—only what the attendings passed on to you. I wanted that."

"It was a teaching place that taught me more medicine than I could get anyplace else, because I was around people who cared about my learning and guided me to have certain standards of how to treat people," said Dr. Earle Robinson. "I was also exposed to a population that was underserved, and I had the ability to provide that service."

*"The Homer G. Phillips physician I knew the best was William Smiley. I always referred to him as 'Dr. Smiley'; I never called him Bill or William, because that would have seemed inappropriate. In 1978, I worked with him on a project, applying for a grant from the Robert Wood Johnson Foundation to convert public health clinics into primary care clinics. He reminded me of what you might call a Southern gentleman: gracious, polite, and dignified, yet also outgoing and engaged—just a wonderful person. I think he contributed quite a bit to OB-GYN at Homer G. Phillips Hospital, but he could also see a bigger picture, and how he could be of benefit to the city, his community, and the community at large."*

—Dr. Clifford Birge, endocrinologist

At its 1937 opening, the hospital had a 76-member house staff, including 32 junior interns. But administrators became alarmed in 1938 when the hospital attracted less than half its intern quota, said the *Argus*, so Mayor Dickmann supplied some quiet funding that allowed Dr. McClellan, the superintendent, "to make a good-will tour of Howard University Medical School and Meharry Medical Center, which furnish 95 per cent of all the Negro internes in the United States." Before his visit, Dr. McClellan checked with

Dickmann and his staff to make sure that women recruits would be acceptable.

His efforts worked. "As a result, the Homer Phillips Hospital has 20 internes this year," continued the *Argus*, "among them three women, the first women internes ever taken in a local municipal hospital." Two of them—Dr. Doris Sanders Moore of Houston and Dr. Maude Sanders of New Orleans—were Meharry graduates, while the third, Dr. Muriel Petoni of New York City, came from Howard. At the time, said the article, there were only 42 Black women doctors in the United States. Dr. Hampton said he was delighted and "in hearty accord with Dr. McClellan's farsightedness" in extending admission to these women.[10]

By 1939, the house staff had grown, and the hospital was accepting half the Black medical graduates in the United States.[11] They had also begun to reach outside the United States for trainees. Their first class of interns in 1937–38 included one student, Dr. E. E. Fuller, from the University of Hamburg in Germany, and Dr. L. A. Smart from McGill University in Montreal, Canada.

Staff in other positions around the hospital also came on board. "My husband John had gotten a B.S. degree in chemistry from a university in Denver, where he grew up," said Mary Ellen Anderson. "His father was deputy sheriff—a white man's job, because he was armed—and he traveled all over the country to bring back people

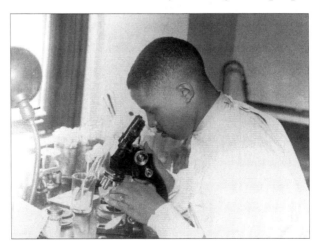

Fig. 3.3: Dr. John Anderson was part of the hospital staff, working as a medical researcher in the microbiology department. Courtesy of Dr. Dale Anderson.

who had violated the law. Imagine: a counselor there told my husband he should go and apply for work in the post office with a degree in chemistry! But Homer G. Phillips Hospital had a lot of publicity throughout the country, and he came here for a job in the microbiology department."

> *"Dr. Smiley was a down-to-earth sort of person—not formal at all—just a likeable person, with a certain ease about him. When doctors appeared on the wards, we were supposed to stand, but Dr. Smiley wasn't like that. Yet he was also very well respected."*
> —Dorothy Jenkins Coleman, nursing class of 1944

Working alongside the attending physicians and trainees was a dedicated cadre of nurses: 78 registered nurses on the floors, 16 head nurses, eight supervisors, four full-time instructors for the nursing school, and—at the top of the ladder—a superintendent of nurses, who had two assistants. Then there were the nursing students, who took courses, worked under supervision in the hospital, and lived in a five-story building behind the hospital on Goode Avenue.

Most new students found their quarters comfortable and even beautiful—in some cases, a dramatic improvement from the tiny apartments or crowded rural homes they had known. Along with the student rooms, mostly singles, the building had a lounge and recreation rooms on the first level. Each floor had a solarium, card room, kitchen, and laundry, with telephones and bathrooms in the hallway. On the ground floor of the residence was a reference library, and in the basement a laundry and ping-pong table.[12]

When Marybelle Barnes first saw the nursing dormitory as a student, she said, "I was excited. I was impressed with the building; it was so nice looking. We had a big living room with a piano in it." Added nursing student Pauline Brown Payne: "When I went there in 1944, it was more or less brand new. You know, it was wonderful. It was clean, and the house mother, Miss Ophelia Clark, kept it quiet. I had a single room on the fifth floor, with a bed, a desk, a lamp, and a chair. That was about it. . . . It was kind of small, but it was nice."

They also had a quality three-year program, taught by experienced nurses, some of whom had moved over from City Hospital #2. Among this group was the redoubtable and timeless Mabel C. Northcross, hired in 1921, who stayed on for decades as the supervisor of the operating room.

But soon there was also controversy. Before 1940, the nursing superintendent had always been a white appointee, most recently Mona McGuire, followed by Jessie Norelius. Finally, the *Argus* had had enough. In 1938, the newspaper first complained that the two white assistant superintendents—Lucy Erdman and Theresa Kneipp—were bossy and arrogant; they added that Ms. Erdman puts "a great deal of racial feeling in her work"[13] and that Ms. Kneipp "regarded her colored associates as 'The Untouchables.'"[14]

Then they took aim at Ms. Norelius, saying that she should not have been named at all, that the city should have listened to a chorus of Black voices strongly backing the appointment of a Black nurse to the post. They scoffed bitterly at Dr. Ralph Thompson, city hospital commissioner, who claimed that not only was no Black woman available but that "the time was not ripe for a colored woman to hold such a position."

In the end, Ms. Norelius left, followed by another white short-timer, Virginia Harrison. In January 1940 a Black director was finally selected: Estelle Massey Riddle, most recently a field agent for the Rosenwald Fund. In 1939, she had made headlines for refusing to take a back elevator at a hotel in New Orleans, where a national nursing meeting was being held. Soon local papers were praising her energetic leadership and new appointments she had made to the staff, including longtime instructor Juliette Lee. The school at last had an "all-race faculty," said one newspaper, happily.[15]

*"In the late 1960s, Dr. Smiley was St. Louis' chief innovator in the health care division of the War on Poverty. He also designed policies and protocols for the St. Louis Department of Health and Hospitals' first maternal-child health clinics. . . . Perhaps even more impressive, Dr. Smiley presided over the establishment of the first family planning clinics in St. Louis, a city known for its conservative attitudes on matters of*

*reproduction. Hardly a word of dissent was uttered as the clinics began dispensing family planning information and counseling, and city officials credited the calm reaction to Dr. Smiley's integrity, reputation, and professional approach."*

— Dr. Will Ross, associate dean for diversity,
Washington University School of Medicine

After a few months, the honeymoon period ended, and newspapers that had been lauding the hospital's construction began reporting its shortcomings. One employee was accused of passing on the names of dying patients to a local undertaker; two residents admitted whispering the names of local "damage-suit" lawyers to accident victims.[16] The *Argus* noted in 1937 that C.I.O. union organizers were targeting the hospital, which they blamed for not hiring enough Black skilled workers.

| Statistics on hospital activities, Homer G. Phillips Hospital, 1937–1944. | | | | | |
|---|---|---|---|---|---|
| | 1937–38 | 1940–41 | 1941–42 | 1942–43 | 1943–44 |
| Admissions (including births) | 10,837 | 12,306 | 12,602 | 11,912 | 11,536 |
| Deaths | 1,114 | 1,025 | 937 | 1,011 | 1,086 |
| Discharges | 9,297 | 11,317 | 11,660 | 11,114 | 10,477 |
| Operations | 1,543 | 1,792 | 1,774 | 3,121 | 2,727 |

Fig. 3.4: This table summarizes activities at Homer G. Phillips Hospital from 1937 to 1944. Courtesy of the Bernard Becker Medical Library Archives, Washington University in St. Louis.

In 1938, the *Star and Times* reported that a model bakery in the hospital worth $10,000 stood idle, while the city spent nearly $6,000 on bread for patients. Superintendent McClellan blamed the Hospital Commissioner Thompson for not supplying a baker to do the work. But Thompson replied in exasperation that they should be blaming the supply commissioner. "I have no more to do with whether an institution buys bread or bakes its own than the elevator boy," he exclaimed. More serious was a story, late in 1937, of a 48-year-old Homer G. Phillips laundry worker, Blanch Marshall, who pricked her thumb on an ironing board. The wound became infected, and a week later she died in the same hospital where she had worked.

Despite its growing pains, by the end of the 1930s, the hospital was clearly a success. In its first year of operation alone, it had treated nearly 11,000 patients who spent almost 211,000 days there—an average of 575 patients per day. In the following year, surgeons had performed 660 major and 702 minor operations, and obstetricians had delivered 1,277 babies. Some 52 physicians and surgeons were on staff. In contrast to the grand jury reports that had repeatedly condemned City Hospital #2, a 1940 report called Homer G. Phillips Hospital "evidently well managed."[17]

## CHAPTER FOUR

# The Diaspora
## Coming to Homer G. Phillips Hospital

*"I was so scared I was shaking in my boots, because when I got to Homer G. Phillips nursing school, I started meeting girls from all sorts of fancy places. Somebody was from the Crescent City, somebody was from the Boardwalk town, and on and on. When we were introducing ourselves, I just said, 'I'm Georgia Rhone from Moro, Arkansas.' And they laughed so hard they almost broke the bed. Anyway, I soon found out that a lot of kids were from little towns like me, basically from the same humble backgrounds."*

> —Georgia Rhone Anderson, 1955 nursing graduate and surgical nurse

MANY NURSING STUDENTS made the harrowing trip to Homer G. Phillips from tiny farming towns in the rural South, from states like Louisiana that offered no real programs for Black people. Some residents found their way there from Eastern states where one or two Black students were admitted to white medical schools but then found no residency slots open to them. Still others walked to Homer G. Phillips from Black neighborhoods nearby or crossed the Mississippi River from modest homes in East St. Louis to a more abundant life over the bridge.

Many of these nurses and doctors—or sometimes their parents—were part of a vast social upheaval: the decades-long Great Migration, which emptied the South of some six million Blacks. These men and women, whose families often worked in rice, cotton, or tobacco fields, took a leap of faith, trusting that unknown cities to the north would offer new and freer lives. By the time this movement ended in the 1970s, wrote historian Isabel Wilkerson, "nearly half of all black Americans—some 47 percent—would be living outside the South, compared to ten percent when the Migration began."[1]

When these children of the South arrived at Homer G. Phillips, especially in the early years of the hospital, they had some adjustments in store. Back home, the rules of segregation were harsh, even brutal, but at least they were clear-cut; in St. Louis, they were often difficult to predict and hard to navigate. Even so, most of the newly arrived Southerners found the city a welcome change. Students from the Eastern states were not as impressed. For some of them, St. Louis was more restrictive, more hostile—at times a racial nightmare—and an uncomfortable blend of North and South.

In many cases, students left behind large families with little money or educational opportunity. Too often, boys who stayed home found themselves chained to the meager land, just as their fathers had been, while the girls worked as virtual servants in their own families and married early to escape. But some enterprising teenagers heard of a St. Louis school—strikingly beautiful yet still, improbably, for Blacks—that offered them the hope of a different life. Somehow, they managed to round up the money they needed from generous grandmothers, hard-pressed parents, and their own jobs so they could travel north, nervous and alone.

They were transplanting their dream "in alien soil," said the poet Richard Wright, "to see if it could grow differently/If it could drink of new and cool rains/Bend in strange winds."[2] While some dropped out along the way or returned home to their previous lives, many found a fresh start and a middle-class future at Homer G. Phillips Hospital.

*"I came from Moro in eastern Arkansas. My mother died when I was 11, and I lived with my grandparents. We lived in the country, where my grandfather, William Smith Jr., had 40 acres of land, and he grew cotton, corn, soybeans, peas, and*

Fig. 4.1: Georgia Rhone Anderson from Moro, Arkansas, graduated from Homer G. Phillips School of Nursing in 1955 and became a surgical nurse. Courtesy of Georgia Anderson.

*beans. We didn't have to buy anything from the store. I was named Georgia for my grandmother, but my uncle gave me a nickname, 'Jack,' because he said I was a jack of all trades. It was my job to milk the cows, feed the cows, feed the pigs, gather wood. During planting time, I drove the tractor; during harvest time, I picked cotton. I pulled corn, I picked peas, I dug potatoes. I did everything."*

—Georgia Anderson

Some Homer G. Phillips students were escaping the desperate lives of their parents—or maybe their parents, like those of nurse Lillian Elliott Haywood, nursing class of 1971, had fled such conditions themselves. In the Alabama countryside, Mrs. Haywood's mother, Emma, was only 13 when she married Benny Elliott, and she had her first baby at the age of 18. Seven more children followed, the last when she was 44. "That's what happened in those days," said Mrs. Haywood. "For the girls, it was 'get married so you can get out of the house.' So, they married the farmers' sons."

Benny, one of 12 children, had five siblings living in St. Louis, and he decided to join them. So, he and his family went north and then economized in any way they could. Emma sewed; when Mrs. Haywood was 12, her mother spent Saturdays ironing for relatives. Benny worked in construction, but he was also a hunter, and on weekends he brought back eggs from a farm in the country. "I would sell the eggs in the neighborhood," said Mrs. Haywood. "I always had a job making money, *always*."

Barbara Jean Bogen Pool, a 1965 graduate, was born in Americus, Georgia, where her father was a day laborer on the farm of a white family; Barbara's mother worked in the house as a servant. "They were plowing from sunup to sundown," she recalled, "but he had sisters and brothers in Miami, and they told him to come down there." Mrs. Pool was not quite five when they boarded the train for their new home.

In Americus, they left behind Mrs. Pool's grandparents, who had their own farm with chickens and two cows. "My granddaddy would milk in the morning, and my grandmother would churn and make butter. Her name was Carnella Dudley, but people called her 'Miss Nella.' They would send their children to ask, 'Miss Nella, Mamma said would you send a quart of milk?' 'Would you send a dozen eggs?' And she always said, 'Oh, sure.' I later learned that a lot of those people were never able to repay her."

Vernell Brooks Brown and Annie Crawford Ward, both in the class of 1962, came from sharecropping families: Mrs. Brown in Gregory, Arkansas, and Mrs. Ward in Aberdeen, Mississippi. "It was just like everyone else," said Mrs. Ward. "They thought they could do better here, and my dad did not particularly care for farming." Where exactly was Gregory? "It's a lot of small places in Arkansas, and folks never heard of most of them," Mrs. Brown said. One day, her parents packed up their four small children and set out for St. Louis on a wing and a prayer.

*"I guess there was a divine influence at work because, in my community, nobody went past grade school. If you graduated from eighth grade, you were through, and the girls started looking for husbands. But my grandfather heard Floyd Brown speak—he was head of the Black Fargo Agricultural School in Brinkley—and he said it would 'make girls and boys better farmers.' I think that hit my grandfather: 'Jack can be a better farmer!' So, he arranged for me to go there to high school."*
                                              —Georgia Anderson

Many Homer G. trainees and students had known segregation and often poverty. Dr. Lee Blount, a St. Louisan and trainee at the hospital, had persevered in medicine because "I wanted a profession that would give me something opposite from what my father did." Every evening, his father came in from his rough, dirty job at the foundry. "The brown skin on his face was gray from the soot and the dust. But his eyes stood out." His father never complained; in fact, he was a quiet man all around. So, Dr. Blount was astonished one day when he heard his father, reflecting on his son's medical ambitions, begin crying, "Those white folks, they're not going to let him be a doctor. They are going to crush him."

In the late 1940s, the family of nursing student Elizabeth Jones, whose father had a good job with the government, moved into the Maple Avenue neighborhood in St. Louis, which was then all white. The end of racially restrictive covenants in 1948 had opened up areas that were previously off limits to Black families—but white residents were not happy. "I remember somebody threw a rock and busted out our window. For a while we had the police canvassing the area," she said.

Barbara Pool was growing up in a segregated enclave of Miami when her parents sent her back to Georgia to stay with her grandparents for the summer. Already, she had forgotten the unwritten laws forged by prejudice in her old community. "I must have been eight or nine years old," she said. "Some kids and I went into the little town nearby where there were stores. I walked into one and strutted back to the ice cream case. At some point, I noticed the other kids weren't behind me; they were up near the front looking at me. But I opened the case to get some ice cream, and the shop-keeper came over and said, '*You*. You can't go in there. You tell me what you want, and I'll get it for you.'"

On another trip back from Americus to Miami, Mrs. Pool was riding in a car with her family when they passed through a town in north Florida. "North Florida was just as terrible as any place in Georgia. And I remember our car started to go *real* slowly, and we saw these folks with sheets on, the Ku Klux Klan. Even though I didn't know a lot about them then, I was very frightened. But we went through, and they didn't bother us."

Richard W. White, a nursing student in the 1967 class, was a ninth grader in Houston when his schoolteacher mother, Hattie Mae White, became the first Black person elected to the school board in 1958. "I was on the telephone talking to a girlfriend when I heard my father holler, 'Come with me.' We went outside and there was a big cross burning on our front lawn. It was more than six feet tall, made of railroad ties that were wrapped in burlap and probably soaked in gasoline. We got the water hose and put out the fire and then knocked it down with a sledgehammer. We didn't call the police."

Marybelle Barnes, who came to Homer G. in 1949, grew up in Louisiana, and her family's nearest neighbors were white. "We used to play with those kids until we started grade school, in separate schools, and then we didn't play anymore. One day, the little white girl came over to our house and she said to us, 'My mamma said to call you Africans.' I didn't know what that was, so when my mother came home, we asked her what Africans were. She said, 'That is where the old folks came from.' That was the first time I heard the term."

*"I knew I was not going to be a farmer's wife. I realized there was no future. This year the crop was good, but next year you'd end up in the hole, so you started over. I didn't want that. What really solidified my thinking was that, during my sophomore year, I met a young man whose mother had recent-ly died, and he was living at home with his father and younger*

*brother. He'd come by the house to see me, and he wore bib
overalls, starched and ironed and creased to the hilt. One day,
I heard him talking to his cousin, and he said, 'I'm going to
marry Georgia, because we need somebody to take care of us.'
And all I could see was me ironing those bib overalls for three
men, and I thought, 'No, that's not going to be the life of me.'"*
                                              —Georgia Anderson

By finishing high school and moving on to nurses' training,
many Homer G. students had gone further academically—in some
cases *much* further—than anyone else in their families. Willa Jean
Richardson Nelson was born in Amory, Mississippi, but her share-
cropper parents left for St. Louis when she was two. Their family,
which grew to four children, lived "in the ghetto down on Thomas
Street near Martin Luther King." They had a run-down house with
a dilapidated porch; when she was tiny, part of it fell on her and
gashed her scalp.

Both her parents were hard workers: her father was a tool-and-
die operator in a mill, while her mother, who had married at the age
of 15, was a maid for a University City family. "My parents were
very much about education," she said. Her mother had longed to
be a nurse, but she had to quit school after third grade, and her
father, an orphan who bounced from home to home, had never
gone to school at all. "He could barely write his name. He would
go different places and remember the streets by the buildings. So, he
made sure that all of us got an education."

Often, parents pushed their children, hard, to pursue the dreams
they had never been able to fulfill. Wanda Claxton Trotter's mother,
a Vashon High School graduate, had completed a practical nursing
program sponsored by the St. Louis Board of Education. "But then
she couldn't afford to pay for the state licensing exam, and she had
wanted to be a nurse as well."

Johnnye Robinson Farrell's father was the oldest son in his family, and when his father died young, he had to quit school to take
care of his siblings. As soon as Mrs. Farrell graduated from Homer
G. in 1968, she headed back to Monroe, Louisiana, where her father was waiting for her at the train station with a question: "Now

you going back to school to become a doctor?" he asked eagerly. No, she assured him, she wanted to be a nurse. But she knew then, as she had known before going to St. Louis, what she had to do for the sake of her self-sacrificing parents. "When they put me on that train to St. Louis with the check for three years of nursing school, I knew in my family there were no failures. I had no choice but to come and be successful."

*"At my high school in Arkansas, I met a young lady who had a brochure from Homer Phillips—and it was in color. I just thought they were the prettiest things I had ever seen, all those pretty girls in those pretty white uniforms. 'Oh,' I said. 'That's what I'll do.' So that's what I started working toward. And that's what I did."*

—Georgia Anderson

In those days before the Internet, it was trickier to know where to find training—so how did people in distant states hear about Homer G. Phillips Hospital? Louise Cunningham, one of nine children, grew up in Westfield, Alabama, in a segregated mill town owned by U.S. Steel. For more than 30 years, her father walked to his job as a laborer, never missing a day's work. "Occasionally, my mother, who was a homemaker, got this bee in her bonnet that she wanted to work, so being a Black female with no skills, she did day work for a white family." During one of those times, Louise's future arrived by U.S. mail. "One summer, this family she was working for went to St. Louis on vacation, and they sent my mother a postcard with Homer G. Phillips on it. From then on, I knew where I wanted to go to nursing school."

In the late 1960s, Johnnye ("Teeny") Robinson Farrell was in high school, thinking about nursing, when her segregated school happened to hire a guidance counselor who knew about Homer G. Phillips Hospital. So, Mrs. Farrell and seven of her classmates were admitted to the nursing school, and six of them eventually graduated. Before she left for St. Louis, her sister—a diehard KMOX listener, who loved the Cardinals games—picked up a troubling rumor.

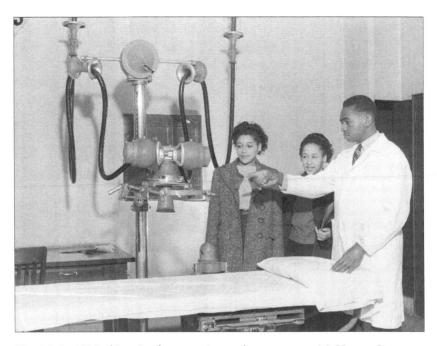

Fig. 4.2: In 1939, this pair of prospective students came to visit Homer G. Phillips Hospital. Courtesy of the Missouri Historical Society, St. Louis.

"'Teeny, they keep talking about closing Homer Phillips.' But my daddy said, 'Don't worry about that. That's where she *wants* to go, and that's where she *will* go.'"

Lula Couch Hall grew up in Little Rock, Arkansas, and if she had been a few years younger she might have made history. In 1957, friends from her school integrated Central High School there, becoming known as the "Little Rock Nine." But by then, she had already filled out the Homer G. Phillips application and gone on to nursing school. "The requirements were very rigid," she said. "You had to have a certain grade point average and be in the upper third of your class. You needed three letters of recommendation. It was just like kids now waiting to hear from college. We all waited to hear from Homer Phillips."

For the medical residents coming to Homer G., the choice was easier. Until desegregation took hold, they had very few choices for training. For Dr. Nathaniel Murdock, who had grown up in

Texas, there were no more than 10 venues nationwide he could consider, particularly for men who wanted to go into OB-GYN. And he had already seen Homer G. Phillips in 1961, while working at Washington University as a research assistant in pathology. "I loved it," he said. "I loved Homer Phillips. It was a big hospital, and it was very, very well organized. At that time, we did more than 400 deliveries a month, which is still a lot, even by today's standards."

> *"In 1949, at the height of my senior year, my grandfather asked me to stay out of school for a week and help him finish picking the cotton, and he said, 'If you do, I'll give you a hundred dollars.' So I did that, but on the weekend he and I had a little problem; he did give me the hundred dollars, but he told me he wasn't going to pay anything else for me. So, I went back to my old school to work and then on to Homer G. Phillips in 1952. I had the tuition, $350, for the whole three years, but I had to ask my uncle to loan me $8 a month for everyday living. The first of every month, I got a money order for eight dollars. To save money, I used baking soda for toothpaste, Vaseline from the units, and zinc oxide as a deodorant. But I still had to buy washing powder, shoestrings, and stockings."*
> —Georgia Anderson

How to get the money together for this new school? For a long time, the cost was just $350 for all three years, but that was still a lot for many families. Rosie Jackson's mother, a young widow with seven children, was determined to help Rosie and her other children realize their dreams. In their hometown of Clarksdale, Mississippi, "we had a grocery store, Mr. Frank's. You could just go in there and get groceries; they would write it down in a book, and when you had money you went back and paid them. My mother always paid, so we never had a problem with getting credit. So, she went into Mr. Frank's and borrowed a hundred and some dollars to send me for the first year."

Charlotte Steel was born at Homer G. Phillips, and she went to nursing school there years later—"returning to the scene of the crime," her mother said jokingly. But her first six months there, she goofed off a little, and she came home with two "D's" on her record. Her mother was irate. "'I'm going to tell you something. I am working at the post office every Christmas to pay your tuition— so you will not make another D. Do you understand me?' And from then on, I did not."

The divorced father of Gretchen Prisby McCullum was a letter carrier in Youngstown, Ohio, but he also invested in real estate—19 houses in all. At the time, he and her stepmother had the help of four of his children, who worked as an unpaid crew to fix them up. "I could cut threads on pipes, I could do electrical work, I could do everything." Mrs. McCullum dreamed of leaving home, but her father would not help. Before she could go to nursing school, she had to spend three years doing domestic work for a white family. The salary was $4 a week, and after paying for a bus pass, she had $3 left.

Money was also scarce for Wanda Trotter's mother, who was divorced with three children to educate. Mrs. Trotter was attending Homer G. Phillips nursing school at the same time that her sister Denise started at Harris-Stowe State College in St. Louis. Still, her mother would not let them work during high school, even in the summertime. "Your job is to go to school," she insisted. "I am your parent; I will take care of you." Instead, her mother worked two jobs: as a silk finisher at a cleaning business by day and as a wedding gown presser in the evenings.

> *"I realized that I hadn't had the same education as others, so I wondered, 'How am I going to compete?' But there were four of us students, and one of the four was always number one in the class. Sometimes it was me; sometimes it was Dolores; sometimes it was Janelle; and sometimes it was Kathleen. But the entire three years, my ranking in class was never less than four. So, I did O.K. When we graduated, I was number two, and number one was Dolores Atwater, who had previously been in college for three years. I felt pretty good about that."*
> —Georgia Anderson

For some nursing students, Homer G. Phillips was familiar territory, because they had already spent time there as patients. Lois

Collier Jackson and her sister were both born there, and Mrs. Jackson had come back as a child to have a huge wooden splinter removed from her hand. Some had also been to Barnes Hospital, where, as a teenager, Mrs. Jackson's sister was treated for pneumonia in the basement ward. "I went to visit her, and I saw water pipes that were leaking. I thought, 'What is going on here? She's sick and all this water dripping?'"

Willa Jean Nelson also had a prior acquaintance with Homer G. Phillips. After a piece of her parents' porch fell on her and knocked her out, they took her there to receive emergency treatment for the cut on her head. "I remember the cold table," she said.

But for those who didn't already know the hospital, getting on the train or bus was tough, as was the seemingly endless trip into the unknown. In 1957, Karole Davidson came to St. Louis from Lima, Ohio, an only child on her first trip away from home. Her mother, the oldest of 17 children who was determined that her daughter would get an education, had made all the arrangements and put her on the bus. "It seemed like it took me three months to get from Lima to St. Louis. I was 19 and I didn't like it at all."

When she arrived in St. Louis, she was shocked by what she found. "Lima was a small town, and I had never seen so many Black people in one place. I was just overcome. I called home long distance and said: 'Mamma, please let me come home. *Please*.' The last time I called, she said, 'If you call here one more time, I'll have this telephone taken out,' and she hung up. It's called tough love. Eventually, I just had to succumb to it, and I finally enjoyed it, stayed, and graduated."

*"My nursing class at Homer G. Phillips, 55 students in all, was devilish. One time, the school had an interns' convention, and our director, Minnie Gore, didn't want us hanging out with those doctors. So that week, one of the instructors gave us a pop test, and of course nobody was prepared for any dumb test. So, half of us didn't pass, and Miss Gore wrote all the parents the same letter: 'If your daughter spent more time studying, her grades would be better.' Well, I'm still number two. Then my grandmother sent me a hot letter: 'What are*

*you doing up there? I didn't raise you like that!' So, I went to Miss Gore's office and said: 'This letter doesn't apply to me. Do you know where I rank in the class? I am also paying for my schooling myself, so if there's a problem, talk to me.' I told her she needed to write my grandmother a letter and explain that this is not me—and she did."*

—Georgia Anderson

From wherever they hailed, the new nursing students found the first days and weeks at Homer G. Phillips to be daunting. Iver Gandy came from Alabama, one of six "Birmingham girls" in the class of 1967. "As we rode down from Union Station in our cab toward the hospital, I saw this inner-city area, and I kept thinking, 'When are we going to where the grass and trees are and everything?' He kept driving, and I saw people's laundry hanging outside; we did that too, but it was in our backyard."

Her trepidation grew when she arrived at school.

We went inside, and we were met by a student nurse who said, "Hello, ladies." I said, "I don't think I like it here. I want to go home." But everyone else said, "Well, we got to try it out." The student showed us to our rooms, and I thought, "Well, it's OK," and we unpacked, but I still felt lonely. I was like, "Oh, my God, what have I done?" And then things began to fall in. The other new students came, and we started saying, "Where you from?" We were meeting each other and forming that bond.

Rosie Jackson arrived on a Monday to begin her education, and she quickly realized that other girls were just as naïve and lost as she was. "I was coming from home for the first time, and there were others—from Mississippi, Tennessee, Kentucky—and they were just as pitiful as I was. We didn't know anything."

Most of the girls were friendly, she added, but some were condescending. "I can remember one girl running down to my room because she heard I was from Mississippi. 'We just want to see what you all look like, to see if you have shoes and clothes . . .' Then she said, 'Oh, you look just like we do.' And I couldn't figure it out. What were we supposed to look like? You never heard people say that Black people from Mississippi had nothing. You never heard them say we were naked."

> *"I never went down to the Fox Theatre, because I knew I wasn't supposed to be there. Later on, it closed and when they opened it back up, Blacks could sit in the balcony. I did go downtown, but at Woolworth's, in my day, you would get your sandwich and then stand because you couldn't sit at the counter."*
>
> —Georgia Anderson

Students from the South often thought St. Louis was a different world. "There was no comparison," said Louise Brown Cunningham, class of 1960, "because Alabama was totally segregated. There were white and colored water fountains. There were Black and white waiting rooms. You know, on the bus, the whites sat in the front and the Blacks in the back. I remember, when I first came, going downtown and sitting at a restaurant counter, eating lunch. I couldn't do that in Alabama."

Still, some trainees found the racial situation all too familiar. Dr. Homer Nash grew up in Atlanta and went to Meharry Medical School in Nashville before coming to Homer G. Phillips in the 1950s for his residency. In Georgia, where his father was a general practitioner, they had lived in a Black enclave and gone to separate schools. "Only people who had to get out and go to work got insulted every day," he said. In St. Louis, he worked in another Black enclave, so he found the city "much the same" as what he had known before.

Other students were horrified by the city's racial divisions. Marybelle Barnes recalls her first trip downtown on the Easton Avenue streetcar. She was with a classmate, Lucy, who was very light-skinned. "When we got on the streetcar, it was full. I was in front of Lucy, and this white man stood up and told her, 'Come on, miss, you sit here.' And Lucy gave him a dirty look and said,

'Barnesie, sit here.' And then she stood over me. He was so embarrassed he got as far away from us as he could."

In Mississippi, said Rosie Jackson, all the Black people knew
exactly where they could go. If you wanted to see a movie, you
went up the stairs in the back, while the whites came in the front.
"It didn't bother me at all," she said. "I mean, that's what we had
to do. It was just the life we lived. . . . I didn't know anything about
prejudice until I came to St. Louis. It was the most prejudiced place
I had ever seen in my life."

In Huntsville, Alabama, where Amanda Daniel Luckett Murphy
grew up, there was certainly prejudice, she said. She recalled the
white neighbor women coming over to have tea with her mother.
"They were condescending. They would call my mother by her first
name while she called them Mrs. Strong and Mrs. Irving. And they
would ask me stupid questions like, 'Well, who are you going to
work for when you grow up?' What they meant was, 'Whose *house*
are you going to work in?' And I felt like, 'You're pretty dumb not
to know that none of my sisters and brothers are going to work in
anybody's homes. Period.'"

In Huntsville, she added, there was an openness to the racism
that made it easier to handle. "People were very upfront about
where everybody stood, and in an average neighborhood it was
highly mixed. There were not these Black neighborhoods and white
neighborhoods, and all of that. St. Louis is the most divided place
I've ever been in."

In 1947, Dr. Frank Richards of Asheville, North Carolina, was a
new graduate of Howard's medical school when he came to Homer
G. Phillips for training. "Absolutely, St. Louis was worse than
Asheville," he said. "I grew up in a segregated town, but it wasn't
as bad as St. Louis. It was terrible."

*"I graduated the last week of August and went home. When
I was getting ready to go back St. Louis, I was standing in
the living room with my grandmother when my grandfather
walked through, and he said, 'Jack, do you need anything?'
I was so shocked, I said, 'No.' But my grandmother said,*

*'Oh, hell yes you do.' So I said, 'I need a hundred dollars.' He reached in his pocket, opened his wallet, and gave me a hundred-dollar bill. I said, 'I'll pay you back.' My grandmother said, 'No, you won't.' After that, my grandfather wouldn't go to the doctor without calling me. He would say, 'Jack, I got a doctor's appointment. You think I need to keep it?' 'Yeah, you need to keep it.' When he got home, he would call. 'He gave me some red pills and some blue pills. You think I need to take them?' 'Yes, you need to take them.' When my grandmother died, my grandfather would not allow anyone to make funeral arrangements until I got home.*

*"One time my grandfather finally said to me, 'You know, girl? You turned out all right.' I said, 'Thank you. And you're partly responsible for it, because I got so many of your traits.'"*
—Georgia Anderson

## CHAPTER FIVE

# "A Special Time and Place"
## The Ville

*"The Ville was a special place and time. You won't ever have
another Ville with the economic and class mixture we had
then. It was also a self-contained community. Everything was
in walking distance: the barber shop, bakery, shoe repair,
restaurants, the Comet Theatre, the Amethyst in the old Poro
building—even a blacksmith shop right behind us. Whatever
you wanted to do was right there."*

> —Dr. John A. Wright Sr., childhood Ville resident and
> Sumner High graduate, Saint Louis University PhD,
> and St. Louis academic leader; his mother worked at
> Homer G. Phillips Hospital

TODAY, TATTERED LACE curtains flutter wildly in the broken-out
window of an empty house in the Ville. Vacant lots and other aban-
doned homes surround it. "It makes my heart hurt when I see the
neighborhood now," said Mary Crawford Lane, a 1951 Homer G.
Phillips nursing graduate, who was born and raised in a four-room
house at 4440 North Market, which she shared with her parents
and 10 brothers and sisters. "It looks like it's just thrown away,
really. To me it's sickening."

In her mind's eye, she can see an entirely different world. When she
knew it—particularly in the 1930s, 1940s, and 1950s—this 43-block
area, tucked in the middle of the Greater Ville community, was a
lively place, full of families, businesses, thriving churches, and over-
flowing schools. "The yards were always slick. We had a peach tree,
so we had our own fruit, and my daddy had a garden," she said.

Fig. 5.1: Dr. John A. Wright Sr., later a respected St. Louis educator, lived in the Ville neighborhood as a child and graduated from nearby Sumner High School. Courtesy of Dr. John A. Wright Sr.

Living in the brick bungalows, small frame homes, and apartment buildings was a diverse blend of residents in socioeconomic terms, who were bound together by race and legal restrictions on social mobility. "You had doctors, lawyers, government workers, maintenance workers, and people who cleaned for families, so you had a mixture of everybody," said childhood resident Victor Roberts. "You might have a lawyer living next door to a janitor, or a doctor living next door to a schoolteacher. It was really a mixed neighborhood at that time."

Whatever their economic circumstances, Ville residents often had the same goals for their children: higher education and upward mobility. Mrs. Lane's father, Charles Crawford, was a school janitor

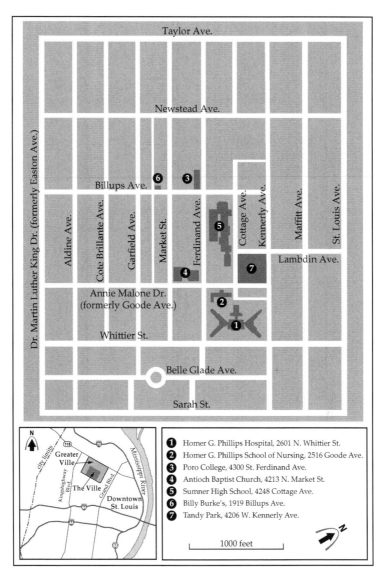

Fig. 5.2: This map shows the location of the hospital within the Ville and the broader community. Map by Chris Robinson.

who worked at Sumner when his children were students there. "He would stand in the halls and just sweep up a storm, making sure you were in class," she said. Her mother, Oliverneze, had a tiny house, but it was always tidy. "Mamma did not tolerate dirt," said Mrs. Lane firmly.

Willa Jean Richardson Nelson, a 1961 nursing graduate, also thought the houses "were nice, upkept places." Traveling from her modest southside neighborhood to the Ville, she said, "was like going to the rich place, from bad to good. The Ville was 'seddity' people—uppity people—that's what my mom said. You could tell because you didn't look the part; you weren't the mink-wearing or glove-wearing type. You felt like the Raggedy Ann. At least, I felt that way."

In the 1920, 1930s, 1940s, and even into the 1950s, it certainly *was* seddity, recalled Mary Ellen Anderson, whose mother stayed on in the 4500 block of Garfield after her children left home. "When she moved there, it was just doctors and teachers and people with this degree and that degree. That block was practically a convention for professionals—and of course people who were property owners. When you owned property, you felt were you above the rest, you know."

And the centerpiece of this vibrant community was Homer G. Phillips Hospital, which attracted many staff members to live nearby and patronize local businesses. "A community needs a hospital like that where people can go, get efficient care, be in good surroundings, and have friendly people with them. I think that kind of institution makes a neighborhood," said Roberts.

> *"I grew up in the Ville. I spent all my early years there, and I lived in three different places. One of them was 4414 Maffitt, the Lincoln Court Apartments. Those were two-room cold-water flats. They had balconies, and in the summertime, people put pallets on the balcony so the kids could sleep outside. Parents in the apartments would look out for each other. If I did something, they would tell my mother. We also had a party line, so you could hear what the neighbors were doing. We didn't realize we were poor until we read about it later."*
> —Dr. John A. Wright

Before it became the heart of the St. Louis Black community, the Ville was called Elleardsville, named for white horticulturist

Charles Elleard, who came from California and created a nursery in the 1860s from a large swath of north St. Louis. By the early 20th century, the Ville had become an area in which Blacks could buy property, and from that point on its appeal grew. "Blacks who initially moved into the Ville saw themselves as being socially superior to the poorer class of black workers . . ." said one case study. "A black managerial class began to establish itself in the Ville, which was fast becoming a desirable residential neighborhood for blacks."[1]

Still, "desirable" was not always an apt term for housing in the Ville or other Black neighborhoods, where overcrowding became a byproduct of segregation. Between 1910 and 1950, when migration from the South swelled the city's Black population, wrote historian Walter Johnson,

> the social and familial life of Black St. Louis was compressed into an area whose population density varied between 200 and 400 percent of that prevailing in much of white St. Louis. . . . [T]he familiar four-family St. Louis brick apartment building was cut up on the inside to accommodate twelve or even sixteen families in two-room apartments, with one room for cooking and eating and one for sleeping, and with no running water, indoor toilets, or reliable heat.[2]

The white landlords who owned many of these buildings garnered rich profits from these buildings, added Johnson. "The artificially created housing shortage enabled landlords to charge higher rents . . . as much as three times the rent for comparable apartments in Black neighborhoods as they did in white neighborhoods. And because their renters had few alternatives, landlords were able to save money by skimping on maintenance. The result was overcrowded, rat-infested, firetrap apartment buildings . . ."[3]

Yet somehow, despite these problems, the Ville was a place of joy as well as exploitation, Johnson said. ". . . as [comedian Dick] Gregory remembered in a chapter of his autobiography entitled 'Not Poor, Just Broke,' these embattled neighborhoods were sites of human flourishing as well as suffering, spaces of joy as well as rage, and places where radical ideas and unaccustomed alliances took root in the 1930s . . ."[4]

But the Depression was hard on the Ville. In fact, it "devastated the Ville, as in-migration continued but economic prospects all but evaporated."[5] Residents tried hard to hold their lives together by doing whatever jobs they could to put food on the table. Thus, the arrival of Homer G. Phillips Hospital—with the possibility for employment, as well as the need for restaurants and other services to cater to staff and patients—seemed like a godsend.

> *"I did first grade at Simmons School, but it was so overcrowded that the Board of Education opened up Cote Brilliante, even though it was west of Taylor. . . . When you think about all the schools that have closed in the Ville: Simmons, Marshall, Turner, Stowe—all those institutions are gone."*
>
> —Dr. John A. Wright

The first elementary school for Blacks was little Elleardsville Colored School #8 on St. Louis Avenue, which was renamed Simmons School in 1890 and completely rebuilt by the turn of the century. In 1910, Sumner High School also moved into the Ville from its downtown location, and the Charles Henry Turner Open-Air School for Handicapped Children went up in 1925. "The teachers were really, really well educated, they had excellent backgrounds, and they were interested in the kids. They wanted to make sure they were learning, and they went overboard to teach kids," said Victor Roberts.

Prominent churches also began springing up, particularly Antioch Baptist in 1878 and St. James A.M.E. soon afterwards. Later on, the area acquired a raft of others, including St. Philip's Lutheran on Annie Malone Drive, Kennerly Temple, St. Matthew the Apostle Catholic—and, oddest of all, a small church cheek-by-jowl with a tavern. "On Saturdays, we could hear the jolly club music," said Georgia Anderson, "and on Sundays, in the club, you could hear the church music because the walls were just that thin."

Key businesses soon arose as well. In the early 20th century, entrepreneur Annie Turnbo Malone began formulating beauty products
and teaching cosmetology to Black women in her five-story Poro

Fig. 5.3: Annie Malone, tenth from right, was with a group of friends,
celebrating a wedding in front of Poro College. April 25, 1927. Courtesy of the
Missouri Historical Society, St. Louis.

College building. Rich and philanthropic, Mrs. Malone donated
the land for the St. Louis Colored Orphans' Home (later renamed
the Annie Malone Children's Home) in 1922. In 1930, the newly
divorced Mrs. Malone moved her business to Chicago, though the
Poro building continued to house a theater and law school.

"My parents lived in an apartment on Cote Brilliante in the
Ville," said Carlene Davis, who grew up at 3903 Finney, down the
street from the attorney George Vaughn.

My mother had been trained as a teacher in Louisiana, but
when she came to St. Louis in the 1920s, there were very few
jobs for Black teachers. So, she went to Poro College and

became a cosmetologist. They had teas on the roof garden at Poro College with all the china and highly polished silver. Mother said Mrs. Malone was a lovely person—soft-spoken, and very refined—and determined to do everything to help Black women be the best they could be.

Poro College also became the site of a law school. In 1936, aspiring Black law student Lloyd Gaines sued the University of Missouri because it had rejected his law school application on account of his race. Finally, the U.S. Supreme Court ruled that the state of Missouri was required to provide Blacks with an education equivalent to whites. In response, the state set up the Lincoln Law School for Black students on the Poro Campus, though Gaines never fulfilled his dream. He disappeared in 1939, possibly murdered, and was never seen again.

*"I was a latchkey child, and when school was out, I'd put my books up and go report to my mother's co-worker, Mrs. Whitsun. Sometimes, I had dinner with her and then I would play outside until my mother came home. Alcohol was always a problem in the Ville, but Mrs. Whitsun's son was the only person I knew then who was on drugs—heroin. I remember that it aged him. He was gray-haired, and he looked old."*
—Dr. John A. Wright

"We had a lot of fun growing up," said Victor Roberts. "We played everywhere. They had a playground at Tandy Center, which is at Kennerly and Goode. There was a recreational center with little wading pools out front and a swimming pool inside. All the kids were mixed together. You might be playing with a doctor's son or a ditch-digger's son, but you made friends with whoever you had something in common with."

On the street or in the playground, there were games of all kinds. "We played the games that children don't even do now, like jump rope and double Dutch," said Alverne Meekins Eldridge, a childhood resident. "I played baseball with the guys, and marbles, jacks, and bolo bat. It was just a wonderful time." Not far away were white neighborhoods, mostly inhabited by working-class German and Italian families, and sometimes the children sneaked down alleys to mingle and play.[6]

In the Ville, neighbors had the rights of extended family, especially when it came to punishment. "If someone saw you do something wrong, they had the privilege to beat the tar out of you," said Mrs. Lane. "Then that person would tell my mamma, and you'd get another beating. That's right. Afterwards, you sat down, and you were quiet. I mean, nowadays they think that's torture, but it taught you respect."

"Parents were always keeping informed from each other," agreed Roberts. "They had their own pipeline. They would call and let your mom know if you were getting into something that you shouldn't be doing, and then you'd be in trouble when you got home. I tried not to get in trouble because Mom was very strict. She had her little cane, and you'd get a few licks that you'd remember. You wouldn't get into that sort of situation anymore."

There was an inflexible etiquette for children walking around the neighborhood: They always, *always*, gave a respectful greeting to adults seated out front. "Folks would be sitting on the porches and reading the paper," said Mrs. Lane, "and nine times out of ten you've spoken to them once that day already. But you got to speak to them every time you pass by. So, you'd say, 'Good afternoon,' and they would say, 'Mm hm.' And I'd be thankful because they wouldn't be saying to Mamma, 'Mary didn't speak to us when she came by the other day.'"

No matter what, you had a firm obligation on Sunday morning. "I don't care if you were out 'til 6 o'clock in the morning; you still had to go to Sunday school. You had to go to church. If you were Baptist, you also went to Baptist Young People's Union and night service," she added.

*"My mother, Elneal Allen Wright, was born in Jonesville, Louisiana, and came to St. Louis in the late 1920s. She was a domestic worker, and then she became a cook at Homer G.*

Fig. 5.4: A member of the kitchen staff at the hospital, Elneal Wright lived with her son John within walking distance in a modest Ville apartment. Courtesy of Dr. John A. Wright Sr.

*Phillips Hospital until she retired in 1963. At first, she worked in the vegetable room, where many of the women worked at that time. It was a big room, and all they did was pick vegetables for the patients. Pick over string beans, pop them, and get them ready to be cooked."*

—Dr. John A. Wright

Like Elneal Wright, some Ville residents worked in the neighborhood, often at Homer G. Phillips or in one of the businesses lining Easton Avenue (later Dr. Martin Luther King Drive). A giant, white-owned cleaning plant hired Blacks; so did some large grocery stores, particularly for jobs stocking shelves.

Local children became patients at the hospital. Alverne Eldridge, who grew up in an apartment on Sullivan Place, got penicillin shots at Homer G. several times a year for strep throat. "I was supposed to get my tonsils taken out, but because it was so crowded, they never had a bed for me, and I still have my tonsils

Fig. 5.5: Alverne Meekins Eldridge, who grew up in St. Louis, graduated from the Homer G. Phillips School of Nursing in 1966. Family members worked at the hospital, graduated from the X-ray technology program, and received treatment there. Courtesy of Alverne Eldridge.

today," she said. Her brother Chauncey was only a toddler when their mother—Celeester Banks Meekins, who didn't own a car—carried him in her arms a dozen or more blocks to the emergency room. "He was forever hurting himself," said Mrs. Eldridge, "and this time he ate some lye from our neighbor. He had ingested quite a bit, and he burnt his esophagus. Dr. [John] Gladney took care of him—and he was a wonderful ENT physician. Chauncey didn't have any lasting damage."

For the Meekins family, like many others, Homer G. Phillips became a family affair. Celeester Meekins was an EKG technician for 22 years, an aunt was an LPN in OB/GYN, a cousin was an RN, and another cousin, Dr. Curtis Franklin, did his residency there. Mrs. Eldridge herself finished the nursing school in 1966, while her sister, Charlotte Meekins Flowers, graduated from the two-year program in X-ray technology.

Sometimes, nurses and trainees received treatment or gave birth at the hospital. In 1950–51, Drs. Dazelle and George Simpson came from Meharry Medical School to do their internship at Homer G. Phillips. That year, Dazelle was pregnant with their first child, and the entire staff was solicitous. "Even the people who worked in the kitchen would always save an extra apple for me, and after I gave birth, every doctor in the hospital came to visit, even the interns on duty. I told George: 'If I keep having all these visits, I'm going to jump out a window!'"

But that feeling—of being part of something important—infused the entire staff. "The attitude of everybody who worked there was that they loved Homer G. Phillips, they were proud to be part of it, and they wanted everybody who came in to be happy there," said Dr. Dazelle Simpson. "It was like one big happy family. We worked hard—we were as busy as I don't know *what*—but we enjoyed it and learned a lot from it."

> "When I was in high school, I would go by Homer G. Phillips and walk in the back door. My mother would be in the dietary department, and I'd go back there to say hello. It was a welcoming place. The cooks would be waving and saying hello, and so would the guy with the meat cleaver. Sometimes, she walked me around the hospital, took me to the office of the administrator, Mr. McKnight, and said, 'I want you to meet my son.' He never seemed like, 'What the hell are you doing here?' He greeted her by name."
>
> —Dr. John A. Wright

On weekends or just as a break from the cafeteria food, which some loved and others reviled, most everyone would pop out for a sandwich or snack from one of the local restaurants. High on the list was Billy Burke's, located on Pendleton, where Ms. Johnson—a moody woman who sometimes displayed a generous heart—would dish up greasy, scrumptious hamburgers and small white containers of delicious ice cream. "She knew we were all poor and raggedy," said nurse Karole Davidson. "When I would go in there and say, 'Ms. Johnson, I've got no money, but I want a hamburger. When I get some money, I'll bring it,' she would give me a hamburger."

Yet Ms. Johnson was unpredictable, admitted Mrs. Davidson.

Some days you would go in there, and she would say, "Hi, baby! How you doin'? There's one of my nurses!" But on other days she was as mean as a snake. She wouldn't even speak to you. But still, one time, my granddaddy sent me a two-dollar bill, but I was so hungry, I wanted a hamburger. I went in and told her my grandfather had given it to me, and I didn't know it, but she saved it for me. Yes, she did. Later on, she gave it back to me.

Whenever the cafeteria served lamb for supper, there was a parade of Homer G. Phillips nurses heading down to Billy Burke's. One of them was Louise Brown Cunningham. "We would walk up there many times and eat one of those greasy hamburgers. I haven't had hamburgers like that since." Even out-of-towners knew about this spot. "Oh, everybody knew about Billy Burke's," said nurse Mary Woods. "I had one friend who came all the way from Chicago. Before she let them take her to where she was going, she had the cab bring her down to Billy Burke's so she could get two hamburgers."

But there were other places to go for food in the neighborhood as well. Sara-Lou, a little more expensive than Billy Burke's, was known for its breaded shrimp. Martin's grocery story had good produce; you could run up a tab at Mr. Ben's. There were confectioneries and mom-and-pop stores on several corners, and finer establishments on Easton Avenue.

When the nurses wanted to see a movie, they would go down to the Amethyst Theatre, where they might face a dilemma: Skip the end of the movie and get back on time, or see the end of the movie and miss curfew. When she was a nursing student in the early 1950s, Georgia Anderson and a group of 10 or 15 friends decided to see *Sudden Fear* there. "We were supposed to be in by 10:00, and the movie was not ending until a few minutes later. We decided we would stay. When the movie was over, we ran right down the middle of the street to the door, which the desk clerk unlocked. Then we just flew in and ran upstairs, and she had to tell the house mother, 'They came in here like a bunch of horses, and I didn't see one of them.'"

For evening entertainment, the area had its share of bars: The Pine Knot, Sorrento, and Ruby's. "We weren't supposed to be in there," said Mrs. Anderson,

> but Ruby let us in to have a drink. Sometimes she'd get jealous, because the guys would be laughing and talking with the students, and she'd say, "You student nurses, you're not supposed to be in here. Get up and leave and don't come back!" But in two evenings or so, we'd be right back. One evening, she called Miss Minnie Gore, our nursing school director, to tell her we were there, and Miss Gore started out, walking down the alley. But Ruby said to us, "You all in trouble now, because Miss Gore is on her way!" And we *ran* out of there! When Miss Gore arrived, we weren't there.

> *"Once my mother became a cook, she worked a split shift. They didn't need anyone past the time when the meals were served, so they sent people home until the next meal. Since most of the folks lived in the neighborhood, they walked home and came back—and that is how they did it in those days. Sometimes, when doctors did the late-night surgeries, my mother had to go over, and she'd take me with her. I would sit in the emergency room and watch them wheeling people in with all that blood. When my mother walked over to the hospital at night, she had a switchblade in hand, popped open, but we knew who the thieves were in the neighborhood."*
>
> —Dr. John A. Wright

In the Ville, residents were never so rich that they minded having a tiny bit extra. "Oh, oh, what we could buy with a penny," said Mary Crawford Lane. "And, I mean, when you would find a penny! I still pick up pennies. Of course, kids nowadays have decided that pennies aren't worth it. But if you get a hundred pennies, that's a dollar. It's still a dollar."

Back then, people were trusting. "I mean, people left their doors open," said Victor Roberts. "You could walk in anybody's house in the whole area. Nobody kept their doors locked—and there were very few incidents of any sort, though anybody could have gone in to burglarize your home."

"The police knew everyone in the neighborhood. They'd say to the kids, 'Get off the corner. You got to get off the corner.' If you didn't, they'd take you and bop you upside your head," said Dr. Wright. "But they had respect. Everyone knew officer Tom Brooks and the others. And when they came around, you knew it was time to do what you had to do. Shape *up*."

As the years went by, the neighborhood changed. In 1948, the U.S. Supreme Court made a landmark decision in a case, *Shelley v. Kraemer*, that originated in St. Louis. A Black couple, J. D. and Ethel Shelley, had bought a small two-story house at 4600 Labadie, near the Ville, in a mostly white area. They didn't know it, but in 1911, 30 out of 39 property owners there had signed a racially restrictive covenant, which prohibited Blacks from living there. A white family nearby, Louis and Fern Kraemer, filed suit on behalf of the neighborhood.

The case made its way through the lower courts to the U.S. Supreme Court, where attorney Thurgood Marshall argued that racially restrictive covenants cannot be enforced by courts under the Fourteenth Amendment. While this decision did not make covenants illegal, it made them unenforceable—which, in effect, rendered them powerless. "The restrictive covenants as we have known them in the United States are dead," said the *Argus*, ". . . surely, surely, a better place in which all men can live together is rapidly drawing nigh."[7]

In St. Louis, a city riddled with some 380 such covenants by the 1940s, Black people were now legally free to leave the Ville and buy any house they could afford. But during the 1950s, the Real Estate Exchange still urged its members to "redline"—and threatened expulsion for those who sold properties to Blacks in white areas. As historian Colin Gordon noted, after *Shelley v. Kraemer*, "the Exchange quickly 'approved a recommendation of the Committee on the Protection of Property that no realtor shall sell to Negroes, or finance any transaction involving the purchase of a Negro of any property north of Easton Avenue and west of Marcus Avenue, nor elsewhere outside of the established unrestricted districts.'"[8]

Yet many of those doctors and lawyers who had been forced to inhabit the Ville or other Black enclaves did manage to step up to fancier homes—and white flight took place on those streets, as well as the city generally. At its high watermark in 1950, the city population reached 850,000, but year by year, it dwindled. And the Ville? The departure of Black professionals left the community to a more limited group of people: those who could not afford to move out.

## CHAPTER SIX

# "A First-Class Place"
## The War and Washington University, 1940–1950

*"The fact cannot be overemphasized that excellence in one's own field, small as it may be, is the best and perhaps the only way in which each individual can help overcome the worldwide problem of racial discrimination. When a Negro or any other minority group member becomes a devoted and competent physician, everyone tends to forget that he is a Negro, but remembers him merely as a good doctor."*

—Dr. Robert Elman (1897–1956), surgeon, professor of clinical surgery at Washington University School of Medicine and head of surgery at Homer G. Phillips Hospital. In 1945, he won the Samuel D. Gross Prize for his groundbreaking research on amino acids through injection, which was said to have saved thousands of starving people in post-World War II Europe.

AT THE START of the 1940s, momentous change was on the horizon in every aspect of life: in international politics, in the national economy, in city government, and in the bustling world of Homer G. Phillips Hospital. In December 1941, after the Japanese attack on Pearl Harbor, the United States was at war. At home, under President Franklin Roosevelt, the dormant economy was coming back to life, and the lean days of the decade-long Great Depression were numbered. In St. Louis, Mayor Bernard Dickmann—a friend and benefactor of Homer G. Phillips Hospital—lost a re-election bid to the less-supportive William Dee Becker.

For its part, the hospital had been thriving. Interns—27 in 1940—continued to flock to it for training, still mostly from Meharry and Howard, but a few from other places, such as McGill and Wayne State. In 1941, said the *Argus*, the 19 interns represented "almost one-third of the Negro medical graduates throughout the United States . . . there being only sixty-two graduates in all." In 1940, a *Post-Dispatch* story featured Dr. Benjamin Kagwa, who had received his medical degree from New York University. He could have trained in New York City but chose Homer G. Phillips for his internship because he had heard that it was "the largest Negro hospital in the world."[1]

Yet behind the scenes, heated discussions were taking place about the future of the hospital. Once the war began, both Washington University and Saint Louis University found themselves short-staffed, as faculty and residents disappeared to join the war effort. So these schools, which had planned to take turns every two years collaborating with Homer G. Phillips Hospital, faced serious and even acrimonious questions about which of them would be involved. At the same time, a grand jury review pointed to the need for a major administrative overhaul of Homer G. Phillips.

In the end, sweeping leadership change occurred, with talented Black administrators as well as distinguished white faculty members from Washington University coming on board. The new head of surgery was the well-respected Dr. Robert Elman, who worked closely with the new medical director and surgeon, Dr. William Sinkler, to create a rigorous, productive program. Meanwhile, the nursing school's new head, Estelle Massey Riddle, would race in like a human hurricane: shaking up the program, launching new initiatives, and tirelessly pleading for money from old friends of the institution such as the Rosenwald Fund.

The nursing program, and indeed the hospital as a whole, was shaken to the core by wartime exigencies, and many nurses were now admitted as "Cadet Nurses," signifying their readiness to aid the war effort at home or abroad. Day by day, the hospital also had to struggle with inequities in staffing and funding: in 1944, it spent $4.86 per patient, while City Hospital #1 spent $6.81.[2] Still, Mary

Fig. 6.1: A well-known surgeon and researcher at Washington University School of Medicine, Dr. Robert Elman (1897–1956) also served as director of surgery and chief of staff at Homer G. Phillips Hospital. Courtesy of the Bernard Becker Medical Library Archives, Washington University in St. Louis.

Vincent Clarke, who had trained at Howard, joined Phillips as a staff nurse during these years and thought the institution was wonderful. "It trained doctors and specialists, laboratory technicians— the whole gamut," she said. "It was a first-class place."

**Dr. Robert Elman**, *a graduate of Harvard and Johns Hopkins University Medical School, "was always a brilliant student," wrote colleague Dr. Peter Heinbecker. Dr. Elman did lifelong work on the function of the pancreas, became known internationally for his work on intravenous nourishment of surgical patients, and wrote a seminal textbook. "In St. Louis, one of his greatest contributions was to the education of colored physicians and surgeons of the Homer G. Phillips Hospital, where he was Chief of Staff and Director of the Surgical Service." Among other contributions to the hospital, he instituted a five-year training program for African American surgeons.*

In 1941, the leadership of Homer G. Phillips turned over completely to a new, often younger, staff. Dr. Sinkler replaced the former medical director, Dr. Henry Hampton. Dr. Oral McClellan, appointed by the previous mayor, was out as hospital superintendent, and the $3,000-per-year job went instead to Dr. Wallace Christian, the urologist who had first interested attorney Homer G. Phillips in demanding a new Black hospital. At the same time, Mayor Becker announced he would submit a bill to the Board of Aldermen asking for a salary increase large enough that these hospital heads could devote full time to their new jobs, without maintaining an outside practice.

This shift in administration was politically motivated, said an *Argus* editorial. "The Negro politicians are hovering around Homer G. Phillips Hospital like varmints around a carcass. We understand that the leading candidates for the positions of superintendent of the hospital and medical director . . . are Negroes who played the prominent part in the election of Mr. Becker." Officially, Dr. McClellan was said to have resigned, but he was not happy. He filed suit against the city for more compensation, charging that while he had received a $200 monthly salary, he had never gotten a residence, lighting, heating, and laundry as the city had promised. A St. Louis court agreed and awarded him $3,161.[3]

Meanwhile, the Rosenwald Fund was quietly making new awards to the hospital. It donated $500 to a scholarship fund so that nurses who wanted more education could borrow money to get it. The foundation also granted $2,500 to the hospital for psychiatric teaching and research, conducted by Dr. Hyman H. Fingert. In 1940, it gave $1,500 to three nurses for yearlong study leaves, and in 1942 it granted scholarship aid to Dr. H. Phillip Venable and Dr. Herbert Erwin.

In 1945, the energetic staff added another new program to the curriculum: the School for X-Ray Technology, under Dr. William Allen. It graduated its first class in 1947, and soon its alumni were populating medical groups around the country. The School of Medical Record Library Science was also established in 1946, and within the first 16 years had 77 graduates. A philanthropic group of women raised funds to equip a medical library at the hospital.

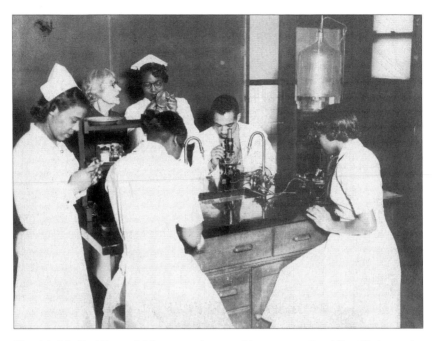

Fig. 6.2: Medical Record Library students and instructors Geraldine Phelps and Doris Mosley were hard at work in the hospital's chemistry laboratory. Photo ca. 1950s. Courtesy of the Missouri Historical Society, St. Louis.

At a National Medical Association ceremony in 1954 honoring him, noted the *Argus*, Dr. Elman "said things that would have cost him his job twenty-five years ago. 'Rigid segregation may lead to disaster. The seriously injured should be treated at the closest hospital, rather than subjecting the patient to the added risk of transportation across the city solely because of the color of his skin.'"[4]

Little by little, however, Jim Crow was starting to wane, and the war helped to diminish its power. On December 7, 1941, first-year nursing student Dorothy Jenkins Coleman was in the nurses' residence along with the other students when they received an urgent summons from the house mother. "She told us what had happened at Pearl Harbor," said Mrs. Coleman. "We didn't even know where that was. But we started crying because we were all worrying that our brothers might be drafted."

Quickly and dramatically, the war transformed life at the hospital. "All of a sudden, interns were turning up in uniform, and we knew they were on their way," recalled Mrs. Coleman. "We were afraid we would never see them again. It was a very sad time." When trainee Jarone Johnson was drafted and sent to Fort Huachuca in Arizona to do medical work at the all-Black hospital, he had to give up his Rosenwald Fund fellowship; so did Dr. William Smiley, who stood in for pathology head Dr. J. Owen Blache when he was called off to service. Dr. James Whittico enlisted and served in the military for four long years.

Civilian Defense also named Homer G. Phillips as a base hospital for Black citizens in case of an air raid on the city. Soon the staff was planning for large-scale emergency services, including a new emergency room in the sub-basement, "which will be able to function for six or eight hours at top speed through the aid of storage batteries in the event electrical service is disrupted," said an *Argus* account.[5]

Budding nurses could train as members of the non-discriminatory U.S. Cadet Nurse Corps. A *Post-Dispatch* story announced the program, saying that 612 nurses would be accepted across the city: 265 at City Hospital #1, 99 at DePaul, 74 at St. Mary's in East St. Louis, 20 at St. John's, and 154 at Homer G. Phillips. Best of all for many nurses, the program supplied a generous subsidy: tuition, books, patriotic blue-and-red uniforms, and a stipend.

The whole emphasis was on speed, since the war effort might need new recruits at any time, so this program accelerated nurses' training from 36 months to only 30. "The government was trying to get us through in a hurry, so we could go over there and help," recalled cadet nurse Gretchen McCullum. "But my boyfriend and I got a laugh out of it, because he was a staff sergeant in the military, and I had a higher rank than he did. I said, 'You're going to have to salute me.' And he said, 'The heck I am!'"

Another cadet nurse at Homer G. Phillips was Pauline Payne, who had three brothers in uniform. She longed to be a nurse, but she had 10 brothers in all, and there was no money for tuition. "There weren't enough nurses during the war years, so they needed to train some to take care of veterans when they came back home.

Fig. 6.3: During World War II, many nursing students were admitted to Homer G. Phillips as "Cadet Nurses," who trained in an accelerated program and declared their willingness to serve the war effort at home or abroad. Some 612 cadet nursing slots were available across St. Louis, 154 of them at Homer G. A group of Cadet Nurses is shown here. Photo from *The History and Development of Homer G. Phillips Hospital*, by William H. Sinkler, M.D., and Sadye Coleman, ca. 1944. Courtesy of the Missouri Historical Society, St. Louis.

And we didn't have to pay—they paid us! I found a paystub from those years: $10 every two weeks. That is what we made." Blanche Tutt, the seventh of eight children, also joined up. "In 1944, I was at Sumner High School, and I had a classmate, Earline, who was sweet as a peach. When Earline decided she was going to be a cadet nurse, I thought, 'Well, I'm going to be one, too,' so I applied to Homer G. Phillips."

Future nursing students were also touched by the war effort. In 1944, Marybelle Barnes lived with her aunt and uncle in Alabama near the Tuskegee Institute campus. There, she often caught sight of the Tuskegee Airmen, who were training to go to war. "Oh, I just thought they looked so good," she says. "They would come on campus and walk around. After they got their wings to become pilots, they received these beautiful blue scarves, which they would wrap around their necks and parade around campus. We had to pick up our mail at the post office, so of course we would pretend to go to the mailbox just so we could gawk at them."

The Ville neighborhood surrounding the hospital also emptied of young men, who learned lessons about equality—and their own abilities—while they were away. In January 1943, Victor Roberts joined the 92nd Infantry, one of two Black Army divisions, and the experience highlighted his education and intellect. "I took the Army general classification tests where they would see what possibilities you have. I was number one in the group taking them, which showed that we could do the same things as others and were going to do just as well."

Still, racial injustice lingered—to cruel effect. After the conflict was over, Blanche Tutt's brothers began coming back from military service. Her 23-year-old sister was preparing to get married, and her fiancé was arriving home shortly for the ceremony. "But she had a ruptured appendix, and the doctor ordered some penicillin for her." A new medication, it was in short supply and very expensive; somehow, her father cobbled together the cost of the prescription. "But do you know what? They gave it to the wife of this prominent person instead, and my sister died as a result. That killed Mamma, when we lost her. Mamma didn't live four years after that."

*"At Homer G. Phillips Hospital, we started out with a truly integrated staff. Fortunately, there were enough trained Negro surgeons in St. Louis to share equally in the responsibilities. Since each surgical ward needed two visiting surgeons, we were able to assign patients to these wards in rotation: first to a Negro physician, then to a white physician. Emergency calls on a 24-hour basis were also handled in the same way. The important point to emphasize is that each of them worked side by side on an equal plane, respecting each other's opinions, interchanging judgments and experiences, and taking over each other's services when either was out of the city."*

—Dr. Robert Elman quoted in the *St. Louis American*, August 19, 1954

Since 1935, leading physicians at Saint Louis University and at Washington University School of Medicine, in consultation with the city health commissioner, had been discussing their role at City Hospital #1 and the forthcoming Homer G. Phillips Hospital. In part their motives were altruistic, wanting to help indigent patients. Further, they felt strongly that Black physicians and trainees needed more opportunities to practice. But they were also drawn by the vast number of cases, some unusual, that would enrich the training of their own residents, interns, and medical students.

In 1938, the head of otolaryngology at Washington University complained to the medical dean, Dr. Philip Shaffer, that "we have not been able to use City Hospital #1 for teaching purposes as planned because of the lack of space. The medical director has asked us to send only one-half as many students as we had expected to teach. We need a service at City Hospital #2 [Homer G. Phillips]. We are prepared to take care of such a service at a moment's notice."[6]

Still, Washington University administrators vacillated for years as to how much responsibility to take. In 1938, Dr. Shaffer wrote to Father Alphonse Schwittala, dean of the Saint Louis University School of Medicine, that their previous two-year rotation plan shouldn't go forward. "One principle we should like adopted is that each assignment of service be on a somewhat permanent arrangement and not subject to rotation. . . . This would seem to be the best plan for the gradual building up of a well-knit, responsible and effective organization in each of the clinical services."

In January 1939, Dr. Shaffer convened an extraordinary meeting, attended by department heads and leading physicians. Dr. Nathan Womack, a surgeon, quickly took a swing at the two-year rotation plan, saying: "It is impossible to work up a service knowing that in two years you have to give it up."

Other racial issues then surfaced, as Dr. Henry Schwarz, OB-GYN, worried that "the white students would not work with Negro interns and nurses." Dr. T. K. Brown noted that "The white students, especially those from the South, resent having Negro interns telling them what to do" and wondered whether both universities might wish to turn over "City Hospital #2 to the colored physicians."

In the end, the University adopted a core goal: a faculty member would direct each Homer G. Phillips hospital service, but these white physicians would work toward enabling "members of the colored medical profession to prepare themselves progressively for administrative medical responsibility." At the urging of Dr. Elman, surgery worked out a collegial plan for working with the Black attending staff: Patients would be assigned to Black and white surgeons alternately, and each would be wholly responsible for that case. And the two-year rotation plan remained, so that Washington University would be at Homer G. Phillips through June 1941.

*"Dr. Elman was an excellent teacher. He came over from Washington University, which had a great reputation as a medical school, of course, and he was very active in what was called non-surgical physiology. He had one of the big names in surgery, so that gave added luster to the internship at Homer Phillips."*

—Dr. LaSalle Leffall Jr., Homer G. Phillips intern and later the Charles R. Drew Professor of Surgery at Howard University College of Medicine

As soon as their partnership began, Dr. Shaffer assigned four Washington University faculty members to direct Homer G. Phillips departments: Dr. T. K. Brown to serve as chief of staff and head of OB-GYN; Dr. Leo Gottlieb to head internal medicine; Dr. Louis Birsner to direct otolaryngology; and Dr. Elman to lead surgery. In one giant coup for the young hospital, Dr. Evarts Graham agreed to become a visiting professor; in another, world-famous plastic surgeons James Barrett Brown, Minot Fryer, and Frank McDowell took part in plastic surgery cases.

Drs. Elman and Gottlieb, both Jewish, were assuming a particularly heavy responsibility, since medicine (120 beds) and surgery (106 beds) were the two biggest services in the new hospital. But they were only the latest in a line of Jewish physicians who were active at City Hospital #2 and Homer G. Phillips Hospital. During the 1940s, Jewish surgeons at the hospital also included Drs. Carl Heifetz, Leo Sachar, Sam Schneider, Major Seelig, Arthur Proetz,

Fig. 6.4: Dr. Evarts A. Graham (1883–1957) was the distinguished chairman of surgery at Washington University School of Medicine and a visiting member of the Homer G. Phillips Hospital medical staff. He was a strong supporter of the hospital and its mission. Courtesy of the Bernard Becker Medical Library Archives, Washington University in St. Louis.

Jacob Probstein, and neurosurgeon Henry Schwartz. "The Jewish community was very intimately connected with Homer Phillips," said surgeon Dr. Frank Richards.

In 1940, a year after he became chief of staff, Dr. Brown wrote a glowing report about the hospital's operation. Altogether, 1,477 babies had been born; 1,033 people had died. Some 660 major and 702 minor operations had been performed, with residents doing 62 percent of the cases. The X-ray department, under Dr. E. W. Spinzig and Dr. William Allen, had seen some 11,000 patients, while the always-busy outpatient department had handled 63,000 visits. The excellent social service department was growing. The noted Dr. David Rioch from Washington University was establishing a neuropsychiatry service, mentoring a talented young Black neuropsychiatrist, Dr. Herbert Erwin, who was a resident in the field.

The faculty coming from Washington University for case presentations and lectures were some of the finest in the United States. Dr. Graham talked about the history of surgery; Dr. Nathan Womack discussed pancreatic disease. Dr. Graham himself solicited noted surgeon Dr. Glover Copher to deliver a Saturday morning lecture series to senior students. Renowned internal medicine head Dr. W. Barry Wood Jr., covered the timely topic of penicillin and its uses. Prominent Black physicians presented, including Dr. A. N. Vaughn on peritonitis.

Under the direction of Dr. Alexis Hartmann, Children's Hospital pediatricians—particularly Dr. Park White—were performing heroic service at Homer G. Phillips. Dr. White, a staunch liberal and civil rights advocate, was a committed staff member and longtime head of pediatrics; he also became a fervent letter-writer, whenever newspapers criticized the hospital. "How easy it is for the 'white press' . . . to demand investigations of Homer Phillips Hospital . . . although the underpaid and overworked staffs . . . are doing a better job of caring for the indigent sick than ever before," he wrote angrily to the *Star-Times*.[7]

Thus, in 1941, when its commitment to Homer G. Phillips should have expired, the university instead decided to sign on for another two years, with an end date of July 1943. Throughout Missouri, patients were becoming aware of the hospital's reputation. A mayor's committee, convened in 1941 to critique the city's public hospitals, could only find one operational flaw: "an estimate that 4 to ten percent of patients admitted are not residents of St. Louis. Patients are said to come from 'hundreds of miles' south of St. Louis."[8]

"*Dr. Elman revolutionized the treatment of ruptured appendix. When penicillin came down the pike, he began to use it in the preoperative management of ruptured appendicitis. He said, 'Well, Whittico, from here on out, we're going to stop just taking patients immediately to the operating room with a ruptured appendix. What we're going to do is correct any deficiencies in electrolyte and fluid balance, and we're going to start a routine administration of penicillin antibiotic for some period prior to surgery.' And that approach was all from Elman.*"

—Dr. James Whittico, Homer G. Phillips trainee and surgeon

Dr. Frank Richards knew Dr. Elman as his chief and his mentor. "He was the greatest. He would come out every Friday to conduct the surgical conferences with our staff, and he helped to train us. He was a wonderful teacher, absolutely terrific. He also helped write articles and books that were connected with the staff at Homer Phillips, and he did a lot of his experimental work with us."

Both Dr. Elman and Dr. Graham became tireless advocates for the hospital. In 1942, they worked closely with the American College of Surgeons (ACS) to secure accreditation for graduate instruction there. They were concerned about support from the city administration, mostly the comptroller, who was "refusing to give the Homer G. Phillips Hospital sufficient finances to carry on as it should as an approved hospital." They also worried about "unfavorable physical, managerial and disciplinary conditions. . . . Much of the trouble in the institution apart from finances is apparently due to the management."[9]

As the two men looked toward the hospital's future, a key goal was locating a capable medical director. "Such a person should . . . have a background of clinical experience, have a flair for administrative work and at least a minimum amount of practical experience," wrote Dr. Graham to the ACS. But the growing leadership ability of Dr. William Sinkler soon allayed these worries. A medical graduate of Howard, he had done all his training at City Hospital #2 and stayed on as an attending.

The staff and University physicians alike respected him. As Dr. Elman said: "Dr. Sinkler, of course, is our real pillar of strength. His official activities, as well as the many hours of time and effort he gives outside and beyond the call of duty, has been the greatest single factor in whatever success has been achieved at the Homer G. Phillips Hospital."[10] Dr. H. Phillip Venable agreed. "Dr. Sinkler brought an entirely new philosophy to Homer G. Phillips Hospital. It was his considered opinion that we must train the young Negro doctor so that in future years he would be able to stand on his own."

Another bright spot was the collegiality of the relationship between the University and the hospital. As Dr. Frank Richards wrote, this connection "should in no way be construed as a strategy

Fig. 6.5: For many former trainees, the Homer G. Phillips Alumni Banquet was the highlight of the year. This dinner was held in 1947; the white-haired man, seated in front, was the hospital's pediatric director, Dr. Park J. White. Courtesy of the Bernard Becker Medical Library Archives, Washington University in St. Louis.

by which Washington University sought to gain absolute control of the various departments or exclude black physicians from positions of importance. On the contrary, the university encouraged the recruitment of black physicians in all staff capacities."[11]

> "A program of rehabilitation . . . we have established at the Homer G. Phillips Hospital . . . I believe is the only one in any hospital in the city of St. Louis and perhaps in the state of Missouri. . . . We learned that nearly one half million dollars are expended for direct relief to totally disabled Negroes in the city of St. Louis each year, and that much of this money could be saved by medical rehabilitation of many of these applicants, a program in which we are now actively engaged."
>
>       —Dr. Robert Elman quoted in the St. Louis American, August 19, 1954

After years of campaigning for a Black nursing head, Black leaders and newspapers had at last gotten their wish. In January 1940, Estelle Massey Riddle came to St. Louis, after serving most recently at the Rosenwald Fund. The eighth of 11 children in a poor Texas family, she had earned a nursing degree at City Hospital #2, followed by a bachelor's and a master's degree at Columbia University Teachers' College, thanks to a Rosenwald grant. No one could doubt that she was eminently qualified for her new job. "We think it not too much to say that Mrs. Riddle is the best qualified woman of her race . . . to man this department," said the *Argus*.

Yet some of the students found her daunting, even imperious. Dorothy Jenkins Coleman, who graduated in 1944, admits to being afraid of her. "I was in the solarium one day, and there was lots of talking going on. Suddenly, someone said 'There's Mrs. Riddle'— but she added a smart word to the sentence. So Mrs. Riddle walked in and said she'd heard that, and she looked at *me!* Well, I was always taught to be respectful of elders, and I would never have done that. I told her I hadn't said it, but I don't think she believed me."

One person who was delighted by Mrs. Riddle's appointment was Dr. Bousfield of the Rosenwald Fund. He had known her when she worked at the foundation, and now he wrote ecstatically to city and nursing officials that her appointment was "almost like a new year's resolution" come true. "Some of us have felt that the whole institution needed 'spark plugging.' It is very likely that this hustling young woman will do just that."[12]

Unfortunately for Dr. Bousfield, he became one target of her hustling. Throughout the two years of her tenure, she peppered him with letters begging him to find Rosenwald Fund support for a variety of causes, particularly scholarships for nurses. He wrote back, unfailingly polite: sometimes parrying her requests, sometimes acceding, and occasionally turning her down flat. Their lively exchange also shows that she was eager for him to come to St. Louis as commencement speaker, conference attendee, adviser, and institutional friend.[13]

Mrs. Riddle surrounded herself with talented staff nurses, among them Hallie Del Wynn, educational director; Juliette Lee, instructor; and Huldah McCarthy, research director. She also hired Mary Vincent Clarke, a Howard nursing graduate with a bachelor's degree from West Virginia State. "I met a friend at West Virginia, Frankie Thomas, who had gone to Homer G. Phillips," recalled Mrs. Clarke, "and she told me, 'Put in an application at Homer Phillips. Ms. Riddle will hire you.' So, I sent my application, and she said, 'Come on.' She was interested in nurses going forward and getting their degrees. She was ahead of her time." Mrs. Riddle was also an indefatigable writer, and in one journal article, she described her success in encouraging staff members to use unpaid summer leave to go back to school.

During Mrs. Riddle's tenure, a nursing student graduated who would break barriers. Velma E. Murphy Jones, a cadet nurse in a class of 40 students, graduated in 1946 and began working at Homer G. Phillips Hospital. Three years later, she and three others became the first African American registered nurses hired at Barnes Hospital; after a promotion, she became the first Black nurse in charge of a nursing division at Barnes, where she went on to work for 35 years.

Beginning in the early 1940s, Dr. Christian was criticized for being old-fashioned and reluctant to change. He nearly lost his job in 1941, and then in 1945 he was asked to resign. His successor was Virgil McKnight, chief clerk at the hospital since 1941. Dr. Sinkler also threatened to resign at the same time—twice submitting his resignation—but was persuaded to remain. At the end of 1941, Mrs. Riddle felt beaten down by her inability to make progress toward improving the nursing school because of a balky administration.

The nurses were also becoming restive about their low pay—lower than that of nurses doing comparable jobs at City Hospital #1—an inequity that Mrs. Riddle had not been able to fix. In 1942, nurses staged a mass resignation, and the city administration raised their wages. A jubilant *Argus* had rooted for their success. "There is no explanation under the sun that can remove the just cause of these nurses. The only explanation . . . would be that 'these petitioners are colored and are therefore not entitled to the same pay and consideration that are given white nurses."[14]

In October 1942, Mrs. Riddle had had enough. She quit and moved to Ohio; her replacement was Henrietta Farrar, a graduate of the Harlem Hospital School of Nursing. Not long after Mrs. Riddle's departure, the nursing school dismissed 10 second-year students—one-fifth of their class—for academic deficiencies. Some 40 nurses stopped work for an hour in sympathy, and the entire class failed to report to work the next day. Soon the city hospital commissioner, cowed by the threat of a complete work stoppage, agreed to reinstate the dismissed students.

> *"'Working together' has also been achieved at the Homer G. Phillips Hospital in the form of a Citizen's Committee composed of men and women, white and colored, lay volunteers from all walks of life, who take time from their busy lives to . . . discuss each month the affairs of the Homer G. Phillips Hospital . . . to go to the city fathers with their findings, [and] to seek improvement for the care of patients. Although only in existence for a few years, this citizens group has achieved a number of objectives, one of which was ferreting out the information that $750,000 remained unspent from a previous bond issue from the city and by getting a judicial ruling which has now made it available for expansion of our hospital."*
> —Dr. Robert Elman quoted in the *St. Louis American*, August 19, 1954

During the 1940s, Homer G. Phillips treated a broad mix of patients, especially in its noted emergency rooms. Some were severely injured in fires or auto accidents. In one case, a three-year-old fell from a burning building. Some of those treated were criminals. Newspapers, white and Black, featured raw tales of dead or dying people transported to Homer G. by ambulance, police, or friends who dropped them off and fled.

Amid these cases were some unusual incidents. In 1941, a 27-year-old woman—a "modern Houdini," marveled the *Argus*—escaped the hospital's fourth-floor prisoner's ward by sliding down a rope sheet 30 feet to the ground, while still wearing her handcuffs.

"She was last seen getting into a taxicab," said the story. In 1942, a Black cotton picker from the Missouri Bootheel, shot in the face by a white plantation sub-boss, languished in prison for six days before finally being brought to Homer G. Phillips for treatment.

In 1949, the *St. Louis American* ran a story about a Homer G. Phillips intern, Dr. J. Smith, who "was saved from serious injury and possibly death, when other doctors discovered a former mental patient who sought to ambush him with a five-inch knife. . . . Noticing her patrolling back and forth, the doctors questioned her. She readily admitted that she was waiting for Dr. Smith and made no secret of her surgical intentions towards him."

Despite the advent of antibiotics, there were far too many cases of tuberculosis, which continued to take a heavy toll in the St. Louis Black community. The *Post-Dispatch* reported that the city had higher rates of the disease than the average for the 15 largest cities in the United States. Mortality among the white population in 1946 was 34.9 per 100,000, but among Blacks it was a startling 151.1 per 100,000.[15]

In the pediatric ward, new cases of polio kept the nurses busy in the days before vaccine. Gretchen McCullum devoted herself to severely affected children confined to the old iron-lung machines. One teenage boy, Rex, was passionately interested in the war effort, but he had few visitors. So, McCullum's own husband began stopping by to update Rex on war news. McCullum herself tried to ease the pain of the iron-lung children by volunteering to put hot packs on them, over and over, to relieve their muscle spasms.

Occasionally, children were injured while they were patients. One little girl wandered up to an open window, covered only with a screen, and pushed. "She leaned over too far, and she fell," says McCullum, "but what was so amazing is she lived to tell about it. It was like she slid down a ladder."

*"One of the first successful thoracoabdominal esophageal gastrectomies in St. Louis was performed at the Homer G. Phillips Hospital nearly ten years ago. Five years ago, the first pelvic evisceration for advanced cancer was carried out at the Homer G. Phillips Hospital; the only others in St. Louis are*

*being done at Barnes. This patient is now living and well and was followed by a number of others, several of whom have also been successfully carried through. One of our white visiting surgeons . . . expressed his sincere desire to be treated himself at the Homer G. Phillips Hospital should he suffer from such a serious type of injury."*
> —Dr. Robert Elman quoted in the *St. Louis American*, August 19, 1954

In 1943, the St. Louis hospital commissioner reported that, at both city hospitals, the patient census had decreased markedly that year. The total patient count at Homer G. Phillips was 207,985, down from 217,230 in the previous year. The number of admissions had also fallen: At Homer G., 208 beds were vacant out of 753, "the highest vacancy in the institution's history." He attributed the downturn to a decrease in the number of indigent St. Louisans, since more had found employment in war production work.

Yet clinical research and training continued to flourish. During the 1940s, three Homer G. Phillips residents engaged in burn research, both at their own hospital and at Washington University, as part of a government contract. In 1947, three senior residents were selected to do research in internal medicine, pediatrics, and general surgery under Washington University department heads. In 1949, under the leadership of Dr. Elman, Dr. Leo Sachar, and Dr. Charles Frazer, a research fellow in cancer surgery, the hospital received a $12,000 grant from the American Cancer Society for work on nutrition in cancer patients. Another grant for nearly $20,000 came from the U.S. Public Health Service for the expansion of mental health services.

Once again, in 1943, the old question came up: Would Homer G. partner with Washington University or Saint Louis University? A year earlier, the ACS had recommended abolishing the rotation system, instead adopting a plan "whereby there could be a definite continuity of the teaching program for the resident staff." Dean Shaffer proposed that Washington University hang on for another year, and Dean Schwitalla agreed. But that year stretched into three.

At a top-level meeting in 1946, department heads discussed the matter and agreed that the hospital was crucial for post-graduate teaching of University students. Anyway, they said, "within a matter of five or ten years [the hospital] would be staffed by colored physicians, in keeping with the original tenets." If staying on would cause a rift with Saint Louis University, however, they would bow out.[16] In the end, Washington University decided that it wanted to stay indefinitely.

Finally, the war ended in 1945, and staff began returning from their service. Business slowly returned to normal, though some of the same problems remained. In the late 1940s, articles appeared in the *Argus* about inequities in pay at Homer G.; interns there received $50 per month, while interns at the white City Hospital #1 received $95. Money was also short in other ways. Dr. Barry Wood wrote to Dr. Bousfield begging for some Rosenwald funds to pay a University internist "with drive and enthusiasm" to take over the Homer G. clinical program—a most difficult task to accomplish with volunteers. With regret, Dr. Bousfield responded that the Rosenwald Fund was fading out of existence, having depleted its funds. Dr. Wood also wrote to the city asking for financial support, but the hospital commissioner replied condescendingly that "traditionally, the Visiting Physicians of the City institutions deem it a privilege to participate in the medical care of the indigent sick."

In 1949, Black attorney Sidney Redmond wrote an inflammatory column for the *Argus* claiming that poor treatment at the hospital had resulted in the deaths of at least two people, including an infant. As Redmond said, "The two white medical schools in St. Louis have used the patients at Homer Phillips Hospital as guinea pigs for years. . . . I know the teachers perform experiments on them that they do not choose to perform at City Hospital #1 . . . numbers have been killed as a result of the treatments, even many more have suffered much pain . . ."

Even the mild-mannered Dr. Wood was angry, and he admitted in a letter to his dean that "it made my blood pressure rise a few points when I read it." For years, his staff and many others at the university had been volunteering their time—even through the difficult wartime years—to help out. An aldermanic hearing on the complaints produced only two witnesses, and a legion of doctors defended the hospital. Both cases were dismissed.

> *"Two years ago, we received a letter from a prominent [white] Texas attorney, thanking the Homer G. Phillips Hospital for having trained their young doctors so well. You see, one of our surgical residents, after his training period was finished, was inducted in the army and found himself in an army surgical center in Frankfurt, Germany. There, he was asked to operate on this lawyer's daughter-in-law for intestinal obstruction, which he did and pulled her through magnificently. . . . When I thanked the white surgeon-in-chief of a large hospital in Fort Worth, Texas, for his liberal attitude in permitting for the first time a Negro surgeon, one of our former Homer G. Phillips surgical residents, to operate in his white hospital . . . he said, 'Don't thank me. I only did what I always do: Give facilities to the surgeons who are equipped to give their patients first-class care. Dr. Griffen is such a surgeon. We are glad to have him work in our hospital.'"*
>
> —Dr. Robert Elman quoted in *St. Louis American,* August 19, 1954

The war had broken down some racial boundaries, particularly after President Harry S. Truman issued Executive Order 9981 in 1948, which decreed that "there shall be equality of treatment and opportunity for persons in the armed services without regard to race, color, religion or national origin." Simply and unambiguously, Truman had outlawed segregation in the military—though implementing this principle proved a difficult, drawn-out process.

That year, Dr. Montague Cobb—an anatomy professor at Howard and a member of the NAACP's National Medical Committee— issued his own unvarnished report on "Medical Care and the Plight of the Negro." Also in 1948, Henry and Katharine Pringle published an article in *The Saturday Evening Post* called "The Color Line in Medicine." Both pieces were scathing indictments of a system in which Blacks were less healthy than whites and had fewer chances to consult Black doctors, who were more likely to treat them well than whites.

Further, Dr. Cobb said, "Negro life expectancy has shown a constant lag of about 10 years behind whites. In 1940, the life expectation of Negroes at birth was 52.26 years for males and 55.56 years for females; that of white 62.81 for males and 67.29 years for females." The Negro mortality rate in that year was 71 percent higher than the rate for whites. "Nearly all diseases which show excess mortality in the Negro are classed as preventable. Conditions like tuberculosis, maternal and infant mortality, and venereal disease regularly show high incidence in any group of low economic status, where there is ignorance, overcrowding, poor nutrition, bad sanitation and lack of medical care."[17]

The Pringle piece agreed, adding that at the heart of the problem lay a shortage of Black doctors. "Only 4,000 Negroes are now practicing medicine, as compared with 176,000 white physicians, and it is estimated that more than 5,300 more are needed to care for the increasing Negro population. The national average today is one colored doctor to every 3,337 Negroes, although the accepted minimum standard is one to 1,500. In Mississippi, the ratio is one to 18,527."[18]

Why weren't there more Black doctors? The Pringles cited a report of the President's Committee on Civil Rights blaming this shortage on "the discriminatory policy of our medical schools in admitting minority students." Only two of the 77 U.S. medical schools freely admitted "Negro applicants, and these are Negro institutions. Many hospitals, vital to the training of all physicians, close their doors to the colored medical graduate. Yet every day, mothers and babies die for lack of proper treatment."[19]

In both articles, Homer G. Phillips Hospital came in for favorable mention as an institution doing its best in a difficult environment. Yet, the tide was clearly turning against segregated hospitals. In his report, Dr. Cobb opposed the creation of any new segregated facilities. It was time, he said, for full and complete integration.

St. Louis was moving slowly toward that goal. In 1944, Saint Louis University began considering the admission of Black students. During mass, the Rev. Claude Heithaus, a faculty member, appealed to 500 students to stand together in ridding themselves of "un-Christian prejudice" and back this proposal. The entire room full of students rose in support. Later, pediatrician Dr. Park White wrote a heartfelt tribute to Rev. Heithaus for his courage.

Gradually, some Black physicians at Homer G. Phillips were joining the Washington University staff. Dr. Sinkler was the first surgeon admitted to the university's surgical faculty. In 1949, four prominent Black physicians—Drs. J. Owen Blache, G. A. Gaikins, E. B. Williams, and Helen E. Nash—were also admitted. A new fellow in surgery was Dr. James Whittico.

The world was changing. But in hindsight, said Dr. Homer Nash, a segregated hospital like Homer G. Phillips really "should never have existed in the first place."

## CHAPTER SEVEN

# Cheating the Grim Reaper
## Surgery at Homer G. Phillips Hospital

*"We had four operating rooms, and of course Barnes had many more. They were better staffed, too, but we had adequate equipment. Don't misunderstand me that Homer G. Phillips Hospital was an inferior little place across town. It was an outstanding facility, medically and socially. The main thing is that it employed so many Afro-Americans."*

> —Frank O. Richards, MD (1923–2014), 1947 medical graduate of Howard University, intern and resident at Homer G. Phillips from 1947–1952, later staff surgeon and head of the surgery department

*"At Homer G. Phillips, we treated the patients like our fathers, our mothers, our sisters, and brothers. We wanted them to live; we didn't want no dead patients."*

> —Dorothy Payne Thornton, nursing graduate of Homer G. Phillips and then a surgical nurse and clinical instructor

A VITAL NERVE center at Homer G. Phillips Hospital was 3 North, the surgery floor. "Picture an X," said surgical nurse Georgia Anderson, who walked the four legs of that X for decades. At the center, just off the elevator, were the four largest operating rooms and a fifth, smaller room for minor procedures. The office of the supervising nurse—for many years, Mabel C. Northcross—was also there, as were lounges, a large recovery room, and a kitchen.

The two legs of the X on the north side of the hospital were surgical wards for male patients; the two on the south were gynecology and genitourinary (GU). After her operation, a tubal ligation patient returned to gynecology on the southwest side, while a prostatectomy case went off to GU on the southeast. On the male surgery side of the floor, patients with infectious problems, such as leg ulcers, were assigned to the northeast side, while non-infectious problems, such as gastric ulcers, went to the northwest. Other floors also sent surgery patients to 3 North. From the fifth floor came orthopedic injuries, as well as eye or ear-nose-and-throat cases; women with breast masses were transported from the fourth.

On each leg of this floor, a long hallway led visitors past offices and a handful of private rooms assigned to patients who needed close attention. At the end of the corridor was an open ward with two rows of iron bedsteads on each side—up to 80 patients in all. Rounding out the varied spaces on each wing were linen closets, utility rooms, and showers and baths.

But the key rooms of all were the ORs—particularly "A," the main operating room, with its balcony viewing area open to visiting medical staff. The room, lined with supply cabinets, was a "restful green," said Mrs. Anderson; the floor was terrazzo. Its centerpiece was the large OR table, flanked by a chair for the anesthesiologist. Just off the OR was a scrub room and a tiny sterilizer nook housing the autoclave and a water bath. "As Dr. Eugene Mitchell, a surgeon, used to say sometimes, they would cheat the Grim Reaper here, because many lives were saved in these four walls," said nurse Zenobia Thompson.[1]

Like most of the rooms in the hospital, the ORs had screened windows—and that was lucky, because in the warm months, they were often open. To everyone's discomfort, the hospital was not air-conditioned, though window units were later installed in some areas. For many years, the dripping-hot medical staff used various ways to keep cool: fans, fans plus open windows, cool cloths on the physician's necks or backs. "Oh yes, we got real innovative," said Mrs. Anderson. "The hospital had an ice plant, where we made our own ice. We had an engineer bring up 50 or 100 pounds of ice and blow fans over it to drop the temperature in the unit."

The floor also had its secrets. Behind the kitchen was the innocently named "prep room." There, the staff took the bodies of dead patients so they could wrap and prepare them for transport to the basement-level morgue.

Fig. 7.1: Later an eminent member of the Washington University surgical staff, Dr. Frank O. Richards (1923–2014) trained at Homer G. Phillips Hospital from 1947 to 1952 and then became a staff surgeon and head of the surgery department. Photo ca. 2005. Courtesy of the Bernard Becker Medical Library Archives, Washington University in St. Louis.

*"Initially, I was interested in OB-GYN, but we delivered so many babies at Homer Phillips that I got so I did not like obstetrics. I said I didn't want to see any more babies born, and I switched into the surgical residency. I liked the act of surgery, and I enjoyed the people in the training program. Many of the fellows who trained at Homer Phillips went on to very prominent institutions. We trained more Afro-American surgeons here than anywhere else in the world."*

—Dr. Frank Richards

Fig. 7.2: A nursing graduate of
the hospital and later a surgical
nurse and clinical instructor,
Dorothy Payne Thornton was
a protégé of head surgical
nurse Mabel C. Northcross.
In fact, some called her "Miss
Northcross the Second."
Courtesy of Georgia Anderson.

*"My mother said I really got started in medicine when I was
a child, because whenever she saw the cat come around the
house with his leg splinted, she knew that Dottie had something to do with it. I had the dog and the cat hopping. When I
got to nursing school at Homer G., I worked on OB-GYN at
first, but I loved the chest. I liked the way we worked around
the heart and the lungs: how you breathe, why you breathe,
how much lung can we leave in or take out."*

—Dorothy Payne Thornton

Why do young trainees choose the highly demanding field of
surgery? It's exciting, said Dr. Earle U. Robinson Jr., whether you
specialize in a single part of the body or not. "For general surgeons,
you get to do something different every day, while in an area like
mine, OB-GYN, you're dealing with one thing," he said. "General

surgeons got to know a little bit about everything, and I got to know all about OB."

Homer G. Phillips was an ideal place to immerse yourself in all kinds of surgery. "Not only did you have a large volume of cases, but you had different types of cases: head and neck, abdominal, extremity, endocrine, thyroid, parathyroid—just everything. And that made it so wonderful," said Dr. LaSalle Lefall, an intern from 1952–53 and later a Howard University surgeon.

The work was also mesmerizing. "I remember the first night I worked on a surgical service, and I looked up and the sun was coming in. I said, 'I'll be damned. I worked all night,'" said Dr. Benjamin Majors, a surgical trainee. "This was very common. But you didn't mind because there was a lot of—not monetary reward—but personal satisfaction that you were becoming a very good doctor."[2]

Surgical nurses also fell in love with the field. "On the medicine floor, patients were always being readmitted for the same chronic problems, but I liked the fact that the surgery patients' recovery was shorter," said Wanda Claxton Trotter. "Surgery was the most interesting of all the services I went through," added Mrs. Anderson. "And *ooh*, I loved doing chest surgery. I could stay in the field all day with a chest case. Those sutures were like poetry in motion. It was fun, fun, fun, *fun*, and I loved it."'

The department even spawned surgical research, said Dr. Robinson. "The surgical service wanted to find ways of caring for patients who were malnourished or needed supplemental alimentary feeding for major surgery. Back then, the surgery residency took maybe twelve people, and after the first year they cut it to four. The people who were cut went into ancillary services, hoping they would be pulled back into the residency. They called it the metabolism service or the research service. In one co-study, they made a baby fluid and a nutritional supplement for surgery."

At Homer G. Phillips, surgeons and nurse specialists had plenty of opportunity to use their skills. By 1940, the surgery service performed some 660 major and 702 minor operations with a post-operative mortality rate of only 7 percent. The total number of procedures soared from there. By the early 1950s, the number of operations had grown to around 8,000.[3] Fully 2/3 of these operations were done by trainees. "This is the policy of the staff in regard to the training of the house staff, that they obtain the majority of operations done in the hospital," wrote Dr. T. K. Brown, chief of staff.[4]

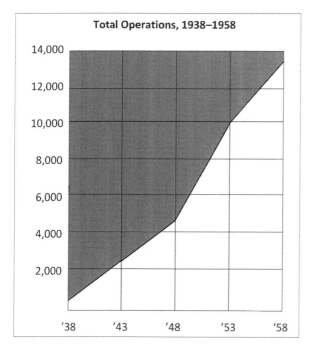

Fig. 7.3: This graph of hospital activity was printed in the hospital's 25th anniversary brochure from 1962. Courtesy of the Bernard Becker Medical Library Archives, Washington University in St. Louis.

By the time the hospital closed in 1979, some 235 residents had finished at least one year of general surgical training: 117 in gynecology and obstetrics, and 90 others in otolaryngology, urology, and orthopedics. Although budding surgeons were exposed to neurosurgery, plastic surgery, and thoracic surgery, they moved on to other institutions for further training in these subspecialties.[5]

*"Dr. Sinkler was my cousin, and he played a part in me going to Homer Phillips. He was also the medical director and eventually director of surgery. He was dynamic; in essence, he was responsible for a lot of the success of the hospital. Of course,*

*we took care of indigent patients, and Dr. Sinkler used to have a saying that if any patient there was not treated like a patient at Barnes or a private doctor, that resident would be fired."*

—Dr. Frank Richards, winner of the William H. Sinkler, MD, Award given by the surgical section of the National Medical Association in 1960

*"Dr. Sinkler was like a general, very professional. When he did something, he did it, and he wanted it done right. He was precise. You just felt like, 'I am with the king. I am with the king.'"*

—Dorothy Payne Thornton

Fig. 7.4: Dr. William Sinkler (1906–1960) trained at the hospital and stayed on to play a major leadership role, becoming medical director in 1941 and surgical director in 1956. He was the first Black surgeon admitted to Washington University's surgical faculty. Courtesy of the Bernard Becker Medical Library Archives, Washington University in St. Louis.

Like so many on his staff, Dr. William Sinkler (1906–1960) had gone to medical school at Howard, graduating in 1932, and then trained at the old City Hospital #2 before moving over to Homer G. Phillips. Afterwards, Dr. Sinkler, who was born in South Carolina, stayed on in town. While building up a successful private practice at Vandeventer and Enright, he trained surgical nurses at Homer G. Phillips as well as Saint Mary's Infirmary, and in 1950 he began instructing trainees at Washington University.

Meanwhile, he took on increasingly significant roles at Homer G. Phillips. In 1941, he became medical director, and in 1956 he rose to director of surgery. "Dr. Sinkler was a hard worker," recalled Dr. James Whittico. "He would operate at one of the other hospitals— People's or St. Mary's—before he reported to work at Homer G. Phillips, and in most instances he'd be on time."

Under his leadership, trainees flocked to the hospital, sending him joyous letters of appreciation for being chosen. "I accept this appointment with infinite satisfaction," wrote Beaumanoir Prophete, MD, who became a St. Louis urologist. "It has been stated," wrote Dr. Richards, "that during his life span [Dr. Sinkler] influenced in some manner one-third or more of the Black physicians receiving post-graduate medical training. . . . Though short in physical stature, he was tall in many other respects. His house officers often referred to him as 'Little Caesar' or 'Napoleon.' Sinkler insisted upon perfection in all areas."[6]

Altogether, Dr. Sinkler was extraordinary, and not only as a surgeon. "I admired him because he was a thinker beyond a medical thinker," said Amanda Luckett Murphy. "He knew about corporations and negotiating and networking and collaborating. I don't know if he had a business degree or not; I never thought about it. But I remember admiring him: that he could do all of these things and still be a physician. He was a bigger-picture kind of person."

Dr. Sinkler also had strong feelings about social justice. As he wrote in one journal article: "The marked, unequal distribution of physicians will be corrected when, and only when, organized groups, both local and national, cease discrimination against our physicians in hospitals, scientific meetings, and in advanced medical training."[7]

*"Dr. Carl Heifetz was a mentor of mine, and later we wrote two papers together. During my training, I remember that he once wouldn't let me operate because I didn't tie a knot right. And I was late for the operation. So, he told me, 'You go treat the burns or something. You're not going to operate.' Things were tough; the surgeons didn't play around."*

—Dr. Frank Richards

*"Dr. Andrew Spencer was in general surgery, and he went on to be the medical director at Homer G. Phillips. He would walk through with his starched white coat, just like you could eat off his sleeve because it was always so clean and neat. It said, 'Miss, I am important.' In surgery, he was precise and real smart—as smart as a whip."*

—Dorothy Payne Thornton

Through the years, the surgical staff at Homer G. Phillips included some wonderful doctors and some characters—occasionally both at the same time. Dr. Walter Young, a fine cardiovascular surgeon, wore a red rose in his lapel every day, as well as an elegant vest and spats. The well-respected surgeon Dr. Leslie Bond, a trainee at Homer G. Phillips, had strong ties to the hospital's predecessor, City Hospital #2, through his father, a 1920s-era trainee. Dr. J. J. Thomas, a general surgeon and "outstanding," said nurse Mary Vincent Clarke, moonlighted in the coroner's office.

Dr. Frank Richards had superb medical skills, "and his skills were matched only by his modesty," said Dr. Ira Kodner, a colorectal surgeon at Washington University School of Medicine. "He advised his students to always be professional, wear a tie." A close friend was north side resident Victor Roberts, who called him "a wonderful man—very outgoing and very friendly. His patients loved him; people would ask for him all the time. They thought he was the greatest in the world." Sheila Bader, god-daughter of psychiatrist Dr. Herbert Erwin, agreed. "He was a physician's physician. Throughout his practice, he was among the most, and for some people *the* most, respected of the Black physicians."

He had enviable surgical technique, such as operating with one hand while holding instruments in the other. "No one could do that but Frank," said Dr. Will Ross, nephrologist and associate dean for diversity at Washington University. "He was the Jackie Robinson of the surgical profession. He was the best in his field."[8] He was also one of the first African Americans to break the color barrier at Barnes Hospital, though he later worried that younger Black physicians might forget those who had made their careers possible. "When I look back at all the battles we fought to get those doors open," he said, "I don't think our youngsters . . . understand how hard it was for us to get into Barnes."[9]

Fig. 7.5: Shown here is a busy surgical suite at Homer G. Phillips Hospital. Courtesy of the Bernard Becker Medical Library Archives, Washington University in St. Louis.

Another brilliant surgeon was Dr. Andrew Spencer, a trainee at the hospital from 1954 to 1959 and later chief of surgery. "He was a genius, but very high-strung," recalled Mrs. Anderson,

and he got crazy on you when you crossed him or did something he thought was unforgivable. One time, he told a senior resident what operation to do on a patient and what technique to use, but the resident did something different. When Dr. Spencer read the report, he made the resident sit for a full day at the patient's bedside. Sometimes, he would walk past you in the hallway and not speak to you. Or he'd cuss you out, then come to your office and say, 'Georgia, how about this?' as if nothing had happened.

He could be quite intimidating, recalled nurse Carol Horton. When he called to talk to the residents, "they stood up straighter. Their whole demeanor changed when they were talking to Dr. Spencer." Once, she faced his wrath after she had spent the entire day changing the dressings of a critically injured patient in the ICU. Briefly, she left the patient's side to go to the office of Georgia Anderson, then the surgical supervisor, where she took a quick bite of a bologna sandwich. "Dr. Spencer came in and jumped all over me because the patient's dressing was soaked by then. I was so angry that I probably could have hurt him. I remember him saying to Mrs. Anderson, 'What's wrong with her?' Then he said to me, 'Calm down. I just wanted to yell.'"

*"Washington University was very good to us and helped train us. Dr. Robert Elman was my chief, and he was the greatest. I was one of the first Afro-Americans, after Dr. Sinkler, admitted to the University's medical school staff. At that time, the St. Louis Surgical Society was not integrated; I was the first Afro-American admitted. And the only way I got in was because Dr. Carl Moyer, who had become chief of surgery at Washington University, said he was going to resign if they didn't take me. He was a terrific guy, very interested in Homer Phillips."*

—Dr. Frank Richards, who served as the first African American president of the St. Louis Surgical Society in 1991. The Dr. Frank O. Richards Medical Student Scholarship Prizes at Washington University honor him today.

*"At first, we had nothing but Black patients at Homer G., and then a mandate came down that we had to integrate. At 2 a.m. one night, I was on duty in the operating room when a*

*white man who had been stabbed came in. I was prepping him
and shaving his hairy chest when I saw that he had tattoos
saying, 'Kill all niggers.' The man survived, and I saw him
again on post-op rounds with the doctors. So, I said to him,
'You want to change that tattoo you got on your chest?' He
said, 'I'm sorry, I'm sorry!' And I said, 'What would you say
about the treatment you got?' He said, 'Excellent,' and I just
said, 'See?'"*

—Dorothy Payne Thornton

Even on the life-and-death surgery floor, medical personnel en-
countered injustice of various kinds. As a young staff nurse, Carol
Horton was working on the surgery desk one day when a Black
surgeon—a former military officer, who demanded respect—asked
her for a patient's record, which was lying on the desk between
them. "I didn't initially know he expected me to pick it up and
give it to him. Finally, he said, 'Would the nurse please give me the
record?' And I said, 'If the doctor wants the record, he can pick it
up.' He told Georgia Anderson that I was a typical 'sapphire,' an
ugly term."

It's possible, said nurse Brenda Pettiway Walker, that the surgeons and other doctors felt frustrated by their forced limitations.
"Most of them came from Meharry and didn't have anywhere to go
as far as learning and becoming physicians because they were not
accepted in white hospitals. Maybe that trickled down."

As a surgical resident at Homer G. Phillips, Dr. Whittico noticed
that his fellow residents were spending much more time doing surgery than their white counterparts at other hospitals. That meant
they were adept in the operating room, but they had less time to
keep up with the latest articles in the surgical literature. Thus, for
two years he ran a journal club to right the imbalance. "We would
meet every Sunday morning in the library at Homer G. Phillips
Hospital, and I would assign four articles to four different residents. It would be each one's responsibility to read that article and
to come report on it. I was pleasantly surprised at the reaction,
because I got 100 percent cooperation."

Fig. 7.6: An ophthalmologist and outspoken advocate of racial justice, Dr. H. Phillip Venable trained at Homer G. Phillips Hospital, became chairman of its ophthalmology program in 1943, and joined the Washington University faculty in 1958. Portrait, Edwyn Studio, ca. 1965. Courtesy of the Bernard Becker Medical Library Archives, Washington University in St. Louis.

Some Homer G. Phillips surgeons, such as brash, outspoken ophthalmologist Dr. H. Phillip Venable, tried to push equality forward. Dr. Venable himself became the first African American member of the Washington University School of Medicine eye faculty. Thanks to an agreement between him and the renowned Dr. Bernard Becker, that department's socially conscious head, Homer G. Phillips eye residents did their first year of training at the university.

*"Mabel C. Northcross helped train me, and once she put me out of the operating room. I didn't do something properly, and she said: 'Doctor, you can't do that in here. Bye!' I didn't have any choice about it. She was Miss Northcross."*
—Dr. Frank Richards

*"Miss Northcross? They called her 'Ole Miss.' I'm in the operating room because of her and her assistant, Miss Bell. They took a liking to me because they saw my ability—the doctors*

*would always pick me—so Miss Northcross just moved me on. She'd say, 'Put on your mask and go in there and do your work.' She was also funny, hilarious. She was always telling us, 'Honey, the doctors don't want you; they got wives at home. So, don't be smiling at them; just do what they tell you to do.'"*
                        —Dorothy Payne Thornton, a protégé of Miss Northcross, called by one nurse "Miss Northcross the Second"

The empress of the operating rooms was Mabel C. Northcross (1896–1987), a native of Humboldt, Tennessee, and a 1919 nursing graduate of Meharry Medical College. In 1921, she came to

Fig. 7.7: The respected and feared nurse in charge of the operating room was Mabel C. Northcross (1896–1987), a Tennessee native and Meharry nursing graduate, who came to City Hospital #2 in 1921 and stayed on at Homer G. Phillips Hospital for nearly 50 years. Courtesy of the Missouri Historical Society, St. Louis.

City Hospital #2 for training and stayed on at Homer G. Phillips for almost 50 years. "Nobody who met her ever forgot her because she was a charming old lady, though not a very physically attractive one. But charming and always polite," said Mrs. Anderson.

It was impossible to guess her age. When Edna Loeb, who was interested in surgery, came to nursing school in the mid-1950s, she heard right away about Miss Northcross and was eager to meet her. "To me she was old, old, *old* at the time, but she may not have been. She may have been in her 50s, but I thought she seemed like she was in her 70s." Dr. Earle Robinson met Miss Northcross on the first day of his internship. "She was a wizened old lady, probably no taller than 5 foot 2, if that. But she was really smart. She had her rules and regulations, and you had to abide by them."

She was also known for her pithy sayings, rhymes, and advice, recalled Laverna Turner Spinks, such as: "You all move like hogs and sheep going to the pasture/The sheep said to the hog, 'Can't you walk a little faster?'" She urged nurses to attend meetings of the operating room nurses' association, saying, "You need to keep growing, and the way you grow is to find out what other people are doing."

The doctors adored her, said Georgia Anderson, because "she pampered and played up to them. She would tell them she was going to do stuff that she knew she couldn't do, but they believed her, and if they asked about it, she said, 'Oh doctor, I'm working on it.'" But sometimes she lectured them, too. On his first day in surgery, recalled Dr. Robinson, "I was in a scrub suit with blood on it, and Miss Northcross said to me, with her heavy Southern accent, 'Doctor, don't you go out looking like a butcher. Get in there and put on some clean scrubs.'"

If a student made a serious mistake, Miss Northcross might resort to corporal punishment. "Like most of us, I got my hands hit," said nurse Richard W. White. "If you gave the doctor the wrong instrument or if you didn't set your tray up right, you had to stand there and *pow*! She would pick up a pair of sterile forceps and hit you on the knuckles." She used those same forceps to pull someone out of the operating theater if she caught them doing something wrong. A stickler for cleanliness, she made the students disinfect

the operating rooms, even the tops of the lights, after each operation. At a time when infections were rampant in ORs, the Centers
for Disease Control stopped by to check for contamination and
rank the hospital. "We came in first," added White.

Other errors led to overtime duty, said nurse Amanda Luckett
Murphy. "Miss Northcross worked us hour after hour, and if she
perceived us to be doing something that was inappropriate, our
punishment was to report back on duty at 3 p.m. to autoclave
things in the operating room or pack iodoform gauze in bottles and
bags. My class actually rebelled, and we got the hours reduced."
On the other hand, said Jobyna Moore Foster, Miss Northcross's
assistant, Miss Bell, "was an excellent instructor, who put you at
ease. She would guide us through whatever we needed to know."

Mabel Northcross didn't own a car, and she took the bus wherever she went. Officially, she lived on the third floor of the nurses'
residence, but she did not spend much time there. "She would leave
home early in the morning, and then she wouldn't get back until
late," added Ms. Loeb. "She lived and breathed Homer G. Phillips
and that operating room. She was dedicated that much, and everyone respected her. Even the interns and residents who rotated
through were almost to the point of saluting her when she passed
by." Added nurse Mamie Walton: "She could run that operating
room in her sleep."

Nursing classes also rotated through the operating room,
and some students chose that high-pressure place for life. Miss
Northcross introduced them to the field with precision and thor-
oughness, while observing them with a keen eye for talent. The
surgical rotation began at 6 a.m. at the cafeteria door, where Miss
Northcross lined up the students and chose what they would eat for
breakfast. "She said, 'You must have a good breakfast, because if
you're going into the operating room, you don't know when you'll
get out to have some nourishment,'" recalled Mrs. Loeb. "Then she
would sit with us at the table and you had to eat the food. She'd
say, 'OK, little lady, you need to eat more. The doctors are not
looking at you. We want you to eat!'"

Next, she would march the students to the OR suite, where they
changed into scrubs and examined the day's schedule. "She'd say,

'I want you to tell me what you think these cases mean. What is an appendectomy? Where will the incision be made?' Then she set up different trays with the surgical instruments and we had to draw them, so that we'd remember them. I still have that notebook to this day, and I treasure it. I learned instruments. Oh, yes."

Iver Gandy had just begun a nursing job at Jewish Hospital in St. Louis, when she stepped on the elevator, and a doctor noticed her Homer G. Phillips pin. "'Mabel C. Northcross,' he said. I asked, 'Did you rotate through the operating room?' And he replied, 'I sure did. You can ask Mabel C. Northcross anything about an operating room, and she can tell you. I wish all my residents had gone through the operating room with Miss Northcross.'"

She had one sweet secret in her life, recalled Georgia Anderson. "We knew the phone would ring every morning a few minutes after 6 a.m., and she would talk real soft. You'd be sitting in the room and didn't know what she was saying. One morning when I was on duty, the phone rang, and I heard her say, 'Oh, oh,' and she looked so sad. I said, 'What is the matter?' and she replied, 'Oh, my friend, he just died.' That's when we knew she had a boyfriend."

*"I don't regret my surgical training one bit. I would rather have been at Homer Phillips than at Barnes, if you want to know the truth. I thought I got better training. Everyone figured we could operate on anybody in town."*

—Dr. Frank Richards

*"The reason why Homer G. was so special is because we were a family. We interacted with our doctors; we got our training from the horse's mouth, as my grandmother used to say. This is why all of us passed the board. When we did things wrong, they corrected us. During one case, the doctor told me, 'If you don't shut up, Dorothy Payne, I'm going to take a suture and put it between your top lip and your bottom lip, which means, zip it.'"*

—Dorothy Payne Thornton

With all the care and precision in the world, patients sometimes didn't make it. Wanda Trotter had a favorite patient, a lovely

35-year-old woman, married with two small boys, who had gall-bladder disease. "She died on the operating table. She was allergic to the anesthesia but not aware of it; when they put her to sleep, she coded two or three times. Her husband was there, along with her parents, and the doctors had to come out and tell them she had passed away. That was traumatic. That was *very* traumatic."

But there were moments in surgery when the nurses knew they had made a difference. "I had one incident when a surgeon told me to give the patient some morphine, though I knew the dose was too high," said nurse Mamie Walton. "I tried to tell him that the dose was off, but he wasn't hearing it. So, I got the syringe, gave it to him, and said, 'You give it. I can't.' He said, 'Well, what's the problem?' And when I said, 'This is over the normal dose,' he looked at it. Now, he had been up all night, so that man was tired. He said, 'Oh thank you, Miss Walton. Thank you.' And we were cool, you know."

To neophyte nurses, the surgical procedures themselves could also be shocking. Mamie Walton was a student in the 1960s when she went on rounds one morning with Dr. Redie Lemons. "All of a sudden, he asked for his chest tray. He had recognized that a patient was in distress, though it wasn't obvious to me. Before I knew it, he had cracked the ribs and was in massaging the heart. It scared the hell out of me! I all but fainted on the floor! I had never seen so much blood. But the man lived. I just wasn't sure that I was going to live!"

CHAPTER EIGHT

# "Killer Phillips"
## The Hectic Emergency Department

*"A few people gave the hospital a nickname—'Killer Phillips'—because it was a trauma center. Everyone knew that if you were shot or cut, that was where to go. We were a leader in trauma."*

—Richard W. White, Morehouse University graduate, 1967 Homer G. Phillips nursing graduate, who spent 22 years working in the emergency room at Homer G. Phillips

IN HIS BRIEF, 1940s-era history of Homer G. Phillips Hospital, Dr. William Sinkler described its large, often frenetically busy emergency department (ED), also known as the receiving room. It "occupies the entire basement of the administration building (with the exception of the morgue)," he wrote. "It includes two fully equipped emergency rooms, a room for contagious diseases and poison cases; one male and one female diagnostic room; two tub rooms, where patients are bathed when necessary; one stretcher room and a waiting room for the relatives of patients or for ambulatory patients who may have to wait their turn for treatment."[1]

Cases ran the gamut from minor complaints to life-threatening injuries. In the late 1940s, for example, newspapers published daily stories of patients who received care or died at the hospital. When two streetcars collided in 1945, the victims were rushed in for treatment; so was a woman, sitting in her living room on Enright, who was struck by a stray shot fired by a policeman outside. A 27-year-old, indicted in a murder case, had his left arm amputated

159

after a fight. Two sibling patients—a four-month-old and a two-year-old—had been bitten by rats while napping.

"Homer Phillips took care of all the shootings, the stabbings, the accidents in the city. If there was any type of trauma, it was brought in, because we were equipped to take care of it," said Dr. Earle U. Robinson Jr. "We had every service covered. If you were in a car accident, we had orthopedics. If you were shot in the chest, we had a chest service. If you were shot in the abdomen, abdominal surgery would care for that. There were four chiefs on four services who were always on call."

Around town, everyone knew the hospital's reputation, recalled nurse Willa Jean Richardson Nelson. "Surgery. Injuries. Accidents. Bullet shots. Cuts. Everyone said they had the best surgeons ever. If you get sick, cut, whatever, go to Homer G. Phillips emergency room. You're going to get good care. The *best* care."

Sometimes police or ambulances, their red lights flashing, rushed people over to the hospital. "Today, you go into the building, walk all the way to the back, and that was the emergency room door," said nurse Lillian Haywood. "I get a chill when I go back there, because I can still hear those ambulances. Just to hear them, you knew something wasn't good."

*"Dr. Andrew Spencer once said that the only way to stop bleeding is surgery. So, he advocated that, if you were shot or stabbed or in a bad car wreck, get to the operating room. In other hospitals, they wanted to do urine tests, type and cross-match blood—and pretty soon, if you were bleeding, you bled out and you were dead. You can take care of the blood work* after *you are in the operating room, so get the person up there!"*

—Richard W. White

On some nights, especially on sultry summer weekends, the ED itself showed grisly signs of the devastating injuries often treated there. "Blood would meet you at the door and go on a trail up to the operating room," recalled Ethel Long, a 1958 nursing school graduate.

Fig. 8.1: The nursing school admitted male students, and Richard W. White, a 1964 Morehouse College graduate, was the second after David Mitchell, class of 1966. A Texas native, he was at work on the morning the hospital closed. Courtesy of Richard W. White.

In 1942–43, nearly 100 patients arrived every day, and on average some 35 were hospitalized. Over the years, the patient load burgeoned. There was so much demand, in fact, that not only were four full-time physicians assigned to the ED, but so was a bevy of interns and residents. In this trial by fire, they had to learn quickly. "We had a terrific emergency department with physicians who really knew their business. When I left, there was no doubt in my mind that I was a good surgeon," said Dr. Benjamin Majors.

Everyone was pressed into service, even those residents heading into other specialties. In the early 1960s, recalled Dr. Robinson, then a resident, "we rotated to the emergency room, because the hospital was always short on staffing. You could be in OB-GYN like me and take call on that service, but they would still assign you to cover nights in the emergency room.

"It could be bedlam, really," he added.

Some nights there'd be a hundred kids in what they called the pediatric convenience clinic, especially in cold weather when mothers were bringing in babies with upper respiratory infections. St. Louis always had an epidemic of asthma because of where it's situated, so some nights we'd see 30 and 40 asthmatic patients. In the emergency room, one side would be for trauma; the other side would be medicine, where you'd have heart attacks, GI bleeding, cerebral hemorrhages, the whole bit. And then half the medicine side was pediatrics, like crush injuries from wringer washing machines. So even though you had several doctors down there, you'd be covering the whole thing.

Nursing students also pitched in to help. "We could go on the wards to work after school, and I think we got a dollar an hour. Eight dollars a shift. We would sign up to scrub in the operating room," said Barbara Pool, a 1965 nursing graduate. "They had a list, and when those red ambulances would come down there, with all those gunshot wounds and everything, the phone in the hall would sound. They would be calling for students to come over and work."

Although doctors and nurses were stretched to the limit, they later appreciated their blistering experience in the ER. "The Homer G. Phillips training was the most rigorous I ever had," said Amanda Luckett Murphy, a 1958 nursing graduate. "They insisted that you do it right. What did you learn? Stamina. Perseverance. Toughness. How to think quickly on your feet because when they said, 'gunshot wound,' we knew the guts were in the hands, and we had to put that patient back together. You had to be able to do that. Tough skinned-ness is not something all people have, but if you came out of Phillips, you really had it."

The word got around that this hospital was not only good but also extraordinarily efficient. "It was the buzzword—'the best hospital, where you got the best care,'" said Jobyna Moore Foster. "We had an excellent supervisor, Mrs. Vivian Bernard, who ran that emergency room like a tight ship. Oh, my, yes. She had doctors

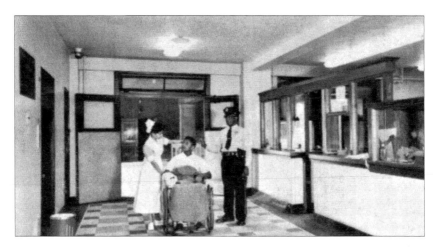

Fig. 8.2: As seen in this photo from a hospital brochure, patients arrived for treatment in the lobby of the Emergency Department near the nurses' station. Guards were always on duty. Courtesy of the Bernard Becker Medical Library Archives, Washington University in St. Louis.

and nurses moving just like clockwork. Mm, hm. Stretcher bearers, ambulance drivers, everybody. They jumped to her music." When patients arrived in the emergency room, "sure enough, they'd take them up to the operating room: prepped, shaved, scrubbed down, dressed, information given—boom, to the operating room. Less than fifteen minutes."

On a Friday or Saturday, Lt. Col. Everett Page, a St. Louis police officer from 1964 to 2003, often dealt with several seriously injured patients. "I would always take them to Homer Phillips because I knew the trauma staff there was the best," he said. "I don't recall anyone dying that we took in there alive. I thought it was just extraordinary that a hospital was able to do the things they did. They took that job very seriously, even to the point that most African American police officers would say, 'If something happens to me, you make sure I get to Homer Phillips.'"

*"There was a man called Chocolate, and he owned a bar down on West Florissant. He was kind of like a gangster, and he got shot on the steps of the federal courthouse with a shotgun.*

*His arm was almost hanging off when they brought him in, and they operated on him for a long time, but they reattached it. I took care of him in intensive care for a couple of days. Then his girlfriend came up and said, 'I'm going to call an ambulance, get you transferred to Barnes and out of this old nasty hospital.' And he laid out and said, 'Bitch, you see this arm? It's working. I ain't going nowhere.'"*

—Richard W. White

Treatment often began in the hospital driveway. "We used the radio to notify Homer G. we were coming in with a serious gunshot wound," said Col. Page. "When we arrived, they were there in the driveway with the gurneys, the doctors, the nurses—the *team*—waiting to start working on these individuals."

Once the patient appeared inside, the admitting department would quickly ask for personal details. "We had to stand at a window, because we were not allowed to sit," said Aretha Johnson Reynolds Price. "The patient would walk in, and we would get preliminary information: name and address, what your problem was at that time. We had employees who were assigned to go to the room to get as much information from the patient as possible, especially the financial side of it, and if they had insurance."

As often as not, added Mrs. Price, there was precious little time for discussion. "If the case was a gunshot wound or a car accident, they would tell us, 'We're not stopping,' by putting up a hand. So, we would get our papers and things and run alongside to try to interview the patient, getting as much as we could. I've also witnessed nurses on top of patients on their way to the elevator, trying to keep them breathing until they got to the operating room."

There were tricks to asking financial questions, she added, since some patients were cagey about what they had:

Mr. Jeffrey Miller was our boss, and he was tough, but one thing he said stuck with me: the art of interviewing and asking open-ended questions. For example, he would say, "Don't ask them, 'Do you have a car?' Ask them, 'What *type* of car do you have?'" I just thought that was so smart. They all said, "No, I don't have a car," because they didn't want to have to pay. The way we looked at, if you owned a home, or if you owned a car, you were able to pay your bill."

Still, all of this took place in the blink of any eye, recalled nurse Mary Crawford Lane. "The emergency department was fast turnover, *really* fast turnover. You did things to help right away. And we didn't listen to no long, tall stories, because the blood don't stop when you tell these long, tall stories."

*"One of our classmates the first year got shot real bad by her boyfriend from high school, but they operated on her all night long, so that she had two big scars on both sides of her neck. Dr. Andrew Spencer did that, along with Dr. Eugene Mitchell. Mitchell was the fastest surgeon I've ever seen. His dexterity in the operating room was just remarkable. Remarkable."*
                                        —Richard W. White

Somehow, most patients made it. "When I was rushed to Homer G. Phillips Hospital," said one-time patient Lamarr Harps, "I had been shot four times. My injuries were in my right leg, left leg, right hand, and in my abdomen. Through all of that, I survived. So you can't say that there's not a God above, 'cause between God and Homer G. I'm here."

"I remember one gentleman came through, who had been shot in the head. I mean, you could actually see brain tissue," said nurse Johnnye Robinson Farrell. "But he walked out; he survived. A lot of times, they would call the chiefs of staff—Dr. Frank Richards, Dr. Andrew Spencer, whoever—and they were successful. So even if people were shot or stabbed, they actually had a very good chance of survival."

Patients seemed to be everywhere. "One day, I was leaving the hospital, going back to the nurses' home, and this fellow walked up to me and said, 'I need some help.' He had been shot in the neck. He had some bleeding, and I took off my nursing apron—my last one—to put around him, so that was a lost apron. I walked him into the ED and left him there, and I heard he survived," said Laverna Turner Spinks, a 1955 nursing graduate.

Still, not all cases were as serious as the shooting victims, and some people were even regulars. "Malina was our weekend drunk who was always being admitted," said nurse Farrell. "She would tell you, 'I'm throwing up my liver.' I mean, she was just obnoxious—and you had to admit her every time. Ask anybody that worked on any of the female floors or in the emergency room: They remember Malina."

Other cases were a sad mixture of medical care and social work. "When wintertime came, we always got an influx of the hobos from the trains," said Richard W. White. "Since they had been outside, they had spider bites that had turned into abscesses. They were malnourished, too, so they were candidates to be hospitalized. We'd get them healthy by the time spring came, and then they were gone. They went back to ride the trains again."

Of course, one never-ending reason for ED visits was the arrival of babies. Women in labor would deliver in the emergency room or in the tub room upstairs, where staff could prepare them for delivery. But sometimes, the babies came too quickly—or maybe the mother's life was at stake. "I saw a doctor do a Caesarean section without any anesthesia—no local, no nothing," said nurse Charlotte Steel. "They just had to go in and get the baby. That was amazing. The doctor said, 'We don't have time. Get the scalpel.' So that's what they did, and the mother and baby lived."

Hardest of all was seeing children with serious burns come in and then stay to undergo painful treatments. "Oh, God. I can still hear it, I can just *hear* it," said nurse Alverne Meekins Eldridge, who did a student rotation on this service. "They would put all those kids into one crib to go into the treatment room for their silver nitrate dressings. They screamed and cried before they went; they knew where they were going—and the screams were so piercing.

"I recall this one kid, about five or six, named Darrell," she added.

He was burned, third degree, from head to toe; I think he was the only one from his family who survived that fire. He kept saying, "My leg, my leg, my leg." So I told them that, they X-rayed that little boy's leg, and it was broken, so he had to go into a cast. But you know what? I don't remember any of the children dying when I was there. The whole thing just broke my heart, and I went back to the dorm and said, "Lord, if you help me get through these three months, you don't have to worry about me working in peds."

*"I remember the first death I saw. We were trying to get this man up to the operating room, but he was shot pretty bad. Sometimes patients connect; they hold your hand. This one said, 'Don't let me die,' and I said, 'Man, I got you.' When we got up to the operating room, he took his last breath. And that just shook me, you know, because I had promised him."*
—Richard W. White

"We worked, we worked. There wasn't none of this sit-down stuff. We really worked," said Mary Crawford Lane. "I just didn't like it when on Friday, Saturday nights, policemen would bring in the DOAs. How can you be DOA running *away* from them? I never could understand that. They're running away, and they get shot in the back?"

Too often, young men incurred these catastrophic wounds in disputes over—or with—women. Nurse Gretchen McCullum felt horrified by such unnecessary loss of life: "One man, and this ain't funny, one man they brought in there was shot two or three times. He ended up dying, because it was just one of them things. I think it was three nights in a row that that happened. And we said, 'They must be making the women mad this weekend, because we really been busy.'"

Pointless loss of life became the constant theme of life in the ED. "There was one patient who would take rat poison, and I felt that she did it to get the attention of her husband," said Aretha Price. "Maybe the fourth time she didn't get there quick enough, or she took too much, and she didn't make it. Some people would come at the same time, maybe on a Thursday or a Friday, and I don't know if this was the time they were bored or wanted to be around people.

It seemed like they would do different things just to be admitted to the hospital."

Young nurses learned about death and the violent ways in which people died. "I remember one patient dead on arrival," said nurse Charlotte Steel, then a student. "The doctor brought us in and asked us, 'Well, what's, what's wrong with this guy?' He was a young fellow, in his 20s, and we didn't see any visible trauma. We all guessed, 'birth defect,' 'heart attack.' Then the doctor said, 'OK, now I'm going to show you something.' He took an instrument and lifted his nipple up. The patient had a gunshot wound hidden right in that area."

Sometimes students had traumatizing experiences. Joanne Allen Love, employed as a nurse during the week at DePaul Hospital, worked weekends in the ED at Homer Phillips, because she enjoyed the excitement and liked the extra money. But she never knew what might happen next. "One time a lady came in and threw this dead baby in my arms," she said. "I didn't know what to do with it. But we got the experience of taking care of trauma. We worked together, and we saved lives. People came in mangled, but they finally went home."

Yet sometimes they didn't. Minervia Bennett Williams was a nursing student when she made rounds one night with the evening nurse. "We got to the room of a seventeen-year-old, who had been shot, and he said, 'I'm not going to be here when you come back.' I said, 'What are you talking about?' He repeated, 'I'm not going to be here when you come back, so let me shake your hand.' I let him shake my hand. We went down the floor, came back, and he was dead."

Why did people die? What allows one patient to make it while another slips away? Brenda Pettiway Walker, a nursing student at the time, loved fixing up ED patients: shaving them, soaking their feet, doing their hair. "They gave the derelicts to me, and I would just clean them up," she said. "But I would come back the next day, and the person would be dead. That happened almost a half dozen times. Finally, the nurse came to me and said, 'Baby, I know that you like to help people, but these folks have been dirty for years.

When you come and bathe them, soak their feet, or wash their hair, you take the dirt off too fast. From now on, you can't do all of that at once. You have to do it in stages.' She was serious, and I said, 'OK.' They didn't die after that."

As always, dead children tugged on the heartstrings most. Yvonne Jones remembered one little boy who choked to death on a hot dog; another one on a penny. "The thing that bothered me most was seeing children brought in who had been burned in a fire—I mean third-degree burns. They brought them in in white sheets, and that has been in my mind since day one," remembered Dr. Lee Blount, a surgeon.

When a person died, the admitting staff had to inventory his or her belongings, bag them up, and make sure that nothing disappeared. "It would be the interviewer doing that with a security guard or a police officer on staff," said Aretha Price. "It was always two people to ensure that no money or any valuables were taken from the patient. I remember one patient who died—a well-known pimp in the city with diamonds in his front teeth. The officer had to hold open his mouth while I counted each diamond to ensure that, when they picked up his body, he had all his diamonds. I'll never, ever forget that in my life. Never."

After a death, the victim's friends and relatives often wanted to see their loved one's body. "A group of Black Muslims got into a shoot-up," said nurse Georgia Anderson,

and one of them was killed outright. Two others were shot real bad, and one of them died. We were scared to death to tell the leader, but Dr. Spencer, the surgery chief, said, "Somebody got to tell him." So, Dr. Spencer and I told him. Then the leader said, "Will the brothers be able to view his body?" And we said, "Yes. But how are you going to do that without disruption?" And he said, "We'll just march around his bed and look." We pulled a bed out in the middle of the floor, and there must have been 100, 150 of them. They marched around that bed, looked at him, marched out, and left. Nothing happened. Nothing. The only thing you could hear was the shuffling of feet.

*"I worked the 4th of July one time. A husband and wife—I guess they got into an argument, and she stabbed him with one of those long forks, but he had enough presence of mind not to take it out. When he came into the hospital, he was holding the fork. Of course, she was crying, 'I didn't mean it, baby,' and all this kind of stuff. Anyway, we got to call the police; you had to call them on any gunshot wound or whatever. And when the policeman came, they were hugging and kissing."*

—Richard W. White

Often, cases ended happily with the patient's physical—and even emotional—wounds healed. Altogether, the Homer G. Phillips ED was often gratifying and always exciting. Prospective nursing students considered that reputation before they applied, recalled nurse Lillian Haywood. "My aunt said: 'Why don't you go to Homer G. Phillips?' I had heard a lot of stories about the emergency room, and they were kind of like horror stories: gunshot wounds and all of that. I didn't really know if I wanted to see that; I just wanted to go where it wasn't as exciting. But I applied and was accepted."

Early on, people from the community would drop by the ED and watch, just for fun. "My grandmother raised us, and on weekends we used to go over to Homer Phillips and sit in the waiting room," said Aretha Price.

This may sound a little different, but it was our form of entertainment. I don't know if we had a TV at that time. We would sit there on those brown, hard benches—almost like the pews you see in church—just watching to see what type of patients they brought in. We saw the walk-ins, and we saw them take people out of ambulances. We never even thought about whether they had diseases that could harm you, like tuberculosis. We might sit there for a couple of hours, and then we would take the bus or streetcar and go back home.

But for staff, there was a whiff of danger, especially when the injured party was a criminal. At the time of his residency, recalled Dr. Robinson, "they didn't have an ambulance service like they have now. Most people transported to the hospital in emergencies who were criminals were brought by police van. Usually there'd be two officers: one driving and one in back. I had some confrontations with patients who tried to accost me, but there was always a policeman in the room when you were sewing someone up."

Once in a while, an encounter escalated into an attack. "I was working 3 to 11 in the emergency room, sitting up at the admission window and waiting on another patient, when a man came up," said nurse Johnnye Robinson Farrell.

He had been drinking, and he was complaining because he wanted to go in right then. I said, "Well, sir, I'm doing something right now. I'll take care of you." Then he said, "Oh, I remember you. You're the nurse that stuck that thermometer down my throat." And he hit me and broke my nose. Well, there were several policemen standing around at the time, so of course he got the worst of it. I was off work quite a while, because they didn't want me to come back until after I went to court. When we got to trial, his family tried to bribe me not to press charges, but he got about 18 months in jail.

In the 1960s, the city invested in a new ED for Homer G. Phillips to update the space, but some of the same problems persisted. "I had worked in the emergency room for no more than a month when my beloved wife found out that there was a shooting in the emergency room, though completely on the opposite end," said obstetrician/gynecologist Dr. Nathaniel Murdock. "The emergency room was a long corridor, probably a half-block long; I really was in no danger at all. But my wife said: 'You know, we really don't need money that badly, so I think you should come out of there.' She didn't just 'think': She was telling me."

But others liked the whole experience. "The very best thing for me was working in the emergency room. I liked the doctors down there, and I got familiar with the police," said Blanche Tutt, a 1948 nursing graduate. "Working there, I saw so many things in life, just out in the raw."

## CHAPTER NINE

# "First-Rate . . . in Every Respect"
## 1950–1960

*"There is no question in my mind: One of the best experiences in my medical life was at Homer Phillips. Why was that? Because of the training we received and the excellent teaching we got from people who were on the staff then, specifically Dr. William Sinkler, Dr. Frank Richards, and Dr. James Whittico. I'm glad I chose Homer Phillips. The internship was first rate, in my judgment, in every respect."*

—Dr. LaSalle D. Leffall Jr. (1930–2019), 1952 graduate of Howard University College of Medicine, intern at Homer G. Phillips Hospital (1952–53), resident at Freedmen's Memorial Hospital (1954–1957), later chairman of the Department of Surgery at Howard and the Charles R. Drew Professor of Surgery

THE DECADE OF the 1950s was a bustling, fast-paced time at Homer G. Phillips Hospital. On the staff side, dedicated Black doctors—working collegially with visiting physicians from Washington University School of Medicine—continued to treat indigent patients and train classes of Black interns and residents, most from Meharry and Howard medical schools. Patients flocked to the hospital in greater-than-ever numbers, often creating an overflow that led to a line of gurneys parked in the hallways.

The torrent of patients was astonishing. In 1950–51 alone, the hospital admitted 17,691 people, including 3,242 newborns, and treated 55,973 in the receiving (emergency) room. In 1952, they calculated

Fig. 9.1: Dr. LaSalle D. Leffall Jr. (1930–2019) earned a medical degree from Howard University in 1952 and did an internship at Homer G. Phillips Hospital from 1952 to 1953. Courtesy of the Bernard Becker Medical Library Archives, Washington University in St. Louis.

their training statistics since 1919 when City Hospital #2, the predecessor institution to Homer G. Phillips, first opened: 620 interns and residents in all, 10 medical record librarians, 55 lab technicians, 26 X-ray technicians, and 479 nurses.[1] Three-quarters of the African American babies in St. Louis were born at Homer G. Phillips.

At times it seemed they handled every kind of case imaginable, from the tiniest babies to the oldest adults. In fact, on January 1, 1950, Mrs. Ophelia Lane of Lawton Avenue gave birth to a son, Leon William Lane, at 12:04 a.m.—the first new baby of the decade in St. Louis. That same day, Henry Houston, a retired railroad worker who was 100 years old, died at the hospital. His obituary said he had been born a slave in 1850 on a North Carolina plantation.

"Homer G. Phillips was a happy place in the 1950s," said nurse Georgia Anderson. "We felt that what we were doing was of value to the community and the world—and it was. We were a proud group."

Yet, as newspapers reported with growing intensity, trouble was brewing for the hospital. A series of investigative committees—grand

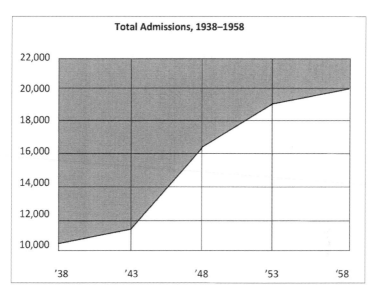

Fig. 9.2: This chart, which originally appeared in a Homer G. Phillips Hospital brochure, shows the total admissions at the hospital from 1938 to 1958. Courtesy of the Bernard Becker Medical Library Archives, Washington University in St. Louis.

juries, mayoral panels, aldermanic inquiries, even studies by the hospital itself—came to two conflicting conclusions. First, they reported that the hospital was overcrowded and staffed by too few people, who were paid too little. But the city's financial planners also declared that, to make its budget balance, the city should be cutting staff at all city public hospitals, including Homer G. Phillips. Worst of all was the dire situation in the cruelly congested mental health ward.

At the same time, another problem was punctuating the decade: a series of deaths among key staff members, each more catastrophic than the last. By the end of the decade, Homer G. Phillips Hospital had lost several leaders who had been mainstays of the hospital's success.

*"I was very pleased with the nurses at Homer Phillips. When we were in training, our professors told us, 'Remember, if you don't have good nurses, it's impossible for you to render the*

*best care possible.' And these nurses were good. They were very good."*

—Dr. LaSalle Leffall, president of the American
College of Surgeons in 1978–79

The first staff death came as a bombshell. By 1950, Henrietta
Farrar had been head of nursing for eight years, replacing the ambitious Estelle Massey Riddle, who had left after only two years.
Mrs. Farrar was tall "and very dignified," recalled Pauline Brown
Payne, who kept a photo of Mrs. Farrar on display for decades after graduation. Mrs. Farrar was kind to her at a key moment, after
Mrs. Payne had injured her back lifting an obese patient. Instead
of insisting that she return to the floor, Mrs. Farrar invited her to
inaugurate a less-strenuous position as clinical instructor, helping
students prepare for the state boards in medicine. The experiment
was a success, and Mrs. Payne's back healed. "I owe so much to
her," she said.

Mrs. Farrar was well-respected, recalled Mary Crawford Lane.
"To me, she was on the ball," she said, adding that students were
a little afraid of her. One night at 2 a.m., Mrs. Lane and her roommate, then students in the Homer G. dormitory, decided to clean
their room. "When we looked up, Mrs. Farrar was standing there
saying: 'Ladies, *ladies.*' Boy, if we could have crawled under the
rug, we would have."

As the new decade began, Mrs. Farrar was earning $366 a month
and living in an apartment in the nurses' residence. "Though she
was not considered a 'popular' executive," said a story in the *St.
Louis American*, "it was known that she had greatly elevated the
standards of the nursing school and was held in high esteem by
hospital officials and those in higher circles in St. Louis."[2]

But in December 1950, she presented a long-overdue bill for
$2,700—payment for student uniforms—to Dr. Walter Hennerich,
hospital commissioner, and John O'Toole, director of public welfare. Confused, they asked her why it had not been paid sooner,
and she explained that she had collected the money from students
as she was supposed to, but it had disappeared from the filing

cabinet where she kept it. Dr. Hennerich impounded her books and discovered, he said, that some $4,900 had gone missing during the previous three years. A warrant was issued charging her with embezzlement.

A few days later, Mrs. Farrar failed to appear for a Saturday class, and staff found her in bed, comatose and dying—the result, they said later, of a deliberate drug overdose. But there was no suicide note, and in letters to her relatives, she had staunchly denied the charges. The *American* was skeptical, asking: "Why should Mrs. Farrar do such a crude thing—receive and keep moneys that would have to be accounted for . . . ? Also, there is the pertinent question going the rounds—were others involved who let her 'take the rap'?" No definitive answers ever emerged.

In 1951, a new director of nursing was appointed: Miss Minnie E. T. Gore, who had previously served as staff nurse, head nurse, medical supervisor, and assistant superintendent of nursing at the hospital. A firm believer in advanced education for nurses, she herself had a bachelor's degree in nursing education, plus a master's degree and some work toward a doctorate. She proved to be a powerful force in the hospital's history. While some students found her daunting or even unfriendly, others described her as strict but fair, and often very kind.

Other new staff members also appeared on the scene, including Juliette Lee, promoted to educational director. "We were afraid of her," said Annie Crawford Ward. "She would set up mathematical equations, and she would make you sit there in a chair and do them in your head. No pencil. No paper. You had to figure it all out. She would say, 'Visualize mentally.' And you're doing this hard math in your head—but you passed it."

*"Dr. Sinkler had graduated from Howard in 1932, at a time of marked segregation. During my senior year in medical school at Howard, he came to speak and said, 'You can get wonderful training at Homer G. Phillips. You'll be able to get experience in surgery in all the disciplines, and I encourage you to come.' So that's where I wanted to go. During my internship, he was*

*the best technical surgeon I saw. He was very good at head and*
*neck, breast, mastectomy, and primarily abdominal surgery."*
                                                    —Dr. LaSalle Leffall

One bright spot at Homer G. Phillips continued to be its hard-
working medical director, Dr. William Sinkler. "He was very brisk
and business-like, and he certainly commanded respect," said Dr.
Homer Nash, then a trainee and later a noted pediatrician. "As
residents, we didn't have much contact with him. If you went to see
him, you had goofed!"

Dr. Sinkler, appointed head of surgery in 1956, was better known
to surgical trainees. "He was a student of surgery, and what I admired about him was that he was a *par excellence* technician. That's
one reason I wanted to work with him," said Dr. James Whittico.
Later, the busy Dr. Sinkler hired Dr. Whittico as an assistant to
make sure his patients were properly admitted to the hospital, their

Fig. 9.3: This class photograph of nurses from 1952 has a signed image of
class member Norris Jackson McReynolds in the middle. Courtesy of Norris
McReynolds.

histories taken, and their physical examinations done; after surgery, Dr. Whittico provided the surgical follow-up.

Perfection was Dr. Sinker's standard, recalled one-time trainee Dr. Clarence S. Avery. "Because he required us to justify our treatment plans and conduct, I went to his office one day to discuss a case. The patient had been shot in the left side of the base of the neck from six feet away with a shotgun, and my prognosis was not an optimistic one. 'You stayed in the Army too long,' Dr. Sinkler told me. 'You do not value human life.' He then reverted to his role as teacher—outlining and explaining treatment which may have altered the outcome."[3]

"I never saw him angry," said nurse Dorothy Thornton. "but when he said 'jump,' everybody jumped. He did it with kindness, though; he was an excellent teacher." On Saturdays, he would initiate new residents into the mysteries of surgery by demonstrating which instrument to use with which layer of skin or which clamp to use on blood vessels.

His career was marked by a series of firsts. He was one of the first Black surgeons to pass the exams of the American Board of Surgery (1947) and gain admission to the American College of Surgeons (1948); the first Black surgeon appointed to the Washington University medical school surgical faculty; and the first Black surgeon to operate at Cardinal Glennon Children's Hospital, Barnes Hospital, and the Jewish Hospital of St. Louis.

All in all, Dr. Sinkler was the person "who really made Homer Phillips shine," said Dr. Leslie Bond. "He was a very staunch medical director, and he would always say, 'You may be treating poor patients, but don't you ever mistreat one of the patients. If you do, you're out.' And you would be out on the streets for two weeks. As interns, we made $30 a month, and they would take out $2 for laundry, which was real skimpy. But if it was found that any house staff member did not treat the patient right, he was still out."

Dr. Leffall agreed. "Dr. Sinkler always told us about treating patients with respect and dignity. I'll never forget when a resident was presenting a patient, Thomas Sullivan, and he said, 'Thomas...' And Dr. Sinkler said, 'You mean *Mr. Sullivan*. Young man, let me tell you this. As long as you're on this service, you never call a patient by his or her first name. It's 'Mr.' this or 'Ms.' That, which lets them know that you're treating them with respect and dignity.' That left a big impression on me, and even today I try not to call you by your first name in front of other patients. You're 'Ms.' This or 'Mr.' that. Treating patients with respect and dignity. No substitute for that. *None.*"

> "*What made Homer G. Phillips so wonderful was not only its large volume of cases, but also the different cases: head and neck surgery, abdominal surgery, extremity surgery, endocrine surgery, thyroid, parathyroid—just everything. They had their share of trauma patients, but that was not the only thing. They had what we called elective cases: cancer of the breast, gallbladder disease, cancer of the intestine, thyroid surgery. We had a vast variety of cases.*"
>
> —Dr. LaSalle Leffall

Other members of the staff were also fine practitioners. One star, hidden from the limelight, was radiologist Dr. William E. Allen Jr., among the first handful of African Americans to take a leading role in that field. An intern at the old City Hospital #2, in 1941 he became director of radiology at Homer G. Phillips, also heading its X-ray technology program. His department averaged 25,000 X-ray exams per year, along with 2,000 X-ray and 100 radium treatments. "People loved him," said nurse Dorothy Thornton. "He was a very good instructor, and he knew his job. He ran a tight ship."

"He was a wonderful person," said nurse Ethel Long. "When we were students, we thought you were just little people there, and someone as important as that might not remember you. But you could pass him, and he would remember your face, maybe even your name, and speak to you very kindly: 'How are you this morning?'"

Another behind-the-scenes person was the hospital's top pathologist, Dr. J. Owen Blache, director of its laboratory, which was chronically underfunded and understaffed. During the 1950s, he

Fig. 9.4: Dr. William E. Allen Jr. (1903–1981) was director of radiology at Homer G. Phillips Hospital, and he founded its X-ray technology program. In 1971, he became the first Black radiologist to join the radiology faculty at the Washington University School of Medicine. Courtesy of the Bernard Becker Medical Library Archives, Washington University in St. Louis.

waged a quixotic battle with the city, begging them repeatedly to allocate more funding. In 1957, for example, he loudly complained "that because of a personnel shortage, the laboratory can maintain only a skeleton staff of technicians on Saturdays and Sundays, available only for handling emergency cases."[4]

Other prominent figures during these years included Dr. James W. Nofles, one of four Black doctors in the country to receive certification in two fields, ophthalmology and otolaryngology. He went on to found and head the Homer G. Phillips' ear, nose and throat clinic. A noted urologist was Dr. Merle B. Herriford, the first Black board-certified urologist in the United States; another was the Haitian-born Dr. Beaumanoir Prophete. In orthopedics, a key figure was a Caucasian surgeon, Earl Holt Jr., who was also on the Washington University medical staff. And internal medicine had Dr.

E. B. Williams Jr., who had trained at the hospital and was "young and talented," said Dr. Robert Elman, named chief of staff in 1952, in a letter.[5]

Fig. 9.5: A group of Homer G. Phillips house officers take part here in an April 1951 interns' convention in St. Louis. The back of the photo lists L. Harris, Lamothe, "Dinks" McMoth, Frank Richards, and Frank Moodon. Courtesy of the Bernard Becker Medical Library Archives, Washington University in St. Louis.

*"I was an intern, so I lived right there on the hospital grounds. It was wonderful, because if you went to your room and got a call, you'd go running on over to the hospital. You were right there. The rooms were spartan. You had a bed, a desk and a lamp, with a common restroom that all of us shared. But that was all we needed. We made $100 per month, and they gave us board, so we all ate heartily."*

—Dr. LaSalle Leffall

Hurrying was what everyone did at the hospital in those hectic days. In sometimes-graphic detail, newspapers reported on the victims of disasters—fires, family disputes, police shootings, auto accidents, animal bites, robbery-related injuries, and various diseases—all sent to Homer G. Phillips. In 1952, 128 kindergartners and first graders were overcome by gas fumes at Dunbar Branch School for Negroes and treated at the hospital. Seven years later, 200 students at Simmons School went to the hospital with stomach upset after eating pieces of "stardust" candy that some mischievous boys had rescued from a dump.

Occasionally, the hospital faced unwelcome publicity for mistakes made by its staff. In 1956, a six-time mother came in, complaining that she was in labor, but the hospital turned her away—and she had the baby in her car, with a policeman assisting. A tragic incident, linked to the segregation of the two city hospitals, took place in 1953, when 18-year-old John Hughes, a light-skinned Black man, was shot near Homer G. Phillips. He managed to drive to the hospital, but once there he was mistaken for a white man and sent 85 blocks south to City Hospital. The staff there identified him as a Black man, and he was sent back to Homer G., but he died en route.

Sadly, there were occasional suicides. In 1950, a 34-year-old woman leapt from the 5th floor window of the hospital. "It looked like to me that on Sundays everything would go crazy. Sundays were like going to the zoo," said Georgia Anderson. "On the third floor one time, I saw this patient who was fidgety. I knew he was an alcoholic, but I didn't think he was in the DTs. I was almost to the end of the ward when he ran past me, jumped up, and leaped out the window feet first. You bat your eyes and say, 'Did that really happen?'"

While that patient died, another was luckier, added Mrs. Anderson. He jumped out the window and fell into a tree, breaking his shoulder. "He started yelling to one of my nurses: 'Miss Cross! Miss Cross! You'd better come down here and get me!' We had to send for the fire department to get him out of there."

Scattered throughout the hospital were prisoners, brought to the hospital from area lockups for treatment. Those needing acute treatment were in beds on the general wards, often with guards sitting constantly by their side; those with less-serious illnesses stayed in the locked ward in the basement. Some prisoners even "swallowed things in jail in order to come to the hospital," said nurse Carol Horton. "They may have swallowed pins or even bedsprings that punctured their intestines. But while they were recovering, they had an opportunity to try to escape." As soon as their guard went to the restroom for a moment, they picked their locks and disappeared—only to be caught and returned a short while later.

"Bernard was one of the chronic prisoners, who did things to stay in jail," recalled Georgia Anderson.

His words were, "Where else can you get three meals a day and people to take care of you?" When Bernard got tired of prison, he would wrap a razor blade in foil and then in a piece of bread and swallow it. Of course, they'd bring him to the hospital, X-ray him, and there it was. Sometimes it would pass right away, and sometimes he'd get to stay a week or two. While he was there, he would pick his locks, get up, go to the bathroom, take a shower, come up to the desk and talk to us, go back to bed, and lock himself back in. Because he didn't plan to go—that's what he said. Why would he leave?

One time, she added, Bernard informed her that he had swallowed a spoon. "I said to him, 'Bernard, you didn't swallow a spoon. Nobody can swallow a spoon!' He said, 'Give me a spoon.' His tray was sitting there, and he reached out and got a teaspoon, put his head back, stuck it in his mouth, and down it went." When the X-rays came back, Bernard did indeed have two spoons in his stomach.

In 1953, Homer G. Phillips installed its first Protestant chaplain: the gentle, well-liked Rev. Guy D. Outlaw, who was joined in 1959 by Rev. Frederick Zimmerman, S. J., the Catholic Chaplain. Rev. Outlaw had a connection to the nursing school as well: His daughter, Juanita O. Long, became its strict but talented educational director in 1961. The *Guardian*, the school yearbook, lauded Rev. Outlaw for his work. "The Chaplain's services to the patients, students, and all who need him are innumerable. He has been a constant comforter and counselor."

During his first eight years at the hospital, Rev. Outlaw paid some 48,000 bedside visits and gave 16,000 holy communions, along with Sunday services and Wednesday vespers for nurses.[6] But a particular focus, said nurse Mary Crawford Lane, were the many derelicts who came to the hospital with dirty, partially bandaged feet. "They let the flies in the wound to make maggots, which would clean it up—and you'd take off the bandage, and it would be the cleanest wound in the world. The next month you'd look for him to come back again with the other foot." The nurses were saddened by this revolving door of poverty, she said, but "the preacher helped us understand that God was still in it. He was in it."

*"If I think about this staff over and over again, as I do now, it was an excellent staff, and I am trying to be as critical as I can be when I say that—because what was the so-called 'downside'? We had very little downside. They really wanted to do well, and they did well."*[7]

—Dr. LaSalle Leffall

Not only was the busy staff involved in patient care, but they were also eager to do investigational work, and some grants in the 1950s helped this research along. In 1951, a group of Shriners—the Order of the Mystic Shrine—gave Homer G. Phillips a welcome $20,000 for cancer and TB research. Later that year, the Shriners made another gift, $15,600, so that the hospital could organize a cancer clinic and conduct research into cancer of the cervix under the leadership of Dr. William Smiley. To celebrate, they hosted a "mammoth parade," said the newspapers, from downtown St. Louis to the hospital building where a program took place on the lawn, with remarks by hospital superintendent, Virgil McKnight.

But that wasn't all. In 1953, the Shriners gave yet another $15,600 to the young Homer G. Phillips Cancer Research Clinic. Already, said Dr. Smiley, the first gift had "made possible a complete unit providing for the examination, diagnosis, and treatment of women having or suspected of having cancer of the female organs." Originally, the clinic targeted Black women, but "precedents have been broken here by the treatment of white patients in the cancer clinic," said a newspaper story.[8]

A 1956 *Globe-Democrat* story gave readers a look at heart research, performed by Homer G. Phillips physicians, using dogs from the city pound. The work was financed by a three-year-old program, the Institute of Medical Education and Research, funded by fees collected from charity patients at the city hospitals; its aim was to create facilities for research and provide fellowships to trainees, some $10,000 worth in 1955–56. Dr. Elman himself led several research efforts, including one on nutritional rehabilitation of cancer patients, sponsored by the National Cancer Institute.

> *"We were young people in medicine, and it was so interesting to us that we had some bad trauma cases—yet those people survived. There was blood everywhere and yet, in those cases, you resuscitated them quickly, took them to the operating room, and we said, 'This is what you get when you have first class surgical care.' We felt so proud to be a part of it."*
>
> —Dr. LaSalle Leffall

During the long-ago days of City Hospital #2, the graduate trainees had launched their own Alumni Internes Association in 1931, but the group languished after two years. They tried again in 1942, under Dr. J. J. Thomas, but the organization went dormant until 1946. The third time was the charm, again under Dr. Thomas' leadership. The group took off, forming scientific committees, even a social committee. At the 1946 convention, 121 attended from 38 states, and in 1947 the group affiliated with the National Medical Association.

Throughout the 1950s, the organization flourished, holding conventions that attracted hundreds of graduates and prominent people as keynote speakers. Not only did Dr. Leslie Bond's father come back each year for the convention, but he also taught his son some history at the same time. Once, the two Bonds were sitting in a night spot, located in the old City Hospital #2 building. "All of a sudden, my father said, 'That was X-ray,' and I thought maybe a little of the Jack Daniels had gone to his head," recalled Dr. Bond. "But no, it was indeed the old hospital, and we were just where X-ray had been."

In 1950, banner headlines in the *St. Louis American* announced that 350 people would attend that year's Alumni Association meeting, "which is recognized as one of the nation's most scientific meetings."[9] Dr. Montague Cobb, eminent anatomist from Howard, appeared as a speaker, while Drs. W. Barry Wood and Carl Moore, distinguished internists from Washington University, headed scientific sessions.

Each year, the meetings seemed to grow in size and excitement. In 1955, the group's tenth anniversary, former president Harry S. Truman was slated to be the keynote speaker. By 1956, some 400 former interns and residents were attending, and a popular surgical clinic took place under the leadership of Dr. Sinkler and Washington University surgeon and Homer G. chief of staff, Dr. Robert Elman.

Other clubs also organized during the 1950s, including the Friends of Homer G. Phillips Hospital, a group aimed at garnering scholarship help for nursing students, and in 1955 the Moms and Dads Club, which assisted students with gifts, including the baby grand piano in the living room of the nurses' residence. A Homer G. Phillips Hospital auxiliary won honors for its work in 1958 from a group of all the regional auxiliaries. Other groups were stalwart volunteers, including Catholic nuns from the Society of Helpers.

*"The facilities at Homer G. Phillips were not as good as in other hospitals, which looked better overall. But in terms of the equipment we really needed, we found it at Homer G. Phillips."*

—Dr. LaSalle Leffall

In January 1950, the *St. Louis American* ran a cheerful report on the hospital's mental ward, 2 South. The writer, who spent 10 days there as a patient to immerse himself in the experience, described the department: 180 patients admitted, with three more coming in each day; 60 percent of them men; and 25 percent of them alcoholics. He also talked about the range of conditions seen there: schizophrenia; manic-depressive disorder; epilepsy; "pervert personalities;" and "psychopathic personalities," including hard-to-treat drug addicts.

He had high praise for the staff headed by Dr. Herbert J. Erwin, who had established the program in 1949 with a $20,000 government grant. Dr. Erwin—a Homer G. Phillips trainee who did postgraduate work at Harvard on a Rosenwald Fund fellowship—was exceptional, probably the first Black psychiatrist in the Midwest. Supervising the neuropsychiatric social service department was Mrs. Fredda Witherspoon, among the first Black graduates of Washington University's social work program. Leading the patients to the sixth-floor gym for recreation was DeComer Lattimore Lacy, an occupational therapist.

In between interviews, the writer spent time in the convalescent room, "where the patients 'live the life of Riley,'" he wrote. "They have a radio, play cards nearly all day, and help with daily chores. The lovely nurses (and they are beautiful) stop in, chat with them, play games and give encouragement in many ways. Sometimes after one has patted some of the older men on the back, and called them darling, the old chaps don't complain for three days!"[10]

But stories in other newspapers contradicted this lighthearted description. In 1950, the *St. Louis Post-Dispatch* noted the death of Mrs. Ossie Eddins, a mental patient at Homer G. Phillips, who died after jumping from a third-floor hospital window. "The window in the bathroom of the medical ward was found open. She had been placed in the ward because of crowded conditions in the mental ward."

"Psychiatry at Homer G. Phillips was not a happy place to be," agreed Laverna Turner Spinks, a 1955 nursing graduate, who was assigned for a time to the psychiatry ward. "We had all types of mental problems: those who didn't talk, those who talked to the wall all day or all night, one teenaged boy who didn't say anything but just sat there and smiled at you. The orderlies kept us nurses safe. You didn't want to be trapped by any of the patients; one caught me in the supply room once, but I managed to get out."

A circuit court grand jury investigation in 1952 found that 2S was "overcrowded with mental patients." It described the problem as "critical" and recommended that arrangements be made for housing the mental patients in Malcolm A. Bliss Psychopathic Hospital.[11] Dr. Hennerich, city hospital commissioner, responded that he had no spots open at Malcolm Bliss for Black patients. "I have more applications from white persons than I can accept," he said.[12]

In 1954, local religious leaders weighed in, complaining about the state of mental health care in the community. One prominent rabbi, Ferdinand Isserman of Temple Israel, also condemned the practice of shackling mental patients at Homer G. Phillips and Malcolm Bliss, describing it as "a 'brutal one' that 'goes against the conscience and compassion' of St. Louis. A nation that did that to its prisoners would be outlawed under the Geneva Convention," he asserted.[13]

Later in 1954, yet another grand jury assailed the packed conditions of Homer G. Phillips' psychiatry wards, noting that they were built to accommodate 65 mental patients but had 220 on the day of the jury's visit. "The conditions must be stated again and again," the report said, "until the public demands a change."[14] By 1955, the city was spending more than $1.5 million a year to care for mental patients at three institutions, including Homer G. Phillips.[15]

In 1957, the Missouri legislature finally cleared the way for the Homer G. Phillips mental health patients to be transferred to other facilities, and by 1959, the transfer was complete. The service at Homer G. Phillips became a consultation service only. "This year marked the end of a service which, for a decade, has made far-reaching contributions to the community and to the nation," mourned the *St. Louis American*.[16] For their psychiatric training, nursing students began living in the nurses' residence at Malcolm Bliss and training there.

Through the years, Dr. Erwin had done his best to care for this mass of patients. His work, said his foster daughter Sheila Bader, "meant that Homer G. Phillips had a psychiatric wing, that people who needed further treatment had a place to get it, and that when these patients went to 2 South or to Dr. Erwin's office on Grand, they would be seeing someone who knew what he was doing, had been well trained and was interested in their well-being."

Dr. Erwin also trained and mentored another devoted psychiatrist, Dr. John Anderson, previously a microbiologist on the hospital
staff. After graduating from Meharry Medical College, he returned
to St. Louis for his internship at Homer G. Phillips Hospital and,
influenced by Dr. Erwin, decided to specialize in psychiatry—a new
field for Black specialists. He became the second African American
accepted into the psychiatric residency program at Barnes, working with such greats in the field as Drs. Eli Robins, Samuel Guze,
and Edwin Gildea. On weekends, said his son Dr. Dale Anderson,
also a psychiatrist, "he would drive me over to the hospital and
do consulting work with patients." Added his widow, Mary Ellen
Anderson, "he saw people coming into the hospital, who couldn't
eat or sleep and were as thin as a bone. The psychiatrist would
work with them, and the next thing you knew, they were gaining
weight and acting altogether different."

Fig. 9.6: Lula Couch Hall
came from Little Rock,
Arkansas, to attend the
Homer G. Phillips School
of Nursing, graduating
in 1959. She then spent
36 years in psychiatric
nursing at Malcolm Bliss
Psychopathologic Institute,
ending as director of
nurses. Courtesy of Lula
Couch Hall.

Student nurses trained on the psychiatric wards, where some were frightened but others gravitated to it. Lula Couch Hall, who graduated in 1959, spent a 36-year career in psychiatry at Malcolm Bliss, beginning as staff nurse and ending as director of nurses. "I enjoyed working with the mentally ill. I liked to be able to talk to them, see them get better, and go home," she said. "And the field of psychiatry has changed a lot. Initially, they were warehousing mentally ill patients, and then they realized that a lot could live on their own with the proper support and supervision."

Another nurse who went on to an illustrious career in psychiatry was Amanda Daniel Luckett Murphy, who came from Alabama to Homer G. Phillips in 1955 and found it "the most outstanding thing in the world." Because of an illness, she missed her psychiatry rotation and had to make it up as the lone student in the class. "It was really exciting," she said, "because I began wondering: 'Wow. How do people think? How does that have an impact on how they live?'" Eventually, she earned a PhD in counseling and psychology, became chief executive for a mental health center in East St. Louis, and in 1980 founded the Hopewell Center (now the Amanda Luckett Murphy Hopewell Center) for patients with mental disorders. By the time of her 2011 retirement, the center had 4,500 patients and 150 employees.

> *"St. Louis was segregated. I didn't find it any more segregated than Washington, D.C., where I had been for medical school. You didn't have any money to go to any restaurants, so you ate at the hospital. About the only time you went anyplace is if you went to a movie. That was about it. If it's segregated, it's segregated. That's what you lived with then."*
> —Dr. LaSalle Leffall

Blacks were forced to squeeze into segregated city neighborhoods, and not just because of housing policies. Quietly, St. Louis was also eliminating downtown and midtown areas that housed many Black residents. In 1939, some 200 or so apartment buildings and houses—most occupied by Black renters—were destroyed in creating the Gateway Arch National Park. During the 1940s, the city began planning for the destruction of the 465-acre Mill Creek Valley neighborhood, which housed some 20,000 people and a host of Black institutions.

The problem, said the well-known urban planner Harland Bartholomew, was that the city was losing too much of its historic industrial core. "Indeed, by the 1940s, three decades of sustained boom activity in the western periphery of the city and in St. Louis County had reconfigured the settled landscape, with nearly all housing and commercial starts clustered outside of the old urban core . . . and it would take a large-scale coordinated effort to reverse the flow of people and investment," noted one study on St. Louis planning and policy.[17]

Key impediments to investment in the city, said Bartholomew, were working-class areas within downtown St. Louis. So, in 1953, the city announced plans for a giant urban renewal project—the country's largest to that point—that would demolish some 5,630 housing units in Mill Creek Valley and create a new industrial zone in their place. The project took place in 1959, and displaced Black residents became the main victims of this redevelopment effort. In fact, "a harshly critical 1964 congressional report highlighted St. Louis public officials' failure to provide adequate relocation assistance to the 4,212 families and 1,331 individuals cleared out of Mill Creek, most of whom ended up in substandard housing on the city's north side."[18]

But after the 1948 *Shelley v. Kraemer* decision, significant population shifts began occurring. More African Americans were moving into the city; from 1930 to 1955, the minority population rose from 94,000 to some 232,000—a 146 percent increase. During the same years, the white population in the city fell from 732,000 to around 650,00, an 11 percent decline. Most were moving to St. Louis County, and many of those leaving were middle- and upper-income white residents.[19]

With each new census, the depopulation of the city continued, fueled in part by white flight. This trend would continue into the future. "The City lost an average of just over 10,000 persons a year between 1950 and 2000, during which time it plummeted from ninth to eighteenth in the national ranking of metro areas," wrote historian Colin Gordon. Thus, not only was St. Louis becoming one of the most segregated metropolitan regions in the country, but it was also diminishing in size and prestige. Of course, these losses meant a steep decline in its tax base, which meant fewer funds available for spending on public hospitals.

Nationally, discrimination was still endemic, but the doors were gradually creaking open. In 1954, the U.S. Supreme Court declared an end to school segregation in its *Brown v. Board of Education* ruling. The next year, the 13-month Montgomery bus boycott began after Rosa Parks refused to move to the back of the bus and was arrested. In 1957, Congress passed the Civil Rights Act to protect voting rights.

Still, the brutal 1955 murder of an African American teenager—14-year-old Emmett Till, a Chicagoan visiting relatives in Mississippi—was stark proof that intense racial hatred lay just beneath the surface. In 1957, when nine students tried to integrate Central High School in Little Rock, Arkansas Gov. Orval Faubus used National Guard troops to block them; in turn, President Dwight D. Eisenhower ordered federal troops in to force the school's integration.

In St. Louis, the Urban League and other groups were also pressing for integration, urging employers to hire Black staff members. Institutional barriers also were crumbling. At Washington University, the first cohort of Black undergraduates matriculated in 1952; a decade later, Dr. James L. Sweatt became the first African American to graduate from the School of Medicine.

And in 1955, Mayor Raymond Tucker declared that patients of all colors must be admitted to both city hospitals. From that point on, any patient living in the western part of the city would come to Homer G. Phillips, while those to the east would go to City Hospital #1. Despite this order, Homer G. Phillips remained largely Black.

*"When I was nine years old, I was coming home from school one day, and there was a little bird in the street, a robin I think, that couldn't move. I took it home and my father said,*

*'Oh, the wing is broken.' He got some wooden splints and a tongue depressor; we splinted the wing and put him on the back porch with a little water and some crackers. After a few days, he was flying around the porch, and then we opened the door and he flew out. I said, 'I am going to be a doctor. I have cured my first patient.'"*

—Dr. LaSalle Leffall

The hospital was training physicians who scattered around the country, sometimes the world, to practice. A growing group of overseas trainees, 44 in 1959, had come to the residency training program from such countries as the Philippines, Turkey, Greece, Italy, Mexico, Japan, and various African nations. But a rising chorus of voices was calling for change: more staff members, especially nurses' aides, and especially a larger outpatient clinic.

The clamor began in 1951, when a grand jury urged the city to enlarge the hospital's basement prison ward, which had only eight beds for a prisoner count that often reached 30 or 40. A prisoner had recently escaped from the hospital, they said, and had killed a nearby grocer. In response, the hospital asked for a large grant, $666,000, to make improvements. In 1952, the mayor proposed a new public works bond issue that included $2.4 million for 200 more beds at the hospital, but the idea was shelved.

Now aldermen became convinced that a new outpatient clinic was vital to the hospital, and they found money from a 1944 bond issue to help supply the needed $1.15 million. Condemnation proceedings got underway to clear an entire city block south of the hospital, 36 buildings in all, so that construction could began. In 1955, they also decided to spruce up the hospital inside. When Mayor Raymond Tucker visited, he said he was "gratified" by the new paint job, lighting fixtures, and tile floors over the bare concrete, plus $60,000 worth of new equipment.[20]

By 1956, complaints of overcrowding and personnel shortages were growing louder. Dr. Sinkler tried to calm the excited aldermen, assuring them that the situation was serious but not acute, and that they only needed around 35 more staff members. But superintendent Virgil McKnight contradicted him, estimating that the hospital needed some 120 more staff members on its nursing service.[21] The aldermen voted to look into the idea of offering free tuition—then $360 for the three-year course of study—to draw more nursing students into the profession.

They also decided to investigate conditions at the hospital themselves, and in November 1956 announced an aldermanic investigation. But before they could begin, a mayor's team—headed by Dr. Frank Bradley, director of Barnes Hospital—announced its own findings: Homer G. Phillips and City Hospital needed $1 million more each year, primarily for 250 new employees. The aldermanic committee echoed these findings: The hospital needed to go up from 915 employees to 1,062. Another grand jury committee in 1957 came to the same conclusion.

Fig. 9.7: This photograph of the Homer G. Phillips Hospital Staff includes attendees (in back, left to right): Drs. Helen Nash (far left), Liwanag Roman (third from the left), Herbert Miller, William Sinkler (fifth from left), Park White (sixth from left), and Neal Middelkamp (seventh from left). November 20, 1957. Courtesy of the Bernard Becker Medical Library Archives, Washington University in St. Louis.

Late in 1957, a *Post-Dispatch* editorial made a welcome announcement: "With funds made available by City Hall, Homer G.
Phillips and City hospitals are embarking on expanded programs
for training nurses, backed by a full-time recruiting system." At
last, the long-awaited $1.4 million outpatient clinic building
was completed in 1959. In 1957, the budget for the hospital had
reached a whopping $4.076 million, with $3.2 million earmarked
for salaries.

But the city budget was under pressure, and in 1958 the *Post-
Dispatch* reported an ominous suggestion by the Board of Estimate
and aldermen: "that either Homer G. Phillips or City Hospital
be closed, and operations be consolidated in one of the institutions. . . . This proposal was dropped, however, because the patient
load at the two institutions is too large to handle at either single
hospital."[22]

> "I loved Dr. Carl Moyer, head of surgery at Washington
> University, because he was one of the leaders in surgical physi-
> ology. He would come over to Homer Phillips, but more often
> we went over to Washington University when he was lecturing.
> He told us about replacement therapy, electrolyte solutions,
> and you had to listen carefully because if Carl Moyer said it,
> that was gospel. You knew you were getting it from the top."
> —Dr. LaSalle Leffall

Washington University physicians still worked collegially alongside Homer G. Phillips medical staff, and in 1950 three won special
awards from the hospital's alumni association for "help in devel-
oping Phillips Hospital and for contributions to Negro medicine":
Dr. Robert Moore, dean and professor of pathology; Dr. Evarts
Graham, professor of surgery; and Dr. Park White, assistant professor of clinical pediatrics.

At times, the School of Medicine threw its weight behind changes it thought were needed in the hospital. In December 1950, Dr.
Moore—a pathologist himself—sent a heated letter to the hospital
commissioner, Dr. Hennerich, to complain that Homer G. Phillips

had only one trained pathologist in its laboratories despite an annual total of 188 autopsies, 2,012 surgical specimens, and thousands of clinical pathology tests.

As a Homer G. Phillips brochure admitted, the School of Medicine still supplied staff to direct its major clinical divisions. But gradually, Dr. Sinkler was working toward his long-cherished goal: grooming African American physicians to take the place of their Washington University mentors.

One of these mentors was still the respected surgeon, Dr. Robert Elman, who continued to serve as surgery head and chief of staff—and also remained wholly committed to equal education for African American students. During a National Medical Association dinner in 1954 honoring his work, Dr. Elman gave a keynote address in which he slammed the idea of segregated hospitals, called for more research opportunities for Black medical students, and proudly described the model rehabilitation efforts at Homer G. Phillips, which had returned 86 long-term patients to useful employment. Most of all, he cited Homer G. Phillips as a key example of white physicians and trainees working on equal terms with their Black counterparts.

"I have a wonderful letter from a white medical student who served over weekends in the emergency room of the Homer G. Phillips Hospital in which he expresses his admiration of the type of care he saw patients receive, of how much he learned, and of the atmosphere of courtesy and cooperation in which he was able to work," he said in his talk.

But in 1957, Dr. Elman died of heart disease. That same year, his stalwart surgery colleague and one-time chief at Washington University, Dr. Evarts Graham, died of lung cancer. For years, Dr. Graham had backed Dr. Elman's efforts, urging surgeons to consult at the hospital and appearing himself for occasional lectures. In 1952, Dr. Graham had written to the Interns Alumni Association with high praise: "I am sure that you know . . . my very high regard . . . for the splendid work which the colored doctors are doing not only at the Homer Phillips Hospital but all over the country. I am particularly gratified at the number of colored surgeons who have been made Fellows of the American College of Surgeons."

These two losses were cruel blows, but the hospital still had Dr. William Sinkler—until he, too, died of heart disease in 1960. Still, by the time of his death, he had scored a long-cherished triumph. "Dr. Sinkler lived to see the fulfillment of his efforts," wrote Dr. H. Phillip Venable in a hospital history. "At the time of his untimely death in September 1960, every Department at Homer G. Phillips Hospital had a Negro as director or associate director. In every instance, the physician was a diplomate of his respective American Board. He was also a member of the faculty of Saint Louis University or Washington University."

The tornado that devastated St. Louis in 1959, sending dozens of Black residents to the hospital with injuries and rendering others homeless, somehow seemed a metaphor for the winds of change that were already churning—and that would swirl around the hospital during the next decade.

## CHAPTER TEN

# Loving the Children
## Obstetrics, Gynecology, and Pediatrics

*"I loved the children. Those summers in St. Louis were terrible, and we had no air-conditioning, except for a couple of units. But the children didn't mind. They could be ever so sick, but after you gave them a dose of medicine, they'd be up shaking the bed rails, wanting to get out and go to the playroom. They would bounce back with the least effort. That just made me love pediatrics, and that's why I specialized in pediatric nursing."*

> —Jobyna Moore Foster, Homer G. Phillips nursing graduate, class of 1957, who worked at the hospital until 1974 when she moved to City Hospital, retiring in 1985

*"When I reached the obstetrics rotation in nursing school, I fell in love with the babies. That became my life calling. I applied for a job at Homer G. Phillips Hospital during my senior year."*

> —Lillian Haywood, St. Louis Municipal School of Nursing, 1971. She worked at the hospital until it closed in 1979

WITH 400 BIRTHS each month, Homer G. Phillips always had a bumper crop of babies. "During my one-month rotation on OB," recalled pediatrician Dr. Mary Anne Tillman, who was an intern and resident at Homer G. Phillips from 1960 to 1963, "I had 100

Fig. 10.1: Born in Detroit, Jobyna Moore Foster graduated from the nursing school in the 31-member class of 1957 and became a longtime member of the hospital's pediatric staff. Courtesy of Jobyna Moore Foster.

deliveries. I guess I could probably still deliver a baby, though I haven't done it for a long, long time."

Many of the mothers came from tough home situations. "They were very rarely middle-class; most were single mothers, and they were undereducated," said obstetrician/gynecologist Nathaniel H. Murdock Jr., an intern and resident at Homer G. Philips starting in 1963. "Accidental pregnancies came to us. There were some who looked down on these people, but I never did. I didn't care whether you were rich or poor. I was going to do the best I could to deliver a good baby for you."

Trainees found excellent mentors in obstetrics and gynecology: Dr. William Smiley, who continued to be a superb surgeon and chief supervisor of the department of obstetrics and gynecology; and Dr. Seymour Monat, section head of the OB-GYN department. "Dr. Monat was much like me," added Dr. Murdock, "kind of no-nonsense but gentle. If you did something he thought you should have done in a different way, he would say, 'Let's discuss this.'"

Fig. 10.2: One of eight children in a St. Louis family, Lillian Elliott Haywood graduated from the St. Louis Municipal School of Nursing in 1971 and then worked at Homer G. Phillips Hospital until it closed in 1979. Courtesy of Lillian Haywood.

Starting in 1966, Dr. Smiley also worked to improve the outcome of women and children as Dr. Monat's replacement to head the local Maternal Child Health Project, a joint venture of the city and federal government aimed at improving the local infant mortality rate. One year after the program began, Dr. Smiley reported to the city's Board of Health that more than 2/3 of the pregnant women in the Jefferson-Cass area had registered at the center—an increase of 29 percent in four years.

Alongside these physicians were seasoned nurses. Dr. Gerald Medoff, later an infectious disease specialist at Washington University School of Medicine, was a young, inexperienced trainee at Barnes Hospital newly assigned to the obstetrics rotation at Homer G. Phillips. "I came in around 11 o'clock one night, and I went to see a woman who was in labor. I did a pelvic exam and said to the nurse, 'I feel a foot.' She was very sanguine, really an expert. She said, 'You've got a breech.' I said, 'What am I going to do?' And she said, 'Try and turn him.' 'What do you mean, *turn?*'

Fig. 10.3: Dr. Helen E. Nash is shown caring for infant patients at Homer G. Phillips Hospital, ca. 1945. Courtesy of the Bernard Becker Medical Library Archives, Washington University in St. Louis.

I said. She said, 'You just do what I tell you to do, and it'll be all right, Doctor.' I delivered a breech, and everything was OK. She was just wonderful."

Dr. Lee Blount, then a trainee and later a surgeon, recalled one evening at the hospital before he had done his obstetric rotation, when he got off the elevator for his shift. "I saw three or four nurses who had delivered many more babies than I was ever going to. A patient was in labor, but the doctor was late getting there because his car didn't start. They said, 'Come on, young Doc.' I said, 'Oh no, I haven't had the course yet!' But they said, 'It's all right. You're going to have the course *now*.' Sure enough, that delivery was my first baby."

Sometimes there were crises to manage. Late one evening, nurse Jacqueline Calvin was on duty as the night supervisor, when she got an emergency call from an obstetrician, who was in the middle of a delivery. "I went running up there, and everybody was upside the wall. The patient was in the center of the room; she had decided she was going to have her baby on the floor, and everyone was scared. I wasn't going to fight this big woman, so I said, 'Give me the sterile equipment.' I put it on the floor and let her squat down there and push that baby out. You know, if you can't fight them, join them."

*"Maternity was 4 South, 3 South was gynecology, and 5 South was pediatrics. On 5S, we had one big ward that held 18 males on this side and 18 females on the other. Then we had these small rooms along the hallway including a diarrhea unit, also called the isolation ward, where there were children under a year of age. The diarrhea would set in and kill them from fever and dehydration. Shigella would be the culture that came back, and they just couldn't thrive."*

—Jobyna Moore Foster

*"Even though it was a wonderful training facility, some conditions were substandard compared to private institutions, and even City Hospital. There was air-conditioning only in the Nursery and in the ICU. The wards were often overcrowded. We would often run out of supplies, equipment, and linen. We had to learn to improvise."*

—Lillian Haywood

The chock-full pediatrics department had every kind of patient imaginable. "The floor was divided up," recalled nurse Martha Jackson Nelson, a 1961 graduate. "One area was for acute care—like the ones who came in with pneumonia. Other sections were newborn, isolation, adolescent, and children who had had surgery. In the ward itself, there were big kids on one side and small kids on the other. We would have a census of 85, 90, or 100 sometimes. Actually, it was a hospital within a hospital because we had all these areas to take care of."

Decades after working on that floor, nurse Louise Brown Cunningham could still rattle off the kinds of cases she saw. "One little boy named Abe was having continuous seizures, but I saw him later when he came back for a follow-up, and he was like a totally different child. I remember a little girl who had burns—and burns *smell*. She would say, 'I stink, I stink.' I also recall a baby who had eczema. His hands were restrained so he couldn't scratch, and they had him lying on X-ray film, so he wasn't able to move and scratch on the bed linen."

Some children were in and out a lot, such as those with sickle-cell disease or the hundreds with lead poisoning, who needed a treatment called chelation. Others were frequent visitors to the ringworm clinic. A few stayed on and on, living their whole lives at the hospital. Two little boys, one named George, were hydrocephalic, and they developed huge heads in those days before shunting was common. Their home was the solarium, where it took two nurses to turn and feed them. "George was well known in the hospital; the doctors, nurses—he knew them all," said nurse Annie Crawford Ward.

The children who died were the most memorable, added Louise Cunningham. "One patient delivered conjoined twins who had died, and our instructor took us to see them. They were joined at the chest and had one set of legs. If it was in this day, when they have ultrasound and all that, they would have known about those babies in advance."

For Laverna Turner Spinks, one long-ago baby still tugged at her heartstrings. A newborn at the hospital, he had serious problems, "but we kept this baby alive for two or three days, and it had been a struggle. I left and went home, and then when I came back to work the next day, he had died. I just said, 'Where did my baby *go?*'"

*"Mary Vincent Clarke was one of our nursing supervisors in the newborn and premature nursery, and we rotated through there and learned from her many kinds of skills: how to feed babies, how to place them in cribs and bassinets, how to diaper them. She was strict, and she made sure you practiced the best procedures. She was great. She was great."*

—Jobyna Moore Foster

*"Mrs. Clarke, the nursery supervisor, and Mrs. Helen Wallace, the head nurse, were excellent teachers. They expected us to give the best care to our patients regardless of their socioeconomic*

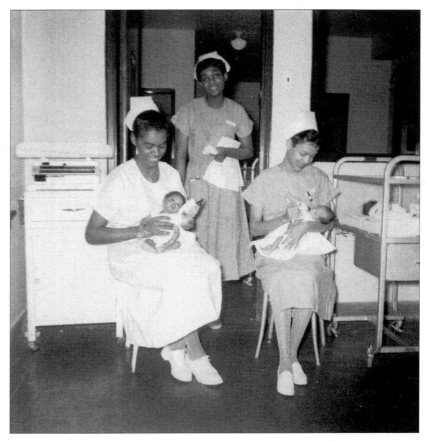

Fig. 10.4: Nurses were busy feeding babies in the pediatric ward at Homer G. Phillips Hospital. Courtesy of Martha Jackson Nelson.

*background. We worked eight-hour shifts, five days a week, and two weekends, with the third weekend off."*
—Lillian Haywood

Until the hospital closed, the supervisor of the newborn and premature nurseries was Mary Vincent Clarke, born in 1913 on a small farm in rural Virginia, where she heard about slavery from her grandmother, who had been 13 years old when it ended. The importance of education passed down through her family. "Mamma would always tell us to learn all we could. She said, 'What you got in your head, no one can take away from you. Study hard.' And they didn't keep us out of school to work on the farm."

One day, she burned her arm, and a teacher sent her to the infirmary for treatment. "This nurse in her stiffly starched white uniform and her cute little cap took care of my arm so effectively that I was truly impressed with her. And I said, 'Well, I'm going to be a nurse.'" Every day, Mrs. Clarke trudged more than three miles to high school and afterwards worked as a domestic for a year to pay for Howard University's nursing school. Her grandmother helped, using insurance she had received for a son who had died in World War I.

After earning a bachelor's degree from West Virginia State College, she began looking for a job, and Estelle Massey Riddle hired her at Homer G. Phillips. As supervisor of the nursery, she was eager for ways to improve. At a conference, she learned of a formula to predict how many diapers they would need for infants—and an accountant at the hospital, who had questioned her earlier orders, was so impressed that he told her: "I had no idea. From now on, whatever number of diapers you order, you will get them."

While she was in charge, she had no patience with students who wouldn't follow the rules. "I said, 'If you're coming over here, thinking you're going to run the nursery, go back to the nursing school and stay, because I'm in charge here.'" She was also determined that her nurses would do their jobs. All newborns had to have a test tube attached to collect a urine specimen, and the report was supposed to be on the chart shortly after birth. But it wasn't always happening on time, and some doctors were vexed. She told the office, "From now on, every baby's going to have that specimen attached to his record, if I have to do them myself." The problem was quickly solved.

With the babies, though, she had endless patience. "I would see her when I went in to do circumcisions, things like that," said Dr. Murdock. "And from my vantage point, she was very, very compassionate."

*"Dr. Helen Nash would come through, and a lot of the nurses were nervous about her questions. She'd want to know why this patient's blanket wasn't a certain way. She was strict, and she could be harsh. A lot of times I would go on rounds with her, but I wouldn't be afraid of her because I knew she wanted us to learn. She wanted us to know how to take care of those children."*

—Jobyna Moore Foster

*"Some people didn't like Dr. Nash because she had her personality. She was one of the first Black doctors, and she did have a rough way to go. But she did have her personality."*

—Lillian Haywood

Another stickler was Dr. Helen Nash, a Meharry graduate and Homer G. Phillips trainee, who became chief resident and then

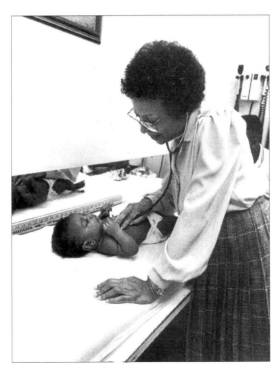

Fig. 10.5: Dr. Helen E. Nash (1921–2012) was a pediatric supervisor and associate director of Pediatrics at Homer G. from 1950 to 1964, and in 1949 she was the first Black woman to join the St. Louis Children's Hospital staff. Photograph ca. 1990. Courtesy of the Bernard Becker Medical Library Archives, Washington University in St. Louis.

pediatric supervisor until 1965. Her career was filled with firsts. In 1949, she became the first Black pediatrician at St. Louis Children's Hospital; she also was the only woman among the first four African American physicians asked to join the Washington University School of Medicine faculty.

When the welfare of babies and children was at stake—as in child abuse prevention or rat eradication—she fought city leaders tenaciously. At Homer G. Phillips, she battled for new incubators and hand-washing facilities. With Mary Vincent Clarke, she also succeeded in making a long-overdue change. "When she got there, the preemie unit at Homer Phillips had a high mortality rate, and she—with the aid of a few others—cleaned it up and got them back to standard of care. Nobody had really paid attention to the premature babies, and that was a great job that she did," said Dr. Homer Nash, Helen's younger brother, also a pediatrician at Homer G. Phillips.

"Helen was a genius," said nurse Mamie Walton. "The woman was so smart it wasn't even funny. She did research on cases. I referred a girlfriend of mine to her, who had two children with sickle cell, and she did research on sickle cell. Those children lived longer than most kids do."

Her tenacity helped pull some patients through crises, recalled Jobyna Moore Foster.

> We had a four-bed ward where we housed our sickest children, and one little girl there had bad third-degree burns. When Dr. Nash made her rounds, she made sure that her dressings stayed wet with silver nitrate, and she would come back to check! She'd put on a glove and pat to see if those dressings were soaked. If not, she would say, "Who is taking care of this patient this morning?" And she would ask to see that person *and* the head nurse. She was tough. But the girl lived; we saved her life.

She was also hard on residents, recalled Dr. Leslie Bond.

One night I was on call, and we had a real busy night with head injuries, diarrhea patients, and everything. I think there were 17 admissions, and I was a bit late getting all of them written up. When we started making rounds with Dr. Nash, I wasn't up to snuff on one baby with diarrhea, and I was duly reprimanded. But when we got to the last patient, a head injury, she said, "*This* is the way a head injury should be followed." That was where I had been all night long, and I thought, "Well, she's fair."

"*Dr. Helen Nash would blast you, like, 'Why is this baby not restrained properly?' She could get on you real hard. Dr. Homer Nash was milder in his conversation and approach to you as a nurse, knowing we were student nurses and doing the best we could. But both were excellent teachers. They wanted us to learn. They would show us different cases: 'Come and see this.' So, we respected them highly, that Nash family.*"

—Jobyna Moore Foster

"*Dr. Homer Nash was a different story. His personality was just totally different than his sister's. You wouldn't even know they were sister and brother. I don't know why she got the rough personality, and he got the gentle giant.*"

—Lillian Haywood

Dr. Homer Nash followed in his older sister's footsteps, becoming a resident at Homer G. Phillips from 1952 to 1955. "My sister Helen had finished her residency and started a practice here, and by the time I finished medical school she was about three or four years ahead of me. She convinced me that this was a good place to come."

In those days, only a couple of vaccinations, primarily smallpox and DPT, were available, so all the other childhood diseases—measles, chicken pox, mumps, and rubella—showed up in the hospital. When they saw children with meningitis, "it was often a

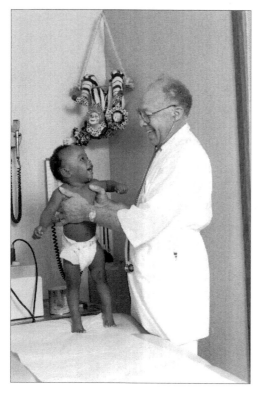

Fig. 10.6: Dr. Homer Erwin Nash Jr. was a respected pediatrician at Homer G. Phillips Hospital, at St. Louis Children's Hospital, and in private practice with his daughter, Dr. Alison Nash. Courtesy of the Bernard Becker Medical Library Archives, Washington University in St. Louis.

little late," said Dr. Nash. "We saw a lot of kids with diarrhea, and they would come in pretty dehydrated, so we had to get them on IVs and culture the stools—do what we could. They all survived. I didn't see severe malnutrition, though a lot of the kids were scrawny. They may have had separated or unmarried parents who were living hand to mouth."

You learned on the job, he recalled, and even a year's experience made a difference in your patient wisdom. As a resident, Dr. Leslie Bond was on the 3-to-11 shift in the ER, when the patient load was the heaviest. "I was down seeing kids there, and I kept sending patients up to pediatrics, until Homer Nash finally called down and said, 'Les, do you know what penicillin is?' I said, 'Yeah.' 'Give some of those kids penicillin and send them to the clinic next week. Don't be admitting them.' Homer was one year ahead of me here at Homer Phillips."

*"Oh, Lord. Dr. Park White was one of our best coming through. He was a friendly, fatherly-like, cheery kind of Santa Claus person. We all loved Dr. Park White. Oh gosh. In making rounds with him, he would show us so many different cases, point out different illnesses, tell us the signs and symptoms for us to look for. We loved to make rounds with him."*

—Jobyna Moore Foster

Fig. 10.7: Dr. Park Jerauld White (1891–1987), a well-known St. Louis pediatrician with a busy private practice, served as Director of Pediatrics at Homer G. Phillips Hospital from 1945 until his retirement in 1966. Courtesy of the Bernard Becker Medical Library Archives, Washington University in St. Louis.

A staff member at St. Louis Children's Hospital and director of the Department of Pediatrics at Homer G. Phillips from 1945 to 1966, Harvard-educated Dr. Park J. White was an unusual mixture of privilege and dedication to social justice. For Dr. Helen Nash, he became an important mentor, and they took up causes together. When poor parents were burning lead-filled car batteries in their kitchen stoves to heat their homes, and the toxic fumes were poisoning their babies, the two went to see the mayor. He stopped the practice of discarding batteries in junkyards where poor people could find them—and infant deaths from that source dropped to zero.

Dr. Homer Nash also knew Dr. White well. "Every Friday," he said, "they had rounds at St. Louis Children's Hospital, actually a kind of lecture, where they presented cases. All the residents went over, though we had to leave one poor guy back to cover the service. Some of the pediatricians we saw presenting were Dr. Neal Middelkamp, and the chairman, Dr. Alexis Hartman. One of our visiting physicians was Dr. Park White, who never failed to come over. He was one of my favorite people. He taught me a lot on rounds, such as not to get angry about the foibles and slip-ups that people did. And I needed to let them go, because I had a few myself."

Everyone remembered Dr. White's kindness, and some still recalled his other interest: poetry. "I loved him. He was a sweet old man, just wonderful," said Martha Nelson. "And I have a book of poems that he wrote." Better still, he wrote a poem in Mary Vincent Clarke's honor. "He was the most learned person I have ever come in contact with. Oh, my goodness. He was a jewel."

*"Dr. Mary Anne Tillman was another one of our favorites. She would almost take you by the hand and show you step by step how to take care of patients: what she was doing, what was the plan. And her bedside manner was the best of all the doctors who came through here."*
—Jobyna Moore Foster

*"Dr. Tillman was the nursery medical director, and her professionalism ensured that our infants received excellent care."*
—Lillian Haywood

Another pediatrician who knew Dr. Park White was Dr. Mary Anne Tillman, who maintained a private practice but also oversaw the hospital nursery until it closed. She remembered him as an excellent teacher who used stories and even humor to make lessons come alive for trainees. In the clinic, they saved big families for him, because he took the time to fully to discover their needs. Dr. Tillman also learned from Dr. Helen Nash, "who taught me that you sometimes have to be forward and assertive to get things done."

Those lessons took hold, said nurse Annie Crawford Ward. "Dr. Tillman was very nice, and you could communicate with her. You didn't feel afraid. But I've also seen her go toe to toe with some of those interns. She had to do that because—I don't know what it is about interns and residents—but they can come in thinking they know a lot, when they don't."

Dr. Tillman had memorable patients, too, including the children who had eaten chips of lead-based paint. They were assigned to the solarium for care, but the staff had to cover the windows with black paper to keep out light that would trigger seizures. Still other children were burn victims, who had stood too close to space heaters in their chilly Mill Creek Valley homes, and their clothes had caught fire. She recalled shaken babies, including one girl whose father shook her as a baby, and she had not talked until she was nearly seven years old.

Who would guess that disposable diapers were the cause of much child abuse? Often, "it was somebody taking care of someone else's child—such as a live-in boyfriend at home who was not working," said Dr. Tillman. They use up all the diapers, and then this child soils over everything. All the diapers are gone, and there's no money to get any more. They just get more frustrated, and they hit the child when they soil their clothes."

But there were also the happy cases, especially the children she saved. One premature baby required a feeding tube, and every other day, when it needed changing, Dr. Tillman had to do it, because the child would stop breathing during the switch. But that baby survived and grew up. "I stayed in contact with her and her two children," she said.

*"We worried about some kids when we saw child and infant abuse, such as cigarette burns on the buttocks. In one case, we had testimony that a child was being abused physically, but the judge sent that child back home—and he came in again with broken limbs. So that was a big question for us: Why would the judge send kids back into those homes?"*

—Jobyna Moore Foster

*"My favorite patient story was a 15-ounce baby girl, born at 23 weeks' gestation to a 15-year-old single mother. I cared for her for four months. At her time of discharge, she was eating baby food and placed on a blanket on the floor for stimulation."*
—Lillian Haywood

When treatment went well, the work in pediatrics was reward-ing, uplifting. But it didn't always go that way; sometimes, there were physical strains. Lillian Haywood had to retire after she was diagnosed with serious nerve damage in her hand. "Do you remem-ber the baby bottles where you'd hit and twist the metal tops? Well, we found out that all the nurses have nerve damage in their hands because of hitting and twisting those bottles."

Along with the draining physical work, they had to watch small children suffer. In the 1940s, nurse Gretchen McCullum recalled working tirelessly in the so-called milk lab, where she washed bot-tles, poured milk into them, and then processed them in a sterilizer. But she also saw sick and dying children with polio, several of them languishing in the old iron lungs.

Older children could also tear at your heart, like the 12-year-old who gave birth. Or the 14-year-old who told Alverne Eldridge that her 18-year-old boyfriend wanted a baby. "I talked to them like they were my children. I said, 'Do you realize what you're saying? You want to give up your childhood, your freedom, and everything?' But she got off that pill anyway." Worse still was the 9-year-old impregnated by her stepfather, along with her two sisters.

Pediatrics wasn't for everyone. Babies with lead poisoning would be crying inconsolably, said nurse Mamie Walton, "and I would rock them and cry with them. The supervisor would come by and say, 'Mamie Walton, how long you going to sit there and rock that baby?'" Another child had been bitten in the forehead by a dog. "I was crying, and the doctor said, 'You going to cry, or you going to hand me sutures?' I thought, 'I'm going to cry.'"

Treating every child well was paramount, but at times nurses had special favorites. For Vernell Brooks Brown, the two children she remembered best were sisters with sickle-cell disease. "They came in all the time, and I could hear them crying. I used to hate that: seeing them in pain." She also met a six-year-old boy whose father was a police officer. Somehow, his three-year-old brother had gotten hold of their father's revolver and shot him. "He was my patient in pediatric intensive care, and one morning around breakfast time, he asked me if he was going to die. I said, 'Of course not! You're doing fine!' About one o'clock he spiked a fever and died. I had to go home, I was so upset. So, I found out that pediatrics wasn't for me."

But other nurses found pediatrics enormously rewarding, especially when they could hand a patient a new life. Lillian Haywood recalled a young, indigent woman who had given birth at the hospital but left her baby blanket behind when she checked out. After work, Mrs. Haywood set out to find her. "I knocked at the door of the address we had for her, and the lady there said, 'Oh, she doesn't live in here. She lives out in the garage.' I went out to the back, and it took her a while to get to the door because she was wrapped in so many blankets. Because of the cold, she had a space heater, and the baby was lying right in front of it.

"I said, 'Honey, why didn't you tell us you were living in a garage?' She said, 'My mother put me out, and this is where I have to live.' I said, 'How are you keeping your milk cold?' She said, 'It's out in the snow.' I went back and reported this to the visiting nurses, and they were able to get her an apartment. We might have saved two lives that day."

## CHAPTER ELEVEN

# "Future Nurses Club"
## Nursing Life at Homer G. Phillips Hospital

*"In Evansville, Indiana, I was in the Future Nurses Club, and I really loved the school nurse; I admired her so much that I wanted to be a school nurse, too. Back in the '50s, there were only two schools that would accept African American people: One was Homer G. Phillips, and the other one was Grady in Atlanta. But they were rioting and marching in Atlanta, and my mother said, 'You're going north.' So I came to Homer Phillips."*

> —Martha Jackson Nelson, nursing graduate of Homer G. Phillips, class of 1961; B.S., College of St. Francis; pediatric nurse practitioner program, Washington University School of Medicine, 1974; she later specialized in sickle-cell screening and education as a Washington University School of Medicine and then St. Louis Children's Hospital staff member

IF PHYSICIANS ARE smart, they value the nurses who work with them. "I have always believed that nurses are the eyes and the ears at the heart of the hospital, because they are the ones truly in contact with the patients," said Dr. Earle U. Robinson Jr., once a trainee at Homer G. Phillips. "I always taught the residents and interns I trained that when a nurse tells you to come, don't turn over and go back to sleep. Come, because she's calling you for a reason."

With its affiliated nursing school, known for its high standards and dedicated staff, Homer G. Phillips had a strong source of fine

Fig. 11.1: This group photo of Homer G. nurses includes Edith McIntyre,
Barbara Young, Ernestine Williams, Nora Smith, Doris Stamps, Anna Parker,
Lorrin Pugh, and Sydney Skipper. Courtesy of Martha Jackson Nelson.

nurses. "Yes," said Dr. Lee Blount, a surgeon. "It had some of the
best nurses. Some of the *best*."

Becoming a nurse at Homer G. Phillips was a three-year journey
that began with a letter of inquiry to the school. Next came the
application forms and tests, then the hoped-for letter of admission.
Not everyone got in. In a 1957 newspaper article, assistant education director Juliette Jones said the school had 135 applicants for
that year but could only take 32 of them.[1] Finally came the heart-
in-mouth trip to St. Louis, most often by train or bus.

The course of study itself, with only a month off in the summers,
was a rigorous program—and not everyone made it. Some dropped
out, dismayed at the hard work; others took flight at the sight of
blood, suffering, or death; still others were asked to leave for bad
behavior or low grades. For the ones who ran the gauntlet successfully, there was a capping ceremony at six months and graduation
at the end.

Along the way, students did have some fun. They enjoyed a dormitory life filled with camaraderie, study, and mischief. In their off

Fig. 11.2: Shown here is a grade report of nurse Yvonne B. Jones, who graduated from the School of Nursing in 1968. The school was known for its tough grading. Courtesy of Yvonne Jones.

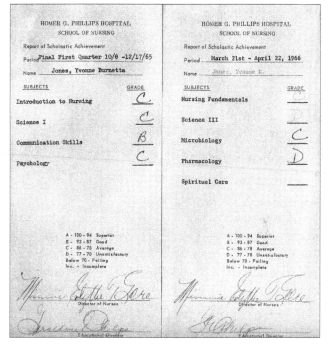

hours, they had a social life that included school dances, trips to area cultural attractions, and dates with young men—which meant an ongoing battle of wits with the housemother as they tried to evade detection (and demerits) when they sneaked in past curfew.

In the end, they all learned how to make a bed with razor-sharp hospital corners and wrinkle-free sheets. They figured out innovative ways to starch their beloved nursing caps. Most seriously, they learned how to treat indigent patients with compassion and respect—then, at times, how to face the death of these patients with courage. The reward was academic and emotional enrichment. "Homer G. Phillips provided an avenue to complete me as a person. It has meant life or death for me," said nurse Ethel Long.

The education they received provided lifelong practical benefits. As soon as they graduated, they were nurses who, because of the school's stellar reputation, were eminently employable. They were young, educated women, capable of earning a good living—and they, often unlike their families, had become solid members of the middle class.

*"My grandfather, Jesse Brown, worked in the coal mines in Kentucky. He scraped up the money to send me to nursing school in St. Louis. He paid for it, all three years—$300 and some. He said, 'Pay me back when you can,' or something like that, but I never had to pay him back."*

—Martha Jackson Nelson

In the 1950s, there were few career choices for women, especially African Americans. "My sister was a teacher, but I knew I didn't want to do that, so I chose to be a nurse," said nurse Joanne Allen Love. A doctor wrote her a letter of recommendation, her minister wrote a second, and a teacher wrote the third. "I was accepted into the school and after that began studying hard so I wouldn't flunk and be a disappointment."

Anita Lomax Hubbard heard of Homer G. Phillips from a cousin, so in 1965 she and two friends in Mobile, Alabama, took the entrance exam. Somehow, her acceptance letter didn't arrive until late August, when she was about to begin junior college. Quickly, she changed course and climbed into a bus for a nervous ride to St. Louis. "I was scared, I was *scared*. I had never been out of Mobile," she said. "My daddy got me on the bus. He was in tears. He kept coming onto the bus saying, 'You OK?' So, you know, it was pitiful."

Since Johnnye Robinson Farrell's father worked for the railroad, she got a free train ride to Missouri in the sleeping-car section. During that journey, her excitement outweighed her homesickness. "I didn't really get sad until I went home for Christmas," she said, "and when I got ready to come back again, I think I cried all the way to St. Louis."

Lula Couch Hall, class of 1959, remembers filling out the application for Homer G. Phillips. "You had to have three letters of recommendation. It was just like kids now waiting to hear from the college of their choice: We all waited to hear from Homer Phillips." When the time came, she took the train from Little Rock and was reassured to meet others who were also headed to the school. "In fact, one of the girls on the train, Yvonne Brown, ended up being my roommate."

As they settled into the dorm, they got to know the young women living around them. A kindly administrator had placed Iver Gandy and her group of "Birmingham" girls near each other, which made them feel at home. As they unpacked, they compared notes on items they had been told to bring, including their church clothes, especially a hat and gloves.

For some, including Ethel Long, raising the tuition money had been hard. Her mother, a maid in an East St. Louis hotel, could not help, so she worked in a small hospital as a nurse's aide until she had saved $300 toward tuition. "I thought I was one of the only nurses there who had paid their own way," she said. "Some of our classmates received scholarships; others were in a two-parent home and could pay that tuition. In nurses' training, we had a month or five weeks off each year for vacation, so I would ask them, 'Could I work those weeks for spending money?'"

Yet Mrs. Long was not alone. Mamie Walton was an orphan, who had worked at the Federal Reserve Bank for a year to save up for nursing school. "I paid in full that first day, so flunking out wasn't an option. Whatever it meant, even if I had to stay up all night studying, that's what I was going to do because I had no backup. It was just me."

> *"I thought the initiation was awful. We all had a 'big sister,' who was an upper-classmate, and I had to go to her room and polish her shoes or wash her shoestrings—whatever she wanted me to do. She would help me, too, if we needed help. But they blindfolded us and marched us around the hospital. Oh, I thought that was terrible! I was so afraid; I didn't know what was going to happen to me. Then I got to do it to the next class that came in, and we did the same thing to them."*
> —Martha Jackson Nelson

Once all the new students had arrived, they faced initiation week, which meant a round of hazing by upperclassmen. "Students in the class of 1967 were called Snoots," said Iver Gandy. "Every time you approached an upperclassman, you had to say, 'I'm Snoot Gandy,' and make a snorting sound. You were also assigned a big sister, and you did favors for them, like polish their shoes or wash their caps. Believe it or not, you *can* make white shoes shine."

Brenda Pettiway Walker, 1968 nursing graduate, recalls being blindfolded and asked to eat "eyeballs," actually peeled grapes. Older students had her touch a hot iron, then asked her to hold it—but they had swapped it for a cold one. "Where I drew the line," said nurse Carol Horton, "was when they put cooked spaghetti on us, like it was worms. My mother came to visit and called me down to see her right on time, because that would have killed me."

Friday that week, she added, was Hell Night, when the older students blindfolded the younger ones and led them to the hospital's sub-basement. "You held somebody's hand while they took you to all these rooms. They said, 'You have to be careful, because this is the morgue,' and you go, 'Oh, my God.' Then they put our hands in something that made you think it was someone's body. It was just, ew, *yucky*."

In those first weeks of school, they learned how to take care of their own uniforms: a blue-and-white-pinstriped dress with sleeves trimmed in white and detachable white cuffs; a stiff, scratchy white collar; a snowy-white bib apron, "starched so stiff you could stand it up," said Ethel Long; white hose and clunky "granny" shoes they had bought in a special department at the downtown Famous-Barr department store. They had gorgeous navy-blue wool capes for special occasions or in winter. Most of all, they had white caps, which they soaked in blue Faultless starch. Behind the backs of the staff, who wouldn't have approved, they flattened the wet caps on their mirrors and let them dry, so they wouldn't need ironing.

"The laundry took care of our uniforms, so we didn't have to do that," said Wanda Trotter. "You'd put them in a duffel bag outside your room on laundry day, and they would bring them back. But you had to take care of your own shoes and white shoestrings, and make sure your white hose didn't have any runs. And they inspected. If you had heavy hips or were a well-proportioned lady, you

Fig. 11.3: This Homer G. Phillips nursing school uniform, which belonged to Lula Hall, included a blue-and-white dress, white pinafore, white cuffs, and collar. Mrs. Hall graduated in 1959 and worked as a nurse in St. Louis until her retirement in 1996. Courtesy of the Missouri Historical Society, St. Louis.

had to wear your girdle so you wouldn't be shaking going down the hallway. Of course, you'd never go anyplace without a full slip on."

The granny shoes earned mixed reviews. "I heard a lot of people say that they were the most comfortable ones they had worn, but they just *wore* my feet. I was almost crying, especially if we had to walk on an incline. My toes would go forward, and my feet would be hurting so bad," said Alverne Meekins Eldridge. "We only had

Fig. 11.4: Here is a group of nurses on the obstetrics service with their instructor. Left to right are: Ruby Patterson, Rubystein Gary, Sarah Jane Banks (instructor), Shirley Smith, Martha Jackson (later Nelson), and (below) Jennye Robinson. They were all wearing their elegant navy blue capes. October 15, 1959. Courtesy of Martha Nelson.

to stay in them for six months, and then I threw those shoes away in the trash. I certainly did."

Early on, incoming students wore some black items as part of their earliest uniform: a black scarf, tied neatly in a bow; black shoes; and black stockings. Those stockings were unpopular, especially among students who couldn't afford garments to hold them up. "I didn't like them because they would fall down," said Mary Crawford Lane, a 1951 nursing graduate, who came from a family of 11 children. Garter belts? "Yes, but you got to buy them, see. And we couldn't, shall we say, afford the niceties."

Never, ever could nursing students hike up their waistbands. "The hem of your skirt had to be exactly 18 inches from the floor," said Johnnye Robinson Farrell, class of 1968. "They would actually take a yardstick and measure if they thought it was too short."

Even jewelry was limited, she added.

I was a senior when I decided to get my ears pierced. I asked one of the doctors, Dr. Gehamy, to do it, and then quite a few other students decided to get theirs pierced, too. Most of us had enough hair to cover our ears, but one had gotten her hair cut—and that's how people found out. Miss Gore called us into her office and admonished us. So we couldn't put earrings in, but we kept the suture thread there so the holes wouldn't close up. Then when we got a little money together, we went downtown and bought us some cheap earrings and put them in on weekends.

Whatever minor quarrels they had with their outfits, "we were very proud of our caps and uniform," said Martha Jackson Nelson. "Very proud. It just made us feel like Florence Nightingale. We had no nail polish, no earrings, not a lot of make-up. And we were not called by our first names, but we were addressed as 'Miss,' like 'Miss Jackson.' It was professionalism."

*"The first year, biology and math were almost exactly what I had in high school, so I felt like I was really prepared. I*

*struggled with pharmacology; I had a hard time with it, and I didn't think I was going to make it. I would go to the pharmacology instructor, Juliette Lee, on Saturdays, and she would tutor me and several others to get through it. I can remember my mother saying: 'She'll never make it. She's afraid of everything.' And I thought, 'I'll show her!'"*

—Martha Jackson Nelson

For nearly all new students, the schoolwork was a challenge, and they knew from the start that not everyone would be allowed to stay. "They laid down a lot of rules, but that was all right for me; I was used to rules. Around 60 of us went into nurses' training in September 1955, and within the first six months, we were down to 22 or 24," said Ethel Long.

Those early months were devoted to such classes as nursing arts in which the starched and polished Thelma McClendon declared that there were three parts of nursing: aspiration, inspiration, and perspiration. The perspiration part came true soon enough as they learned to make the beds, bathe the patients, and empty the bedpans. They also took anatomy and physiology to learn the nerves, the blood vessels, and the systems. Pharmacology taught them to calculate dosages.

After a few months, they could go on the hospital floor, doing such basic tasks as taking temperatures. "We had to start sticking an orange or a grapefruit to learn how to give shots," said Johnnye Robinson Farrell. They also had to keep the patient units—each with its iron bed, chair, and night table—in order. "We started out washing those old, rusty beds," said Jacqueline Calvin. "I got left behind one day at lunchtime because Mrs. Theresa Vaughn, our instructor, didn't feel I had gotten enough rust off that night table. Oooh! I was so angry."

The transition from high school to nursing school, with lots of homework, was a shock. "I was scared to death," said Annie Crawford Ward. "The instructors were hard, and so was the amount of work they required of you. I told my mom, 'They expect too much,' and she said, 'Well, just do the best you can.'" Over time, they came to realize that some of the toughest teachers were actually fair. "Juliette Lee was stern, but as I look back, that was necessary, and she became one of my favorites," said Ethel Long.

Roommates studied together, and sometimes students buoyed each other up. "Charlene Luckett from Mississippi was one of our super-duper smart classmates, at the top of the class; if she didn't pass the test, nobody was passing it," said Carol Horton. "Her room was next to mine, and I can remember her knocking on my wall and saying: 'Are you up studying?' 'Yeah,' I'd say. 'No, you're not. Get up and study!'"

Sometimes, students made trouble. Johnnye Robinson Farrell's suitemates sneaked off with food from her care packages. Edna Loeb's messy roommate earned her demerits, despite her own neatness. "One girl who was sent home would get up on Saturday mornings and bounce the basketball down the hall to wake

Fig. 11.5: Nursing students were taking part in a science class at Homer G. Phillips, while instructors demonstrated with a skeleton and anatomic models. Photo ca. 1960. Courtesy of the Missouri Historical Society, St. Louis.

everybody up," said Martha Jackson Nelson. "She was smart as a whip, and she said that sending her home was the best thing they did, because she is a doctor now. Two others would run down the hall, streaking, and they didn't care who saw them."

One night, Charlotte Steel got sassy with her mother over her extravagant purchase of a $45 housecoat. "When she got the bill, she called me, and I decided in my infinite wisdom to hang up on her. About an hour later, the buzzer in our room rang, and I thought there was probably a boy downstairs to see me, so I brushed my hair and put on a little lipstick. When I stepped off the elevator, I saw my mother's bag. She had come all the way from East St. Louis to scold me because I had hung up on her."

Those who made it through the first six months took part in a solemn capping ceremony, often held in the nursing school itself or in the old Kiel Auditorium, in which they recited the Florence Nightingale pledge. "That was the night when we got our Florence Nightingale lamp, with the little candle," said Iver Gandy. "And then you got your cap. I felt on the top of the world receiving it."

One person who was not thrilled with his cap was a male classmate, Richard W. White, who wore his own student uniform: a smock and pants. "My mother and father came for the capping ceremony, and when they gave me the cap, everybody laughed. Some of my classmates talked about having me put it on, but I said, 'Never.'"

> "In the third year, I studied hard, because I wanted to graduate, and I wanted to pass state boards. That was my goal. We took these National League of Nursing tests every so often, and if you didn't pass those, that was an indicator of how you were going to do on state boards. And when I take the state boards, I didn't pass pediatrics, though I came close. So I studied and went back, and I almost made a perfect score. I had to, because I wanted to prove to my mother that I could do it."
> —Martha Jackson Nelson

Over the next two years of nursing school, students gradually took on more responsibility. "In the second year, you actually

Fig. 11.6: These are three male nursing graduates, left to right: David Mitchell (class of 1966), Calvin Rice (class of 1968), and Richard W. White (class of 1968). Courtesy of Meredith White.

started doing patient care, like taking vital signs," said Johnnye Robinson Farrell. "Next, you could change IVs; give shots; and draw, pass, and pour medications under supervision. You felt like you were becoming a nurse."

As they rotated to different areas of the hospital, students also began deciding what to specialize in—partly a process of elimination. "What attracted me to surgery was seeing these patients on other floors worry people to death. 'I need a bedpan, I need this or that,'" said Rosie Jackson. "I knew early on I wouldn't be able to handle it. I was not calm enough to get up and assist you when I knew you could get up and do it yourself. You know, if you need the bedpan, go to the bathroom. Get up and go."

All the while, they continued taking classes from various teachers, some deeply respected and a few not at all. In the former group was Thelma McClendon, known behind her back as "T-Mac." "She did not play, so you did not play around with T-Mac," said Jacqueline Calvin. "She just walked in smiling, and you didn't cheat. When she'd walk out of the room, you would sit there quietly and do your test."

"The first thing we learned was how to wash our hands," said Louise Brown Cunningham. "I can never forget that. Mrs. McClendon lined us all up and had each one of us wash our hands for her, and then she showed us the correct way to do it. She said, 'Your hands are ten avenues to infection.'" Martha Nelson learned how to prepare a water pitcher. "I'll never forget her saying to me, when I had filled it completely with ice: 'Well, where's the water going to go?'" Privately, T-Mac was compassionate. Aware of Mamie Walton's precarious financial situation, "she would give me shoes and clothes. She was a sweetheart. She just said, 'Here, take this.'"

Still, she could be tough. "If your cap was not starched and creased just right, she'd just squash it on your head," said Charlotte Steel. "Yes, she was a hard taskmaster," said Karole Davidson, "because she liked perfection. When we made beds, you had to miter the corners just so, and if they weren't just so, she would snatch the sheets and tear the bed up. Oh, my Lord, have mercy!"

Another star was the pleasant Theresa Whiteside Vaughn, who injected humor into her teaching. Or Eleanor Bell, an OR instructor. "Before we could scrub in the operating room, we had to learn what was on the trays for different types of surgery," said Louise Brown Cunningham. "Ms. Bell would open up these trays, and we had to draw the instruments on each one, then we put them into a notebook for future reference."

For Minervia Bennett Williams, Juliette Lee "was brilliant, probably the best teacher there. She is the reason that I know medicine backward and forward today." Lee blended tough classroom teaching with kindness, but she was determined that her students would master the hard math they needed. One Sunday, she captured them for extra work, recalled Laverna Turner Spinks, saying, "You are not free today. You belong to me."

Barbara Pool remembers Doris Mosley, chemistry and anatomy instructor, who was about to send her progress report home with a "D" from Mosley's course. "I requested a conference with her, and I was just crying. She reached over and handed me a box of Kleenex, so I would wipe my eyes—but the grade went home. So, I saved up three quarters and called home on a pay phone, and I told my mamma that grade was coming. She didn't get hysterical; she just said, 'You do the very best you can.' And no other D went home for anything; in fact, I was an honors student."

Juanita Long, formerly in the military and later the nursing director, inspired fear with her stern manner. One day, she called Charlotte Steel into her office. "I was trying to figure out what did I do? So, she said, 'Sit down, Miss Wyatt.' I was thinking, 'Oh my goodness, this is serious.' Then she leaned over and said, 'What size are you in the waist?' I said, 'I beg your . . . ?' and she said, 'Well, I think you're probably like a 23 or so. What's going on is that we want you to be the page at the Coronation Ball, and we need someone who will fit into the uniform.' I could have just fallen off my seat."

*"The house mother, Nannie Whittico, lived in an apartment on the first floor of the building. She was a sweet little lady, but she didn't take any stuff; she would get on you. But every night she would fix up a cart with snacks and put it in the hall; you could go down and get fruit or graham crackers."*
—Martha Jackson Nelson

Nursing students lived in the five-story nurses' residence at 2516 Goode Avenue, just a short walk by land or tunnel from the hospital. Most were in single rooms, though there were some doubles. "Every morning, they would ring each room around 5:00 or 5:30," said nurse Norris McReynolds. "We'd get up and shower and go through the tunnel to the hospital to eat breakfast. From there, we would go to the ward for a pre-conference and then on to give morning care to the patients."

They used that same cafeteria for lunch and for dinner, three years straight. "In general, the food was OK, but there were two things I didn't like," said Martha Nelson. "One was grits; I had

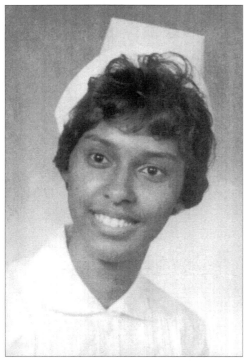

Fig. 11.7: Martha Jackson Nelson graduated from the Homer G. Phillips School of Nursing in 1961. She continued on to become a nurse practitioner and worked in sickle-cell screening and education at Washington University School of Medicine and St. Louis Children's Hospital. Courtesy of Martha Nelson.

never had them before, and we had them morning, noon, and night. I had never had lamb either, and oh, that lamb was terrible. So, my mother would send me a little money, and I would save it up. Whenever they had that lamb, I would go to Billy Burke's for a hamburger. Sara-Lou was known for its breaded shrimp, and that cost a little more. I really had to save up to go get shrimp."

The dorm was comfortable, with a large lounge and recreation rooms downstairs, as well as a prayer room named for house-mother Ophelia Clark. There was a basement rumpus room, and each floor had a solarium, laundry, and kitchen. But it lacked air-conditioning and could be brutally hot in the summers. Students tried everything—fans, wide-open windows, cakes of ice—to keep cool, and they even climbed out to the roof for a breath of fresh air. In the winters, they opened their windows and kept perishable foods outside as a kind of homemade refrigerator.

To give them a taste of St. Louis life and some new cultural experiences, the school sponsored trips to local attractions: Forest Park,

Fig. 11.8: Nursing students shown here were in formal dance attire at the Masonic Hall. Standing, left to right: Fredericka Cooper (Jr.), Jeanette Walker (Jr.), Anna Walker (Fr.), Barbara Stevenson (Sr. and Queen of the dance), Lillie Jones (Sr.), Georgia William (Sr.), Martha Jackson Nelson) (Jr.); and sitting, left to right: Florence Matthews (Fr.), Loretta Stewart (Fr.), Delores Graham (Fr.), Sandra Nelson (Fr.), and Barbara Young (Jr.). November 28, 1959. Courtesy of Martha Nelson.

the Muny, the St. Louis Symphony, basketball games, and skating rinks. Occasionally, there were special treats, such as a Marian Anderson recital in 1943 and later an Elvis Presley concert. At the school, there were Valentine's Day dances, a George Washington tea, and proms.

> *"St. Louis was much larger than Evansville. They had service cars, which I was not familiar with, that ran up and down Easton [later Dr. Martin Luther King Drive], and all you had to do was flag them down. And even riding the bus, we did not have to sit in the back; we could sit anywhere. But I was pretty much confined around the hospital. I went to Antioch Baptist; there was a movie theater in walking distance. I didn't venture out much. My circle was right there."*
> —Martha Jackson Nelson

Monitoring the students were house mothers or matrons: Nannie Whittico, mother of Dr. James Whittico; Ophelia Clark (known as "Muff" behind her back); and Bertha Gilkey. "They were kind," said Ethel Long, "but they had a lot of rules. Men were not allowed to go above the first floor, and we had to be in by curfew, which was 10:15 on weekdays and 11:00 on weekends." From their desk by the front door, the house mothers watched the comings and goings, sometimes questioning young men who came to call. They used a buzzer system to summon students downstairs to meet their dates.

"They would lock the dormitory at 10:15," said Mary Crawford Lane, "and they didn't mean 10:16 either. Sometimes we had to run to beat that curfew, before they could lock the door. If you missed, you had to ring the doorbell and explain to Miss Clark what happened. . . . Oh, my land! I didn't do that because I didn't want her to be telling my Mamma!"

Demerits became an unwelcome fact of life, said nurse Edna Loeb. "If there was an assembly in the morning, you'd better be there two minutes ahead [and] not two minutes after, or you would get a demerit. If your instructor reported you as being late to class, you got another demerit. And they would punish you if you got too many. Rather than having free time in the evenings you were grounded."

Another check on student behavior was the presence of staff in the dorm, among them Minnie Gore and Mabel C. Northcross. Miss Gore understood the girls' need for food after 9:00 p.m. when the cafeteria closed, said Georgia Anderson. "Her housekeeper, Miss Dean, always had a big bowl of fruit out for us to eat. We could knock on Miss Gore's door, and she would say, 'Come on in. Let's see what we can do.' She would always have eggs, so you could make omelets and bacon, grilled cheese sandwiches, and what have you."

Life in the dorm was fun, added Edna Loeb. "Before lights out, we would talk for hours about where we came from, who our families were, that kind of stuff. Those who wanted to participate in the Friday and Saturday night card games—poker, bid whist— sometimes played all night long." Students took those games

Fig. 11.9: Five nursing students were polishing up a dance routine in their spare time. March 1959. Courtesy of Martha Nelson.

seriously, said nurse Claudine Johnson. "I played one time and reneged on a hand. I thought they were going to throw me out that fifth-floor window. I said, 'Never again!'"

> *"After I graduated, I stayed on to work, and I lived in the dormitory with another classmate from Texas. You got free room and board if you stayed a year, and I saved all my money and bought a car. But I moved out of the dormitory when a nurse took her life there. It was the 4th of July weekend, and her family kept calling. I would go to her door and knock, and she wouldn't answer. When she didn't show up for class,*

*the house mother came and opened the door, and that's when*
*they found her. She was involved with one of the interns, and*
*she was working on labor and delivery when his wife came in*
*and delivered a baby. So I never wanted a doctor; I married a*
*postman. No, I didn't want one."*

—Martha Jackson Nelson

The young nursing students attracted a swarm of potential suitors: firefighters and police officers, college graduates and postal workers, doctors and trainees. "They would warn us about the doctors, not to get too involved, that it made a bad nurse-physician relationship," said Ethel Long. "But they were young, good-looking guys, and we were young, cute chicks—so people are people, you know." Added Mary Crawford Lane, "There was a wall between the dormitory of the nurses and the men, but you'd meet the residents on the ward. Once I was dating three of them, and they were all named John!"

It was risky to date the trainees and doctors, because some were privately married. "Our instructor, Doris Mosley, talked to us about the doctors," said Jacqueline Calvin. "She said, 'When you come to school, you will see the doctors with wedding rings on, but in a couple of weeks they will take them off. If you ever want to know about somebody, come to me or to Miss Gore, and we will let you know.'"

Mabel C. Northcross seemed to know when OR nursing students were preoccupied by young men. During her training, Georgia Rhone Anderson was daydreaming about a young man during her work. "She said to me, 'Miss Rhone, you hear me? Your mind ain't with you, and it ain't been with you for three days.' I laughed so hard I almost got hysterical. I told her, 'You know what, Miss Northcross, you're right!'"

She also was brutally frank with young nurses who were making eyes at the doctors, she added. "'Honey, you might as well quit grinning at that doctor. He doesn't want you. He got a girlfriend.'" Or the tiny, wizened Miss Northcross might say to them, "He got a wife. And he'd take me out before he'd take you!"

Still some students seemed to court trouble by sneaking in late at night through the tunnel and then quietly up the stairs. "I wouldn't risk it," said Ethel Long. "No, no. It would be putting your whole life on the line." Still, following the rules still gave them time for fun. On dates or double dates, nurses would go to the movies, to Gaslight Square in the Central West End, or to Peacock Alley, a jazz club located in the old City Hospital #2 building on Lawton.

A handful got special dispensation to marry during training. "Our class was the first that they allowed to get married," said Alverne Meekins Eldridge, class of 1966, "and I was fortunate to

Fig. 11.10: Nursing students could climb to the dormitory roof for sunbathing or conversation. These four were (left to right): Willa Jean Richardson, Maxine French, Loretta Butler, and Fredericka Cooper. Photo ca. 1959. Courtesy of Martha Nelson.

get married at the beginning of my senior year." But the administration may have been keen observers of relationships. "Curtis is my
ex-husband, and we got married while I was still in school, though
I was about to graduate," said nurse Carol Horton. "I had to ask
Miss Gore for permission—and her response was to save enough
money for the divorce."

> *"My first choice was adult medicine, and I don't know why I
> chose adult medicine, because those patients were older, and
> they were sicker. Instead, I got my second choice, pediatrics.
> And that's where I stayed and ended up becoming a pediatric
> nurse practitioner through the Washington University pro-
> gram. It was a good thing I didn't get my first choice."*
> —Martha Jackson Nelson

Old and sick or young and sick, patients still died during treatment, and student nurses had to get used to the sight and sadness
of death. "My first patient that I lost was a lady who died in child-
birth, and she had twins," recalled nurse Dorothy Thornton. "They
put the babies in an incubator, and then we worked on the mother. I
just thought about the fact that those kids were going to be without
a mother, and I dropped a couple of tears."

During a terrible heat wave in the summer of 1966, Wanda
Trotter took care of a female patient who came in desperately ill
from heat stroke. "That was the first person I had seen to pass
away, and you're learning something new, but yet you're scared to
death and sad. They taught us to bathe the body and make sure the
dead patient was presentable for the family, and they also taught us
to hold our emotions in. But still I was saying to myself, 'Oh, my
God, this patient is *dead*.'"

Occasionally, that first experience with death nearly ended a
young nurse's career. "I had a patient in his early 20s who had been
shot, but he was doing very well," said Brenda Pettiway Walker.

> But the next day, the bed was gone, and they told me he had
> died. So I went into the room where the body was, and that

was the first time I had really faced death. I stood there looking at this man and everything about him was perfect, but he was dead. Then the nurse came in and said, "He's still your patient. Get him ready." We had to bathe him and put the tags on him, and I had such a horrible feeling that I ran out of the hospital up to my room, where I started packing my suitcase and crying: "I cannot do this. How can people in their 20s just die like this?" All of a sudden, I looked up and there was Miss Gore, who seemed like she was seven feet tall. At the time, I wasn't even a hundred pounds.

She said, "Pettiway!" I said, "Yes, ma'am." She said, "What are you doing?" I said, "I'm going to leave. I can't take this. I don't understand death." She said, "You can't go. Your room is the only room in this whole dorm that I can show people. Whenever anybody wants to come and look at a room, I bring them to yours." Then she smiled and said, "I want you to realize one thing, and that is that you do not give nor take life, you only preserve it." Then it just clicked for me. She said, "Take a few minutes, get yourself together, and go back over there with your patients."

Ethel Long had nearly the same thing happen, with the same results.

I was feeding a patient, and she ate a spoonful of oatmeal; she could only mumble, because she had had a stroke. And then she stopped talking. So I called my instructor, and when she saw the patient, she said, "Miss Shelton, your patient is deceased." I stared at her. She looked me in the eye and said, "Miss Shelton, your patient has died." When I tried to follow her out of the room, she said, "You can't do that. You have to stay with the patient until the doctor pronounces her." I had to stay with this patient who had died, 30 to 45 minutes.

Well, I had to decide then, that I was not going to leave school, because there were other students who cried and said they were going to go home. I decided that my only other options were working for a private family or running an elevator. So, I had to stay, and it was all right. But it was the first time I'd seen anyone die. You never forget it. I have not forgotten it, and that's been about 60 years ago. I remember her. I remember where I was. I remember where I was standing. By her bed. And the direction her bed was.

*"I was so excited to have made it—I had proved my mother wrong! My parents came to my graduation, which was at Kiel Auditorium, from Indiana. We all wore beautiful white uniforms, and they had to be a certain length. Miss Gore, the director of nursing, checked all of us to make sure they were the correct length. Some of the nurses had shortened theirs, and she made them let theirs out."*

—Martha Jackson Nelson

At graduation, proud parents or other relatives came to St. Louis to join the celebration. The ceremony took place in various venues—Christ Church Cathedral downtown, Kiel Auditorium—and the students wore pure white uniforms, fitted by the Famous Barr department store. How did they feel that day? "Relieved," said Lois Collier Jackson, "because it had been tough."

Annie Crawford Ward had her mother and sister there. Even though her father was working construction out of town and couldn't make it, "he told all his buddies, and some of them came, too. He told them I was graduating from Homer Phillips, and that was something." Even the Army cooperated. Alverne Meekins Eldridge's husband, Raymond, got a day pass from Fort Leonard Wood to attend.

For Louise Brown Cunningham's graduation, Estelle Massey [now Osborne] had come back to be the speaker. "I've never forgotten what she spoke about. Her subject was 'On Beyond Zebra.' She said the alphabet ends at 'Z,' but we need to go on beyond Z. She was telling us to grow, to do more and more. I guess I took that to heart, because I did go on beyond the diploma, and I ended up with a master's degree."

Students knew what they had ahead: state boards, a firm choice of specialty, the hunt for a job. But they had passed a giant milestone, and they had their diplomas in hand. "Lord have mercy," said Rosie Jackson. "I was so glad to get across that stage."

## CHAPTER TWELVE

# The Final Era
## The Long Path to Closing, 1960–1979

*"The medical director was Dr. William Sinkler, who was a sur-
geon by training. The hospital administrator was a man named
Virgil McKnight. Things were physically well maintained, and
there was a strong culture there. For a young, impressionable
person like me who had not seen Black people in authority, it
was a very positive experience."*

> —Dr. Donald M. Suggs, oral surgeon, who trained at
> Homer G. Phillips Hospital, later worked there for
> several years, and became president and publisher
> of the *St. Louis American* newspaper, which he
> purchased in 1980

IT WAS 1960, and Dr. Sinkler—"nationally known surgeon and medical director of Homer G. Phillips Hospital since 1941," mourned
the *St. Louis American*—had died after his second heart attack.
Right away, administrator Virgil McKnight named an interim replacement: Dr. Herbert Erwin, head of the hospital's Department
of Neuropsychiatry since 1942 and associate medical director since
November 1959, when Dr. Sinkler suffered his first attack. The new
head of surgery was the talented, outspoken, and often abrasive Dr.
Andrew Spencer.

The hospital was changing again, as was the temper of the nation. The civil rights era was dawning, and incoming students were
caught up in it. "In 1961, the year I graduated from high school
in Miami, that's when things just started to explode with all the
protests and marches," said nurse Barbara Pool. "The leader was a

Fig. 12.1: A trainee at Homer
G. Phillips Hospital and then
a St. Louis oral surgeon, Dr.
Donald M. Suggs became the
publisher and executive editor
of the *St. Louis American*
newspaper. Courtesy of Dr.
Donald Suggs.

canon in the Episcopal church, Theodore Gibson, who was president of the NAACP down there. The powers that be threatened to
put him in jail if he didn't turn over the rolls of the organization,
but he wouldn't do it. We had bus sit-ins, and rather than allow us
to sit wherever we wanted, they stopped the buses from running."

Yet political change was coming. The Democratic Party's hold on
Black voters tightened under President Lyndon Johnson with the
passage of the landmark Civil Rights Act of 1964 (Title VI), prohib-
iting discrimination in employment and barring segregation in public
places. The next year, President Johnson signed two more bills that
were critically important to Black voters: the Medicare/Medicaid
Act of 1965, followed by the Voting Rights Act, which eliminated
discriminatory barriers that prevented Blacks from voting.

The National Medical Association (NMA), a group of Black
physicians, strongly supported the Medicare Bill, and in 1968, St.
Louis surgeon Dr. James Whittico invited President Johnson to

address the national NMA convention in Dallas. But in the middle of the president's address, Dr. Whittico heard a commotion in the hallway: His own father, Dr. James Whittico Sr., a staunch Republican, was loudly protesting the president's appearance. "He was demanding to know what on earth was happening to the National Medical Association that it would let a Democratic president speak to them," recalled Dr. Whittico later.[1]

Through the decade, all the turmoil began to diminish, and by the time nurse Carolyn Spencer graduated from high school in 1969, her hometown of Mobile, Alabama, was relatively quiet. "It was getting better, and by then people were not rioting or anything. The integration came about so subtle. I went to a segregated high school, and my younger brother was the last one in our family to graduate from a segregated school. But my sister, the youngest of us all, graduated from an integrated Catholic high school."

Now the tradition-bound Homer G. Phillips School of Nursing was feeling pressure to modernize. Carol Horton, a 1968 graduate, recalled the advent of pantsuits as nursing uniforms. "They were so cute! But Miss [Minnie] Gore did not approve of ladies wearing pants. At that time, we had a lot of things to do on the floor, like getting under the bed, and pants were really more indicated than a dress. So, she couldn't turn the tide, even though she wasn't happy about it."

Momentous changes were also occurring in the world of Black hospitals, much affected by the integration of nearby all-white hospitals. A decline in their number, which had begun during the 1950s, continued and even accelerated. By the early 1960s, only some 100 remained in existence countrywide, and they were disappearing at a rate of two to three a year. In St. Louis, two of the three Black hospitals closed during the decade: St. Mary's Infirmary in 1966 and People's Hospital in 1967. Slowly but surely, Homer G. Phillips Hospital was becoming an anomaly. In 1967, the *Journal of the National Medical Association* ran a story calling its fate "nebulous" and citing "clashes of opinion" over its future.

What factors were causing this decline in the once-thriving world of Black hospitals? One was the end of segregation. "Civil rights legislation increased the access of black people to previously white health-care facilities. Consequently, Black hospitals faced an ironic dilemma: They now competed for patients with hospitals that had once excluded patients and professionals," wrote historian Vanessa Gamble. Black physicians were also leaving behind the all-Black hospitals to practice in formerly all-white hospitals. "As Black physicians have successfully struggled for and gained entry into the mainstream medical profession, Black hospitals have become marginal to their careers," added Gamble.

One other factor was the economics of health care, which had changed completely. "Medicare, Medicaid, and third-party payment . . . made it economically possible for African Americans to look beyond black institutions for treatment," wrote Gamble. "With the gradual erosion of residential segregation, middle-class patients have moved from the neighborhoods in which Black hospitals exist. Black hospitals have been facilities that treat, for the most part, poor people who are uninsured or on Medicaid. The situation has become especially critical as Medicaid reimbursement has fallen farther and farther behind the actual costs of health care." [2]

Yet even in this new, more open medical landscape, some things—especially disparities in care—hadn't disappeared. In 1965, newspapers reported that Dr. Seymour Monat, head of obstetrics and gynecology at the hospital, was engaged with the city of St. Louis in a fight against its high death rate among African American newborns. At the start of the decade, "St. Louis had the highest Negro infant death rate of 10 major cities in the United States. This amounted to 45.5 deaths per 1,000 births. . . . The doctor said the main reason for the high Negro death rate was lack of adequate prenatal care."[3]

Something else that hadn't changed at the hospital was its chronic need for money. The physical plant needed work, and Dr. Monat, also the chief of staff, wrote to the St. Louis hospital commissioner that there was a "chronic deficiency" in key positions, including anesthesiology, radiology, and pathology—and that was having a corrosive effect on the quality of the hospital.[4]

*"The Homer G. Phillips alumni annual meeting was like the
highlight of the year. I think people felt much more connected
because the options were more limited. And those connections
just lasted. Even people who left St. Louis would come back,
so it was a very tight-knit group."*

—Dr. Donald M. Suggs

An early death knell for the hospital sounded in May 1961,
though its timing was oddly ironic. St. Louis aldermen asked the
city to submit a plan for consolidating the two city hospitals and
closing Homer G. Phillips. But word of their intention got out just
as a memorial service for Dr. Sinkler, a staunch advocate for the
hospital, was taking place; the 16th national meeting of the Homer
G. Phillips Interns Alumni Association, was also in session, and
it had brought dozens of alumni to town. So, a large, boisterous
meeting sponsored by the Mound City Medical Forum and the

Fig. 12.2: The St. Louis City Hospital, often called City Hospital #1, was
located at 1515 Lafayette in south St. Louis. After two previous buildings were
destroyed by fire, this one was constructed in 1907 and closed in 1985. Photo
ca. 1976. Courtesy of the Bernard Becker Medical Library Archives, Washington
University in St. Louis.

Interns Association convened at Antioch Baptist to oppose any notion of closing.

Graduate physicians explained to the *St. Louis American* why they were against the proposal. According to internist and one-time Homer G. Phillips trainee Dr. R. Jerome Williams, "the idea of consolidating the two hospitals has been presented each year for the last six, but it never got as far as it has this time. . . . [The] main objection to the plan is the fear of loss of jobs for Negroes."[5] At the time, reported the story, the hospital employed 1,000 people, most of them Black, while City Hospital #1 had 1,100 staff members, all but a handful white. Astonishingly, one-third of all city jobs held by Blacks were the ones at Homer G. Phillips.

One point in favor of consolidation, said the same story, was the falling patient load at Homer G. Phillips. Recently, the hospital had reduced its bed capacity from 700 to 600, and the daily census hovered around 450. By contrast, City Hospital #1 had 907 beds, with a census of 450 as well; by opening a then-vacant wing, its total capacity could rise to 1,057 beds.

Why was the Homer G. census dropping? One problem was that *de facto* segregation continued at both city hospitals, despite the city's 1955 integration decree. The *American* blamed "the prejudiced attitude of some police officers who by-pass the hospital and take white patients miles out of the way to City Hospital #1." Perhaps the constant pressure on the hospital to keep costs down was also a factor. "A doctor stated that hospital officials were so inclined to economize that they neglected patients and sent them home before they fully recovered."

This talk of closing began to slow down improvements to both hospitals. In 1962, Homer G.'s Catholic chaplain, Father Fred Zimmerman, and the Protestant chaplain, Rev. Guy Outlaw, complained bitterly that their chapels had become bedraggled, even embarrassing. Tucked away in a sixth-floor alcove, above a broken elevator, these sanctuaries had pigeons roosting in the pews and, on one memorable morning, a drunken man stretched out across an altar. They had been promised new quarters on the first floor, but city officials were dragging their feet, unwilling to make a change until the hospital's future was secure.[6]

Rumors of closing persisted. In 1964 huge headlines in the *American* announced, "Homer Phillips Closing Issue Becomes Alarming." The Interns Association was so distressed that its board convened in St. Louis to discuss the problem. Fanning the flames were the actions of city officials, who met in private with Saint Louis University and Washington University administrators to discuss the hospital's fate. No one from Homer G. Phillips Hospital was in attendance. "Like two old warriors conquering a helpless city," wrote Dr. H. Phillip Venable savagely to the *American*, "they participated in secret sessions to divide the 'spoils.'"

As time wore on, the city took no action, but the community continued to push back hard against any thought of closing. The stalwart Interns Association adopted a resolution pointing out that more than three million patients had been treated at the hospital since its opening, 214,942 of them during the 1963–64 fiscal year. That same year, days of service at Homer G. were 171,699, but only 170,192 at City Hospital #1. Yet there was a disparity in total salaries: $4.03 million at Homer G. and $4.5 million at City Hospital #1. "While Homer G. Phillips was giving more service," reported the *American* pointedly, "its operating costs were $924,080 less than those of City Hospital."

Highlighting that discrepancy was a confidential study, commissioned by the city in 1961 from a respected consulting firm, but only acquired by the *St. Louis Post-Dispatch* and made public three years later. Its findings were a bombshell. The "long-suppressed management survey . . . described patient care and emergency room service at City Hospital as inadequate but said Phillips Hospital operated effectively despite staff shortages," it noted. One example of this efficiency was its surgery department. "Approximately the same amount of surgery is performed in the five operating rooms at Phillips as is performed in the eight operating rooms at City Hospital."

Further, the report castigated the salary structure for physicians and recommended "a program to develop an interest in Phillips internships among medical students," adding that the hospital needed "about 20 interns instead of the single intern it has now. Unless the trend with respect to house staff is reversed, the hospital may lose its accreditation."

In response, an embarrassed Mayor Raymond R. Tucker announced that the hospital would not close, and the city would take steps to strengthen it by initiating "a vigorous recruitment program to obtain an adequate number of interns." Sadly, that effort never materialized. One bit of good news for the program: the salary for interns increased from $2,814 a year to $4,157 a year in mid-1965.[7] Still, these salaries were far below those at other hospitals.

*"I went to dental school at Indiana University in 1953, and afterwards I had several options, but I had never had a Black teacher in all of my education, and I had a close friend whose father had trained at Homer Phillips Hospital. So, I learned about it, and the Black physicians in charge, and I was excited by the possibility. I had a good experience here. The physicians were very helpful—they taught me a lot beyond the formal dental program. I was in the operating room, and they taught me anesthesia. It was a very collegial environment at Phillips."*
—Dr. Donald M. Suggs

As always, hospital life was a mixture of daily achievement and occasional dramatic episodes. The Shriners, long generous to cancer research at the hospital, continued to make gifts, including another $4,800 in 1960, for an overall total of $61,600. The $1.27 million outpatient clinic, so long in the offing, finally opened in 1961, with an eye clinic highly prized by Drs. H. Phillip Venable, J. W. Nofles, and Samuel Canaan.

In July 1961 came an incident that made banner headlines in the *American*. An alcoholic and former mental patient, Richard "Dynamite" Shackelford, strolled into the emergency room, grabbed a pistol from an officer on duty, and began firing. While 15 bystanders scurried for cover, more officers arrived on the scene. In the ensuing gun battle, Shackelford was killed and two officers badly injured.

But in October 1962, happiness reigned as the hospital celebrated its 25th anniversary with medical programs for the community, a silver anniversary banquet at the Jefferson Hotel, and an outdoor ceremony on the hospital's front steps. At the banquet, U.S. Rep.

Adam Clayton Powell of New York was the keynote speaker, and more than a dozen groups important to the hospital's history were honorees: among them, the National Medical Association and the School of Nursing's Alumni Association.

Into the 1960s, newspapers continued to report occasional incidents at Homer G.: two employees caught embezzling money and a student suicide. More often, stories concerned patients treated there after fires, accidents, or robberies. In 1964 alone, the papers ran nearly 200 accounts of such cases, including a 6-year-old, hit by a car, with a fractured skull; a 2-year-old who fell out of a first-floor window; and a 63-year-old laborer killed by a falling girder.

In 1965, one story praised the surgical accomplishments of Dr. Andrew Spencer, who "joined the faculty of the [Washington University] Medical School in 1959 [and] holds the highest academic rank of any Negro on the University's medical faculty."[8] Recently, said the article, "Dr. Spencer has performed fifteen successful operations in which he used open-heart massage, saving the lives of the patients." Spencer said that his hard work was well worth it. "Those fifteen persons that I saved are the parents of a total of forty-five children. You can understand what it means to these people to be walking around today."

*"During the late '60s and the '70s, the world was in turmoil: The Vietnam War, women's liberation, the Civil Rights movements. We got scruffed up in all of that. I was at that age in life when you think you're really going to matter; I thought we were going to change the world."*

—Dr. Donald M. Suggs

As the national civil rights movement shifted into high gear, protests began in St. Louis as well, and some Homer G. Phillips staff members played a part in them. Carol Nelson Williams's late husband, Dr. Jerome Williams Sr., was active in the local civil rights movement. In 1963, she says, he helped organize physicians to demonstrate against the Jefferson Bank and Trust Company, accused of racist hiring practices. "He felt that everybody should have opportunity," she added. "It was his personality to be involved."

Johnnye Robinson Farrell, a 1968 nursing graduate, was riding
the bus home after school in Monroe, Louisiana, when

> one of my classmates sat just before the back door, and the
> driver wouldn't pull off until she moved. She said, "No, I'm
> going to sit here." So, we all decided we had to support her,
> and we told the driver that if she had to move, we needed
> our money back. He called police, and they were angry—but
> this was right after the 1964 Civil Rights Act, and they had
> no choice but to let us stay where we were. The high school
> principal called my parents, and they were in support of our
> resistance.

For some of the Homer G. nurses, busy with their studies, the
civil rights demonstrations and even the death of Dr. Martin Luther
King Jr. were events they watched on television. But the temper of
the times—the sense that African Americans could move forward—
gave them even more reason to succeed. "It just instilled in you the
fight to do better and to be the best you can," said nurse Yvonne
Jones.

> *"I remember the nursing staff—dedicated people, mostly
> women. There was a kind of rectitude."*
> —Dr. Donald M. Suggs

During the early 1960s, Miss Minnie Edythe Todd Gore—a large
woman, described by some as "stately" and others as "statuesque"—
was still in charge of the nursing program. Most nursing alumnae
remember her with great respect, but other students found her
daunting. "Oh, my God, I was scared of her. I was never called to
her office, which was a good thing! If you were called to the office,
you were in trouble," said nurse Wanda Trotter.
Parents must also have cringed at the sound of her voice, said
nurse Dorothy Payne Thornton.

> I was a mischievous thing, and whenever I did wrong, she
> would call my mother and say, "Ms. Payne?" And my mother

would say, "What did she do this time?" One time, a bunch of us were at a movie, but it wasn't done by our 10:15 curfew, and we stayed anyway. When the movie was over, one of us rang the doorbell of the nurses' residence, and then all the other nurses ran past the house mother. The next day, Miss Gore said to us, "Miss Gilkey didn't see everybody, but she knew that Miss Payne was in the group." I said, "Oh, Jesus."

Fig. 12.3: This reception was held for Minnie Edythe Todd Gore (1909–1983), longtime nursing director at Homer G. Phillips and, from 1969 to 1973, at the Municipal School of Nursing, the merged school of Homer G. and City Hospital #1. Miss Gore is seated and dressed in white. Courtesy of Jobyna Foster.

Miss Gore was strict yet motherly to the students, said nurse Georgia Anderson. "On Sunday mornings, she sometimes said, 'OK, everybody's who's going to church, get dressed in uniform.' So here we were with Miss Gore, all starched and dressed—she even washed and starched her shoestrings—and she would have on the navy-blue cape with the red lining, thrown back. So, we had our capes thrown back, too. We used to laugh that she looked like a duck with all her ducklings behind her."

When Jacqueline Calvin was in nursing school, a fellow student was shot by her boyfriend, and Miss Gore asked Ms. Calvin and her roommate to appear on the female medicine floor at 11:00 that evening to care for the patient. Nervous and upset, they arrived—only to find Miss Gore and another staff member there already, in full uniform. "They didn't throw us out there; they were waiting for us. It made us feel good," she said.

At a time when some administrators didn't like the idea of male nurses, Richard W. White—only the second male graduate of Homer G. Phillips nursing school after David Mitchell, class of 1966—found Miss Gore very supportive. "Miss McFarland, a very strict person and very old school, protested me taking OB-GYN. But Miss Gore said, 'He's a nurse. How is he going to know about it when he gets to the state boards?'"

In 1966, the mayor invited Miss Gore to serve on a committee to study how Homer G. Phillips and City Hospital #1—neither eligible for Medicare reimbursement because their staffs and patients were not sufficiently integrated—could make changes that would allow them to qualify. Three proposals emerged: first, merge the two schools of nursing; second, faithfully follow city guidelines to take all patients from the south side of Delmar to City Hospital #1 and those on the north side to Homer G. Phillips; and third, merge the medical staffs. Proposals one and two were implemented.

*"I met the other day with some nurses from back in the day, and it was people who were really very conscientious about their work. If you weren't then, I don't think you were acceptable to the group. As you and I know, that is noble work."*
—Dr. Donald M. Suggs

In May 1967, the Homer G. Phillips Hospital School of Nursing and the St. Louis City Hospital School of Nursing merged to form a new school, the St. Louis Municipal School of Nursing, located at 1621 Grattan Street on the city's south side. Even the uniforms would be different: green-and-white pinstriped dresses with white collars and cuffs, plus a green bib and a newly designed cap. The

Fig. 12.4: This is a composite photo of the 1966 nursing graduates from the
Homer G. Phillips Hospital School of Nursing. Courtesy of Jobyna Foster.

old uniforms from Homer G. Phillips went to a school of nursing
in Africa, along with the books.

Through the years, Homer G.'s highly respected nursing school
had graduated 1,037 nurses; in 1967, the 1,000th graduate, Mary
Lillian Wright from Tennessee, was honored with a bronze plaque.
By comparison, the old City Hospital Training School had 1,164
graduates, including 55 men, before the merger.

Andrea Sims graduated from the new school in 1972, and she
recalled some racial tension as the Black and white students tried to
blend. "A number of white people there were resentful. I overheard
a conversation when we were getting ready to have elections for
class officers. These white students were talking about whether they
wanted a male or a female, then they got real quiet" and used a
racial slur, "jigaboo," to indicate that they didn't want any African
Americans in office. Ms. Sims quickly asked her Black classmates

whom *they* wanted to nominate, and, as a result, "the president and treasurer of the class were Black all three years."

In the new Municipal program, said David Baltzer, who did his nurses' training there from 1972 to 1975, student time was equally divided between City Hospital #1 and Homer G. Phillips, except for the psychiatric rotation that was still at Malcolm Bliss Hospital. His class began with 120 students, an all-time record, half of them Black and half of them white. "One-third of my class, uniquely, were men," he says. "Many were returning medics from the Vietnam War who wanted to have a professional license to do things they had done in the field."

For some of the students, comparing the equipment and supplies at Homer G. and City Hospital was an eye-opening experience. "City Hospital always had the best equipment, the best supplies. Homer G. got what was left over," said Lillian Haywood, "and we saw that during our training." While City Hospital had the newer IV bags, Homer G. had the old bottles, she said. While City Hospital had plastic syringes, Homer G. still had glass ones that needed sterilizing. City Hospital also got computers first.

As Baltzer began his training, Miss Gore was still director of the school, though in 1973 she and a colleague were summarily dismissed by the hospital commissioner, who claimed that Miss Gore had allowed the staff member to attend school on city time. Miss Gore countered that at least 20 other instructors and hundreds of city employees were doing the same thing. The two women protested the firing, but they were never reinstated; in 1981, in a secret settlement made public by the *Post-Dispatch*, they were awarded $125,000 amid allegations of racial discrimination.

Immediately, Geraldine Phelps, previously associate director of education, took over as acting director, becoming the permanent director in 1976. Soon she had to fend off a threat to the school's existence. In a 1975 letter to the *Post-Dispatch*, she listed ten reasons why the school should continue, including its record of achievement and the high demand for its 180 students.[9] But in 1976, the city decided to close the school, which graduated its last class in 1981.

Fig. 12.5: In this photo are two graduates of the combined Homer G. Phillips and St. Louis City Hospital School of Nursing programs. Courtesy of the Missouri Historical Society, St. Louis.

*"Remember this: Homer Phillips was the most powerful and most respected institution for African Americans [in St. Louis]. Not only was that felt by the professional class, but it was also felt by the community. I think the history of Homer Phillips Hospital, and its ultimate decline as a medical institution, is sort of the parallel story of the African American community in St. Louis: a diminished Homer G. Phillips and a diminished African American community."*

—Dr. Donald M. Suggs

For some years, the once-reliable pool of talented African American medical students from such schools as Meharry and Howard had been drying up. Increasingly, these interns and residents, who had been forced to find training at a handful of Black hospitals, could now attend programs at formerly white institutions across the country. Homer G. Phillips had to scramble to fill its classes and began to accept a large number of foreign-born trainees from various places: Africa, Cuba, Germany, India, Iran, Jamaica, Japan, Mexico, South America, Turkey, and particularly Haiti and the Philippines. In 1960, half the residents at the hospital were born outside the United States.

"We stopped getting the primary students," said Dr. Frank Richards, surgeon. "When integration came, Black students began to come to Barnes or other white hospitals for training. They did not come to Homer Phillips. So, we began to lose our supply."

The shortage of residents had a major, and sometimes catastrophic, impact on the hospital, since there were often not enough physicians present to care for the critically ill. In his annual pediatric reports, Dr. Park White lamented the shortage. "Although the Executive Board has made efforts to attract senior students at Howard and Meharry and other schools to Homer Phillips Hospital, we still need many more interns than apply," he wrote in 1959. "Funds have not yet been obtainable from the City to provide better housing accommodations, etc., for those who are married, or stipends which compare favorably with those offered elsewhere. Without our 'foreign' residents, our situation would be tragic indeed."[10]

This shortage made Dr. White reflect, in his 1962 report, about the rising child mortality rate at the hospital—from 1.19 percent in 1960 to 1.27 in 1961—and wonder whether some of that was due to a personnel shortage. "Certain deficiencies were apparent—such as inadequate follow-up notes on one infant with congenital heart disease and heart-failure," he wrote. "It is, of course, lamentable if even one death can be directly traced to house-staff shortage."

Those international students who came to Homer G. Phillips felt grateful for the opportunity. Dr. Gracy Thomas, later on the staff of the VA Medical Center, trained in radiology under Dr. William Allen. "He was such a kind and hardworking person," said Dr. Thomas, who had graduated from Kottayam Medical College in India. "I feel honored to have worked and gotten training under such a wonderful person. I have only great memories about Homer G. Phillips Hospital."

One recruitment problem, as Dr. White noted, involved the shockingly low wages for these residents. While other programs paid up to $6,000, Homer G. Phillips could only afford $2,800 a year. Alarmed, the Interns Association made a donation that increased pay by $100 per month, and with that managed to attract 16 new interns. But the city health commissioner prohibited this new stipend because City Hospital #1 interns were not receiving the same thing.[11]

The city had a knack for finding ways to cut corners with residents. In 1963, two resident physicians in the Homer G. emergency room staged a three-hour strike on the night shift after the city hospital commissioner abruptly discontinued overtime pay for trainees—some $200 per shift. Huffed the commissioner to the *American*: "It is not the standard practice in this country or this city to pay over-time salary to Interns and Residents. Normally, extra duties are considered an important part of their training program."

Just as the number of trainees declined, so did the number of patients, a trend that accelerated after the enactment of Medicare for seniors and Medicaid for low-income patients. Because these were federal programs, the law insisted that hospitals accepting Medicare or Medicaid not discriminate on the basis of race. "Overnight, a large portion of HGPH's clientele achieved the power to choose any hospital, and many chose more adequately funded private hospitals over HGPH," wrote author Daniel Berg.[12]

Still, Homer G. Phillips served a wide population. In 1961–62 alone, said a graduate brochure, there were 19,565 admissions, 104,629 patients seen in the clinic, and 103,599 patients in the Emergency and Admitting departments.

*"It was a much different community in those days. There was much more cohesiveness. Some of the streets that are now in shambles were then very nice neighborhoods, because everybody lived together. So there was a kind of camaraderie."*
—Dr. Donald M. Suggs

The hospital's problems continued into the late 1960s. "As the years went by, the reputation started falling down some," said one-time neighbor Victor Roberts. "They used to have incidents during the weekends where people would get into fights, and Homer Phillips was known as having to take care of all those people." The magnificent building also began to decline. "The funding wasn't there, and they couldn't keep it up. The building just went completely downhill."

Some Black officials accused the city of deliberately causing the hospital's deterioration. Leroy Tyus, 20th ward committeeman, opposed Raymond Tucker for re-election in the 1965 mayoral race and supported Alfonso J. Cervantes because, he said, the conditions of the hospital are "deplorable," and it was being "victimized by a planned program of decay."

Also in 1965, a personnel matter at Homer G. Phillips made banner headlines in the *American*, when Dr. Andrew Spencer—who in 1964 had become acting medical director of the hospital while still head of surgery—was abruptly fired by the hospital commissioner for holding a second job as clinic physician and for behaving insubordinately to his bosses. However, Dr. Spencer's supporters believed that what really triggered his dismissal was that he was a whistleblower who complained publicly about substandard conditions and equipment at the hospital. His complaints, in fact, had led to the formation of a new organization that held meetings at Antioch Baptist Church: "Save Homer G. Phillips Hospital."

Even the election of new mayors, all of whom promised change at the hospital, didn't quell the drama. Year by year, the city—pressed for money—kept trying to chip away at the hospital's program. In 1967, Dr. Seymour Monat threatened to quit his job in obstetrics when the city floated the idea of eliminating the hospital's obstetrics unit. Amid the resulting outcry, Mayor Cervantes admitted sheepishly that "I don't believe [this move] is logical any more. I question whether it would go through because of the uproar."[13]

Meanwhile, the neighborhood around the hospital was beginning its long, slow decline, added Roberts. "After a period of time, the neighborhood went downhill, and now it looks as if it's been devastated. On the streets where there were once very nice homes, there's nothing but vacant lots or homes that are vacant." Nurse Gretchen McCullum recalled her growing feeling of unease on the street. "People were selling dope on the corners, and that scared me to death. A lot of times I would go home, and it would be after dark; I'd wait for the bus out there on the corner. And I had to stop doing that; I had to tell my husband to come and pick me up. Ain't standing on the corner no more, you know."

In 1966, Jean Taliaferro Williamson came to Homer G. as a clerk-typist in the payroll office, and she could already "see how the neighborhood was on the decline." But nobody seemed to care, and nobody tried to intervene. "I don't understand; you have people who are supposed to be introducing laws that could help maintain the neighborhood, because a neighborhood don't maintain itself. It's terrible with the vacant brick buildings they have in the Ville. It's a disgrace. I'm going to put it that way. It's a *disgrace*."

> *"I think what happened in the Civil Rights movement is that you germinated a new spirit in the community. So, a community that for the most part had been passive about its segregated public accommodations and all of that, suddenly, at least to an activist group, was taught to see things that for a long time had been accepted in a different way. They started to challenge some of those things."*
>
> —Dr. Donald M. Suggs

The infuriated Dr. Spencer fought his dismissal all the way to the St. Louis Civil Service Commission, which vindicated him, ordering him restored to duty and awarded back pay. However, he never regained his acting medical director post: Instead, that job went to a rival and critic, Dr. H. Phillip Venable, an ophthalmologist who had joined the Washington University faculty in 1958. Since 1943, he had been ophthalmology chairman at Homer G. Phillips, where he had served his own residency and later trained some 100 ophthalmology residents.

"Dr. Venable was an outstanding ophthalmologist, very knowl-edgeable about the field," said Dr. Garey Watkins, who came to Homer G. Phillips as an intern in 1971. "He also had a social conscience, wanting to give back to the Afro-American commu-nity and train Afro-Americans to go throughout this country. But he wanted you to do the work, and every doctor had to look like a doctor. We had to wear a shirt, tie, and long white coat. He said that when we left Homer Phillips, we represented the program, wherever we'd go. So, everyone could tell that you were one of Dr. Venable's residents."

Both in his public and private life, Dr. Venable was contentious. Wishing to live outside the city, he had purchased a building lot in the Spoede Meadows subdivision of Creve Coeur; however, the city used the power of eminent domain to take Dr. Venable's property and use the site for Beirne Park, named for the former mayor who led the fight to acquire the land.

But in 1967, Dr. Venable himself was out as acting director after having vociferously objected to the proposed transfer of the OB-GYN department from Homer G. Phillips to City Hospital #1, arguing that Black women used these services more than whites did. He also charged the city with dirty-dealing: that the transfer of obstetrics was the opening salvo in an attempt to close Homer G. Phillips. The *St. Louis American*, which once more used ban-ner headlines to report the latest firing, said: "The Pot Boils Again at Phillips Hospital."[14]

After Dr. Venable's departure, the city finally appointed a per-manent medical director: Dr. Eugene Mitchell, a St. Louis native and product of the Homer G. Phillips surgical training program. He was also a member of the St. Louis family that had since 1912 published the powerful *St. Louis Argus* newspaper; during the 1970s, he tried to juggle a medical career with leadership of the *Argus*. In 1973, the city also appointed a new administrator to replace the retiring Virgil McKnight, who had held the job for 32 years. Now, the job went to John P. Noble, formerly an officer of the Forsyth County Hospital Authority in Winston-Salem, North Carolina.

Fig. 12.6: Dr. Eugene N. Mitchell (1934–2012), a general
surgeon who had done his residency at Homer G. Phillips
Hospital, headed two major St. Louis institutions. After Dr.
Venable's departure in 1967, he was medical director at the
hospital, and in 1971, he also assumed control of the *St. Louis
Argus* newspaper, which his grandfather had founded in 1912.
Photo from *The Guardian* (hospital yearbook), 1968, in the
Collection of the Smithsonian National Museum of African
American History and Culture, Gift of Pauline Brown Payne.

*"Back then, I thought the Washington University people were
there by virtue of their rank, position, and status, but in retro-
spect, I think some of it was almost condescending. That was
not true in every case, but some. Because I gave anesthesia
there for a period of time, I could see a kind of inappropriate-
ness in addressing the nurses or in the regard they had for the
patients."*

—Dr. Donald M. Suggs

Meanwhile, other local institutions were losing faith in the hospital. "Following the death of Dr. William H. Sinkler in 1960," wrote Dr. Venable in a later hospital history, "the relationship of Homer G. Phillips Hospital to Washington University began to deteriorate. The university withdrew its complete affiliation, for the city leaders were unable to provide some of the sophisticated research equipment requested."[15]

In 1961, the hospital shut down its anesthesiology training program, created by Washington University doctors in 1958, because the city wouldn't fund an adequate staff. "The program was intended to stabilize the anesthesia situation at Homer G. Phillips," said Dr. Robert Dodd, Washington University anesthesiologist. "After our training program was established, the death rate connected with anesthesia and surgery was comparable with the best institutions in the United States."

Some improvements to the hospital were also sidelined amid the recurring disputes. Elevators were frequently out of order; lighting in many areas was poor. In 1967, the *American* reported that the pediatric department, long a squalid place in the summer heat, was not going to receive $75,000 for air-conditioning, even though it had been allocated. Some suspected that the pediatrics department might be the next one slated to move to City Hospital #1.

Oddly, the city did make other upgrades to the hospital, even as talk of mergers and closures continued to percolate. "When I started in 1966, they were trying to remodel the hospital," said Jean Williamson. "In some of the areas, they did not have tile on the floor, and they finally started putting tile in some areas. It seemed like they were in the process of closing the hospital after they made some improvements."

Other enhancements came along, such as a new cobalt lab in 1969 and the long-delayed expansion of the nursery in 1971. Yet some staff members still felt that City Hospital #1 got more. "Sometimes we would laugh and joke about stuff that we had to work with, whereas at City Hospital they were given something different," said nurse Andrea Sims. "But just before we closed, we had a new cardiac intensive care unit built, and they had just finished remodeling the emergency room."

Even so, some began to notice a gradual change in where Black patients chose to go. "My retrospective impression is that there were relatively few at City [#1] right up until the 1960s; there was a tendency for Afro-American patients to go to Phillips and the whites to go to City. But by the mid-1960s, some black patients preferred to come to City [Hospital] #1 because they thought they were going to get better care there," said Dr. Clifford Birge, an endocrinologist, who was an intern at City Hospital #1 in 1961 and chief resident and instructor there starting in 1969.

One problem was the resident situation, added Dr. Birge. "City #1 had the advantage that the two universities supported services there, and because of their support, full-time people were assigned to the hospital faculty. They were better able to recruit residents for training." In 1965, the advent of Medicare, which required the active participation of attending doctors in the patient's care, was also a problem at Homer G. Phillips, where many part-time private physicians were in charge. "So, private attendings would come in and sign the resident's note, and Medicare said 'No. You've got to really show evidence that you've examined the patient and gotten involved in the care; otherwise, we're not going to reimburse you,'" he said.

At Homer G. especially, salary scale was a major issue for trainees. Officially, city employees were supposed to live in the city, unless the hospital could obtain a waiver for that physician. "And the top salary you could be paid in the city was $25,000," added Dr. Birge. "The whole time I was at City [#1], Washington University supplemented my salary to bring it up to whatever level I would be paid there, as an instructor, assistant professor, or whatever."

*"Dr. Eugene Mitchell, medical director of Homer G. Phillips Hospital; Dr. Donald Suggs, a dentist and [Joint Board of Health and Hospitals] board member; Mrs. Marian Oldham, and other black members of the board charged that the City Administration had broken an agreement which would have given Homer G. Phillips an extra $500,000 for work at the hospital. Dr. Mitchell said that it had been agreed that if City Hospital got $1,000,000 in federal funds, then an additional*

*$500,000 in funds from a 1966 bond issue would be transferred to Homer G. Phillips Hospital. . . . It was charged that Homer G. Phillips was being discriminated against. Dr. Suggs said he was outraged by the development. He threatened to resign."*
—*St. Louis Post-Dispatch*, January 29, 1970

During the 1970s, as the city budget was growing tighter, the $15 million subsidy it provided to the city hospitals seemed increasingly unmanageable. Thus, the city engaged in almost nonstop debate about their future and commissioned a series of studies to decide what to do. In 1976, a study by two outside consultants—one white, one Black—said Homer G. Phillips could close, with services consolidated at City Hospital #1, if its clinic and emergency services were left open. But this recommendation was not enacted then because of divisions on the Board of Aldermen and the city's Board of Estimate and Apportionment.

All the while, the hospital continued to attract publicity, some good—but much negative. A 1970 banner headline in the *St. Louis American* announced that: "CRIMES ADD TO THE ILLS AT HOMER G. PHILLIPS HOSPITAL." Security was becoming a major headache for the city, and the staff of 11 round-the-clock guards at the hospital began to seem completely inadequate. Cars were sometimes vandalized; there were thefts from patients. As the city dawdled about providing more personnel, the sheriff threatened to hire a larger staff himself.[16]

Clearly, prisoners admitted to the hospital also needed better, more humane treatment. In 1973, a pregnant woman prisoner was chained to her bed, even though she had been sent to the hospital because of complications in her pregnancy. A priest assigned to the hospital reported "an obvious case of cruelty," he said. One prisoner had "run afoul of immigration authorities [and] was so tightly chained to his bed that the cuffs were digging into his legs." The patient, whose feet were grossly swollen, was being treated for severe frostbite of the feet.[17]

Then-Mayor John H. Poelker admitted in 1975 he could not rule out the possibility that Homer G. Phillips Hospital might be closed as an economy move. With this threat looming, the campaign to save the hospital intensified, aided by the local Black newspapers. A major supporter of this campaign was the *St. Louis Argus*, one of three weeklies serving the Black community—and perhaps it was not coincidental that Homer G. Phillips' medical director, Dr. Eugene N. Mitchell, was president, publisher, and treasurer of the *Argus*.

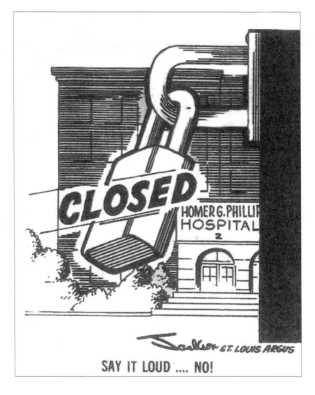

Fig. 12.7: For years, the *St. Louis Argus* newspaper campaigned editorially to keep Homer G. Phillips Hospital open, and it ran a series of caustic cartoons, including this one from March 27, 1975, aimed at stirring up public support. Courtesy of the Missouri Historical Society, St. Louis.

Dr. Mitchell, a talented surgeon, could only be at the hospital part-time because of his newspaper duties. Yet he was an ardent supporter. In 1972, he claimed that the city had been shortchanging the hospital for years and said, "this year marked the first time in history that the institution is operated on an equitable monetary basis with City Hospital No. One . . . [and] that due to the lack of funds in prior years, parts of the hospital have deteriorated and it will take some time for things to be back to normal."[18]

Another nail in the hospital's coffin was struck in 1976, when Washington University School of Medicine said that it "could not affiliate with Phillips unless some changes were made, and it had complete control over the facility's medical operations. The announcement, representing the university's first public statement on the controversy, was a strong point in favor of making City Hospital the sole general hospital. The university has affiliation with City Hospital already . . ."[19]

In 1977, Mayor Jim Conway took office on a platform of promises that included keeping Homer G. Phillips open. Ominously, a new comptroller, Raymond Percich, took office the same day, declaring in his inaugural address that "I won't spend any more money, even for one year, to perpetuate the dual hospital system that we have."[20]

*"Closing Homer Phillips Hospital is a saga in itself. It was the most powerful and most respected institution in the Black community. And that was felt both by professionals and people in the general community. And when it closed, that created a big political crisis."*

—Dr. Donald M. Suggs

Soon Conway appointed a new task force headed by Dr. Kenneth Smith, who had spent time at Homer G. Phillips as a second-year medical student and later became professor of neurosurgery at Saint Louis University Medical School, to study the city's health system. Another member was Dr. James Whittico, a surgeon at Homer G. Phillips Hospital, who had previously headed the Joint Board of Health and Hospitals. Conway, who had opposed the closing of the hospital during his mayoral campaign, now said he would endorse whatever the committee recommended.

When he was first elected, said Conway, "A lot of people wanted to retain Homer Phillips as a private hospital, but they still wanted the city to underwrite it. The dilemma we were faced with is that we were running a huge deficit trying to keep two hospitals open. This was a huge drain on the city's budget, and it limited a lot of other things we needed to be doing."

At the end of five months. Dr. Smith reported that citizens overwhelmingly believed that, as a long-term solution, the city should replace both of its public hospitals with a brand-new, modern facility, likely containing around 800 beds and costing some $45–70 million. "The people we've talked to say that the city of St. Louis—a city of about 500,000 people—doesn't need two hospitals, especially when they're old, half-filled and don't have air-conditioning," said Dr. Smith.

This committee had gathered a host of experts from the medical community in St. Louis, said Conway. "I had them take a good hard look at the situation, and Dr. Smith was really a person that, if he believed in something, would put a lot of strength behind it. But he wasn't the only one. When the committee did all of its studies and recommendations, it was almost unanimous. It wasn't a case where it was the African American docs against the other docs, because many of the African American docs were for it, too."

With any such construction years away, Conway wanted to proceed on a merger right away, and in 1978 he appointed a 22-member task force, again headed by Dr. Smith, to plan the details and financing of the new hospital. At the same time, the Health and Hospital Board, an advisory group, recommended that City Hospital serve temporarily as the one general hospital for the city, since it was twice as large as Homer G. and had better facilities. Still, as late as February 8, 1979, reported a newspaper story, Conway was saying, "I don't know how many times I have to say it, but I'll say it once more—Homer G. Phillips Hospital will not be closed."[21]

Soon another pressing question arose: If the city's $25,000-a-year limit on salaries for city employees did not change, said hospital officials, the city hospitals might soon face a crisis, since physicians could easily make double or triple that amount elsewhere. "We're going to have to declare an emergency," said Dr. Smith. "There won't be any doctors to take care of patients."

Meanwhile, alarmed Phillips supporters were staging demonstrations at Conway's office. On January 31, 1979, nearly 50 were arrested after Conway refused to meet with them. Others attended noisy town hall meetings to pepper Conway with questions. Activist

Fig. 12.8: Residents of north St. Louis marched to City Hall to protest plans to eliminate some services at Homer G. Phillips Hospital. February 9, 1979. Credit: *St. Louis Globe-Democrat*. Photo courtesy of the St. Louis Mercantile Library at the University of Missouri–St. Louis.

and comedian Dick Gregory also came to town and expressed support. "There were times when I would get threats, and usually I knew when threats came to the office, because there would be police cars in front of my house," recalled Conway. "I always let the police know, and my driver was an accomplished person with firearms."

By August 1979, it must have been crystal clear to anyone reading the *St. Louis Post-Dispatch* that Homer G. Phillips was doomed. Laboratories had moved in January. Conway had just announced his intention to remove inpatient care from Homer G. Phillips and consolidate it into "a single, more efficient operation in the City Hospital complex," said one article, which noted that City #1 had "strong, around-the-clock staffing by interns from Washington and St. Louis universities' medical schools." Yet the same story also listed some of the alarming defects of City #1:

(1) City Hospital is actually several old, seedy-looking buildings situated near a run-down housing project; (2) Many patients in the general medical wards are alcoholic, overdosed on

drugs, diabetic, or some combination of the three, doctors say. Contrary to some popular beliefs, more than 60 percent of the patients—even before the merger, are black; (3) The hospital has old-fashioned open wards with no air-conditioning and little privacy for patients; dozens of them share one bathroom; (4) Inside, the buildings are depressingly drab. More important, the needed repairs range from broken elevators to obsolete plumbing and electrical systems.[22]

At the start of August 1979, Homer G. Phillips Hospital was still running, though worried staff members couldn't help but ask themselves: "How long?"

## CHAPTER THIRTEEN

# "Unbelievable"
## August 17, 1979

*"August the 17th: When I think about it, it was unbelievable. We couldn't believe that it was happening. I got into trouble for running though the building alerting folks. They brought in the police and they started locking us up. I was arrested for peace disturbance. They put me in a paddy wagon, took me downtown, and booked me, but I was right out. You know, I've always been a warrior, and I have always loved nursing. And Homer G. strengthened me; it gave me a life that I could reflect back upon with a sense of accomplishment."*

—Zenobia Thompson, who graduated in 1965 and
worked there from 1965 to 1967 and 1977 to 1979

ON THE MORNING of August 17, 1979, Dr. Mary Anne Tillman was on her way to Homer G. Phillips Hospital when she heard breaking news on KMOX radio. "One of the announcers said, 'Something must be going on over at Homer Phillips. We see all these police over there,'" she recalled. "But by then I was already there. They had cut off the switchboard, so the staff of the nursery couldn't call me to tell me not to come to work." As she was walking inside, a policeman drew a nightstick on her.

Nurse Richard W. White was already there. He had worked the night shift in the emergency room, and around 6:30 a.m. he noticed Major Charles Wren, a policeman who often stopped by, walk in the door. "He told one of the nurses, 'This is the date.' We said, 'What's happening?' And he said, 'Well, we're moving out the few

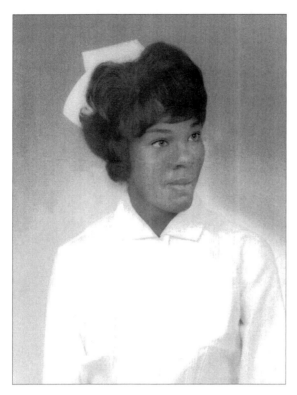

Fig. 13.1: A St. Louis native and 1965 graduate of the Homer G. Phillips School of Nursing, Zenobia Thompson was working at the hospital in the late 1970s when she joined the "Save Homer Phillips" effort. Courtesy of Zenobia Thompson.

patients you have. They are closing the hospital today,'" recalled White.

As White walked to his car in the parking lot, he could see what was happening outside. Mayflower vans were waiting. Helicopters were circling overhead. On Kennerly, along the north side of the hospital, was a busload of officers, and on each corner was a police car. Not far away, White spotted policemen on horseback.

Iver Gandy was on her way into work when she heard a helicopter overhead and assumed it was the KMOX radio helicopter reporting on an accident. "I wondered, 'What is it doing in our neighborhood?'" she recalled. "As I got closer, it sounded like more than one, and then I saw a mounted policeman. So, I'm thinking, 'What in the world is going on?'"

As the *Post-Dispatch* described the scene, "the transfer began when 120 officers equipped with riot helmets and night sticks

Fig. 13.2: As time went on, the *St. Louis Argus* kept up its drumbeat of support for the hospital, as in this cartoon from April 8, 1976. Courtesy of the Missouri Historical Society, St. Louis.

arrived at the hospital about 8 a.m. . . . . The police deployed in near-military fashion, taking up positions at the building's entrances and stretching a 'riot line' of about 40 officers along Kennerly Avenue . . . facing a group of encamped protestors."[1] The removal of patients, using vans and ambulances, took about three hours to complete.

Altogether about 100 protestors were on the scene, as many had been for weeks, and Dorothy Thornton was among them. "Oh, girl, I cried when it happened. In fact, we were defying it. I was one of those who lay on the ground to keep the ambulances from taking our patients. We had a human barrier going. Then I looked up and saw those wheels get this close to me, and I thought about my three boys. I said, 'I'm sorry. I got to break this line, because these people are going to run over us.' There were trucks and ambulances and dogs—and they were holding the dogs back."

*"Even though at school we had referred to Homer G. Phillips as the 'Painful Palace,' I came back in 1977. And a lady named Annie Jackson in the X-ray department asked me if I would come to a meeting to save the hospital. And I said, 'Well, if you think I could be of any help, I certainly could be glad to come.' So, I went to the meeting, and that's how I got involved in the struggle to save Homer G. Phillips."*

—Zenobia Thompson

Even though the exact date of the closing was a surprise, staff members knew the end was coming soon. Just the day before, a number of elderly patients were shifted from the hospital to another facility, and police removed two protestors—State Sen. Gwen B. Giles and Pearlie Evans, an aide to U.S. Rep. William L. Clay—who tried to stop the transfer. Both women were members of the Ad Hoc Committee to Save Homer G. Phillips Hospital and Other Public Hospitals, a group that had been holding a 24-hour-a-day vigil to prevent any shift of services. "I'm no criminal," declared Mrs. Evans then. "The criminals are sitting in the mayor's office."[2]

Another visitor on August 16 was State Sen. J.B. "Jet" Banks, who learned that the ad hoc committee would seek an injunction the next day to keep the city from removing any more patients. Banks said he would contribute to the legal costs. But Dr. R. Dean Wochner, city director of health and hospitals, told reporters that the transfer of patients had already been occurring, little by little, since August 2, when he had declared that no new patients would be admitted in order to speed the consolidation. Thus, only some 60 to 75 patients were left in the hospital. Still, the ban on admissions did not apply to the emergency room or clinic, both of them slated by Mayor Conway to remain open.

The ad hoc committee had formed in December 1978, under the leadership of concerned citizens and staff, including Zenobia Thompson and organizer Walle Amusa. At the start, their major focus was on the fiscal 1979–80 budget. "When they began to put the budget together, that was the flashpoint," said Amusa. "Because everybody knew that if you didn't have Homer G. Phillips in the budget, essentially you're shutting the hospital down." Then comptroller Raymond Percich, who was from south St. Louis, made a quiet threat: if they put any money for the hospital in the budget, he was not going to sign anyone's checks.

Despite the efforts of elected African American officials, added Amusa, the budget passed without Homer G. Phillips funding. "So, after July 1, there was no more money to pay the staff, and they were being issued letters of transfer to City Hospital #1. Then the community responded, putting up barricades around the hospital; families came and put up tents. I'm talking about hundreds of people. From July 1 to August 17, Homer G. Phillips was surrounded."

At one point during the long struggle—which involved demonstrations, petitions, and sit-ins—nurse Georgia Anderson was arrested along with some 46 others. "Mayor Conway had said he would talk to a group, so around 12 of us went down to City Hall. We sat there, and we sat there, and someone from his office kept coming out and

Fig. 13.3: In 1979, with the closing of the hospital approaching, the *Argus* editorial cartoons became more frequent and biting, as in this one from February 8, 1979. Courtesy of the Missouri Historical Society, St. Louis.

saying: 'The Mayor will see you in half an hour. The Mayor will see you in 15 minutes.' Then it got to be 6 o'clock, and someone came out said, 'The mayor has left the office and won't be able to see you today, so you all have to leave.' And we said, 'We came to see the mayor, and we're going to stay until he sees us.'"

Around 9:00 p.m., the police came and told them to get off the floor where they were sitting. "We said, 'No, we're not going to get up. You're going to have to take us out.' So, the police took us on stretchers all the way down to the ground floor, put us in the paddy wagon and across the street to jail. Then we got to singing and beating on the walls and the rails and just being a nuisance. They kept us until 1 or 2 o'clock in the morning and told us to go home. We were never really booked, but I can tell everybody that I went to jail for Homer Phillips."

*"I grew up in north St. Louis on 5600 Grand, and my parent were both laborers. I was very passionate about becoming a nurse, and I was very proud to be a part of Homer G. Phillips. In 1962, during my senior year in high school, I worked at Jewish Hospital as a tray girl in the dietary department, because money was always tight. I would work there for a dollar an hour, and I thought that was hot stuff, you know. In the summer, when the full-time girls went on vacation, I would step in and work twelve hours, so I could pay my way to nursing school: $395, including uniforms, room and board, everything."*

—Zenobia Thompson

Once closing day was over, the city felt gratified by the results, said Conway. "We knew that we had to be very careful when we made the transfer of personnel and equipment, and it really took a lot of planning. I sat down with the key people and made sure it happened *bang*, *bang*, because if there was any delay, we would be facing thousands of people and screaming and hollering. So, they developed a good plan, got everything in place, and fortunately no information leaked out."

On August 17, things went like clockwork, he said.

It was almost funny, because we started to move, and it caught everybody off guard. When protestors began to show up, we already had a jump on them. People said we had helicopters flying around, but they weren't from the city; they were the news media flying around, capturing the action by video. But actually, it went very smooth, and I guess that surprised everybody, that we could do something as delicate as that and make it happen with minimum disruption.

Fortunately, no one was injured, but there was some collateral damage, said the nurses. What would happen to people who only felt at home around Homer G.? wondered Iver Gandy.

One of our patients was Norman, the asthmatic. As a nurse in the ER, I was so impressed that he wanted to pay us back. He would tie a handkerchief around his nose and sweep the emergency room, empty the trash, and just kind of hang around. He had a place. The social worker said he had somewhere he could go at night, but I think he liked being around us because we looked out for him. The women in the kitchen would feed him, or we would see that he got a meal. The other person was Redcap. You know those sticks that have a point on the end? He would pick up paper. You would see him picking up trash around the hospital.

*"Being a nursing student at Homer G. Phillips wasn't easy. It wasn't really easy from the jump. I sometimes wonder why was that? It was very rigid rules, curfews. It reminded me of Victorian times, when I think about it. They intended for you to stay on the straight and narrow, even with all that was going on around you. But I was determined to be a nurse. Wasn't nothing going to stop me. Nothing's. Going. To. Happen, you know."*

—Zenobia Thompson

Was it time to close the hospital? The physical plant, furnishings, and equipment clearly needed updating. "If you wanted a nice bed and nice facilities, you'd go somewhere else," said nurse Jacqueline Calvin. "But if you wanted to be taken good care of, then I didn't think the care had deteriorated." She still took good care of her unit. "We made rounds with Mr. Noble, the administrator, one day. He dropped a cigarette on my floor and put it out. And I said, 'Pick it up.' The administrator with me almost had a fit. But he said, 'She is right. Give me an ashtray.'"

The patient census remained low, now that the day of segregated hospitals was gone forever. "We had lost our patient base, because the girls could go anywhere to have their babies, and we didn't have enough patients to keep the facility open," said nurse Lillian Haywood.

Still, some were embittered that Homer G. Phillips had closed but not the equally rundown City Hospital #1. As Dr. H. Phillip Venable said: "Homer Phillips had everything, but the only thing against [it] was that it was Black. . . . And Homer Phillips was much more recent. Homer Phillips was in good shape. They had just spent two million dollars renovating our emergency room. . . . If we had been a white institution, we wouldn't have had any problems."

Ella Bolden Brown, a 1947 graduate of the nursing school and staff member at Homer G. Phillips from 1947 to 1979, also felt that it was the better hospital. "We assumed that because of the economy, the city could not afford two city hospitals, and of course we all know that if it was a choice between Blacks and Whites, you know who was going to go. . . . Our hospital was the more modern, the more recently built, better equipped—we found out after we transferred over to City Hospital."[3]

Others were simply saddened that a piece of history—and their own past—was gone. On the final day, as the last patients were being removed, obstetrician/gynecologist Nathaniel Murdock recalled that he was "crying, hugging, and everything. I thought it was a horrible thing to do. They should have kept it open so we could serve that population. I didn't think that Barnes, Christian, DePaul, could absorb some of the things we had."

Fig. 13.4: By August 9, 1979, when this cartoon appeared in the *Argus*, it was plain to nearly everyone that the hospital would close. Courtesy of the Missouri Historical Society, St. Louis.

Fig. 13.4: By August 9, 1979, when this cartoon appeared in the *Argus*, it was plain to nearly everyone that the hospital would close. Courtesy of the Missouri Historical Society, St. Louis.

Throughout the Ville and the entire African American community, there was deep sadness. "It broke our hearts," said Rev. William Gillespie, longtime pastor of Cote Brilliante Presbyterian Church. "It was a sad day in the life of St. Louis when Homer G. Phillips Hospital closed."[4]

Still others were philosophical. "Why do you need two hospitals doing the same thing? I mean, it's a waste of money, waste of time, and a waste of talents, spreading them thin instead of getting them all together," said Dr. Homer Nash, pediatrician. Added clerk Jean Williamson: "The era had come to an end. All good things come to an end, and that's life."

*"Homer G. Phillips was a free institution and public. Now, a lot of cities did not have public institutions like that. We fought for a long time to get the hospital, before Homer G. Phillips was killed on Delmar. But afterwards it became the*

*standard thing for health care. Then Homer G. Phillips was*
*just one of many public hospitals—and now there are hardly*
*any left."*

—Zenobia Thompson

After closing, Homer G.'s administrative staff stayed on for a
time to tie up loose ends, as the emergency room and clinic kept operating. On August 31, 1979, noted St. Louis native Dick Gregory
came to town and joined ad hoc committee protestors on a march
from the hospital to City Hall. At an intersection in downtown
St. Louis, protestors blocked traffic, and police arrested 72 people,
including Gregory. Later in 1979, another noted activist, Angela
Davis, spoke in St. Louis criticizing cutbacks at Homer G. Phillips.

Over time, more and more equipment left Homer G. Phillips for
City Hospital #1, despite a march to the governor's office in Jefferson
City, as well as unsuccessful efforts in court to secure injunctions. A
Campaign for Human Dignity formed and began working tirelessly
to try to reopen the hospital; other support groups also sprang up,
including the Ministers to Save Homer G. Phillips Hospital.

Meanwhile, Mayor Conway had been receiving reams of letters—
some supporting, but most opposing—his decision to close Homer
G. Phillips. "Thanks for nothing St. Louis' mayor, sir," wrote Dr.
Jennifer Griffith. "As one of the many 'helpless' professionals
temporarily oppressed, depressed and unemployed by your recent
financial and/or political merger of the city's hospital facilities, I
take this means of voicing my opinion though it is shared by many
more voiceless than I," said another letter-writer.[5]

In April 1980, a dispute flared over the city's failure to pay physicians in the Homer G. ER, because Comptroller Raymond Percich
believed "many are being paid for work not performed."[6] After
they had gone unpaid for six weeks, some staged a walkout that
went on for weeks more. In early May, the emergency room and
clinic were cutting hours and services, but a month later the city
and doctors finally came to a settlement, and the city even agreed to
allow physicians to be paid $25,000—still the city's salary cap—for
working fewer than 40 hours a week.

Fig. 13.5: By the time this cartoon ran on January 29, 1981, the incumbent mayor, James Conway, was facing a challenger in the Democratic primary: Vincent C. Schoemehl Jr., the 28th ward alderman, who was promising to reopen Homer G. Phillips Hospital. Courtesy of the Missouri Historical Society, St. Louis.

Inevitably, the Homer G. Phillips controversy began to affect the 1981 mayoral election. First, Vincent C. Schoemehl Jr., the 28th ward alderman, handily beat incumbent James Conway in the Democratic primary, in part because Schoemehl promised to reopen Homer G. Phillips Hospital. Then, in the general election, he also trounced Republican Jerry Wamser, a lawyer, who had said, "the city cannot afford to shift the services to Phillips from City. Indeed . . . the financially pressed city may have to get out of the hospital business altogether."[7]

In 1982, Schoemehl proposed a $64 million bond issue—but it needed a 2/3 majority and instead garnered 55,583 yes votes to 48,813 nos. Why didn't the bond issue pass? The reason, said Schoemehl, was that Black aldermen representing the north side— particularly Freeman Bosley Sr. and Clifford Wilson—opposed it, "and their opposition created some level of doubt in the black community." Bosley launched his campaign for mayor the day after the bond issue failed. "I sent him a set of keys and said, 'You open it,'" recalled Schoemehl.

After that, said Schoemehl, he gave up, and in 1983 he announced plans to close City Hospital #1, which happened in 1985, along with the Homer G. Phillips emergency room. The Municipal School of Nursing had already closed in 1981. "I wish the bond issue had passed. That is my biggest regret," he said. "I believe it would have succeeded as an independent institution and interrupted the decline of the city." Further efforts by Zenobia Thompson, Walle Amusa, and others to pass a one-cent sales tax for the hospital also failed, and the hospital remained shuttered.

*"[The long period of protest] wasn't frustrating; it was a time when I was at peace. I was happy that I was struggling. I was happy that I understood how to respond in an intelligent, human way."*

—Zenobia Thompson

For years, the Homer G. Phillips Hospital building—named a St. Louis landmark in 1980 and placed on the National Register of Historic Places in 1982—stood vacant and decaying. "I saw it when it was empty, and when we thought it was lost. I went in it with the paint peeling, windows broken out, and what have you. It was heartbreaking," said nurse Georgia Anderson. "We were living in that building and we loved it. It was just part of your heart," added nurse Lillian Haywood.

Then a miraculous rebirth took place. In December 2002, after a lavish $42 million renovation spearheaded by developer Sharon Thomas Robnett, the building re-opened as a 220-unit facility, Homer G. Phillips Senior Living Community. Dr. Dazelle Simpson and her granddaughter got a sneak preview of the new facility just before its grand opening. "I had been upset that the hospital closed," she said, "but impressed with what the developers had

Fig. 13.6: About 100 people on foot and in cars paraded with hand-lettered signs from Homer G. Phillips Hospital to City Hall in observance of the one-year anniversary of the closing of its acute-care facilities. Young protestors Jolene Cotton (4) and Tiffany Hudson (2) joined the ranks of the demonstrators in the march on August 17, 1980. Credit: John Dengler, *St. Louis Globe-Democrat*. Courtesy of the St. Louis Mercantile Library at the University of Missouri–St. Louis.

done with the facility. They took time out to show us every bit, and it brought back a lot of memories."

What memories they were: of the crowded receiving room, of police officers bringing in bloodied patients, of sirens wailing in the background. Of the wizened but wise Miss Northcross; the tough but kind Minnie E.T. Gore. Of long wards, mitered sheets, rusting iron beds. Of extraordinary surgeons in the operating rooms, of babies born, and the homeless coming in from the cold. Of staff lives that began in poverty and ended in middle-class careers. Of patients who walked out the door, whole again. Of a long era that began with starkest segregation and ended in hope. Of the dedicated family that was Homer G. Phillips Hospital.

Every nurse or physician who worked at the hospital agreed that they were delighted to see it remain standing. "I am very proud of having been at Homer G. Phillips," said nurse Norris McReynolds. "My niece once called me, and she said, 'Were you happy there? Because all you talk about is Homer G. Phillips.' Yes, I was very happy there—*very* happy.

"And now, it has risen up out of the ashes, like a phoenix. It is still there."

# ACKNOWLEDGMENTS

I WOULD FIRST like to acknowledge Dr. Will Ross, nephrologist and head of diversity at Washington University School of Medicine, who is a wise and incisive collaborator. During conversations about the project, he gave me excellent advice, helped me navigate relations with the nurses, and suggested sources for me to consult. This project was greatly enriched by his participation, and I give him my sincere thanks.

Another fine collaborator and the author of this book's foreword is Dr. Eva Frazer, an internist herself, who is also the daughter and goddaughter of Homer G. Phillips-affiliated surgeons. Eva graciously shared with me some interview suggestions as well as video interviews she had done with staff members at the hospital; she and I did a few interviews together. She and Dr. Ross also read the draft of this book and made helpful comments.

I owe a great debt of thanks to the dozens of nurses, physicians, and other staff members who made themselves available for lengthy, in-depth interviews about their lives, their education, and their careers. All of them were helpful, but even within this talented, thoughtful group, a few stand out. Time and time again, I found myself calling upon Georgia Rhone Anderson—a Homer G. Phillips nursing graduate, a surgical nurse at the hospital, and a wonderful storyteller—for details of hospital history, especially during the 1950s. Mrs. Anderson also took me on a guided, well-narrated tour of the Ville. Dorothy Thornton, Martha Nelson, Lillian Haywood, Zenobia Thompson, Jobyna Foster, Carol Horton, and Lula Hall were also particularly helpful. Special thanks go to the presidents of the Homer G. Phillips Nurses' Alumni Association: Dorothy Thornton, Jobyna Foster, Yvonne Jones, and others.

Other interviewees included doctors, former politicians, and political organizers, as well as former Ville residents. Among this group, I would like to specially mention several people, including Dr. James Whittico, who was nearly 100 when I first spoke to him. Still, he had an astonishing memory and gave me several interviews before he died at 102. Much valuable information also came from historian and educator Dr. John Wright, who grew up in the Ville, as did one-time hospital neighbor, Victor Roberts.

Along the way, a number of people helped with this work. A magnificent research assistant—Jon Lee, then a graduate student at Washington University—dug out materials, especially articles about the hospital from the *St. Louis Argus* and *St. Louis American*. His predecessor, Kenyon Gradert, was also very helpful. Jennifer Arch, also from the English department, was an excellent transcriptionist and even stepped in once to help with an interview. Designer Chris Robinson did a fine job of creating a Ville neighborhood map.

Information on Homer G. Phillips and his death came from several places. In St. Louis, I am grateful to the medical examiner's office for the lengthy report on his death; to the St. Louis Police Department for the voluminous police report; and to Kathy Grillo, Records Manager for the Circuit Clerk's Office, for her assistance. The court records in the Homer G. Phillips case had been missing for decades, but she was able to supply the records from George Vaughn's trial. Claire Marks, archivist at the State Historical Society of Missouri, supplied boxes of material that I viewed at the St. Louis office, where the staff was very helpful.

In Sedalia, I had enormous help from Marge Harlan, formerly the president of the Rose Nolan Black History Library; Stephanie Sneed of the Sedalia Public Library; and Rhonda Chalfant, Pettis County historian. Staff members at the Pettis County Courthouse were also gracious in helping me access the ledger books with records of legal matters.

Previous histories of the hospital have also provided a great foundation: the chapter by Dr. Frank Richards in *A Century of*

*Black Surgeons: The USA Experience*, published in 1987; a brief history by Dr. William Sinkler; and *The History of Homer G. Phillips Hospital* by H. Phillip Venable. Much information has also come from two films: *A Jewel in History: The Story of Homer G. Phillips Hospital* (Chike C. Nwoffiah, Mukulla J. Godwin, Florence Stroud, 1999) and *The Color of Medicine: The History of Homer G. Phillips Hospital* (Joyce Fitzpatrick, executive producer of the film, with Becky Robinson and Nikki Woods, 2018).

Throughout this project, a number of archivists have also given me great assistance: Stephen Logsdon, Philip Skroska, and Martha Riley at the Becker Medical Library of Washington University School of Medicine were extraordinarily generous with their time, going to great trouble through months of research to find elusive photos or information; so was the archival staff—particularly its head, Molly Kodner, and longtime archivist Dennis Northcott—at the Missouri History Museum. Lauren Sallwasser, MHS associate archivist for photos and prints, and Jason Stratman were extremely helpful and accommodating. Other archivists I relied on for information included Seth M. Kronemer of the Howard University Law School and Calvin Riley of the George G. Vashon African-American Museum. DeLisa Minor-Harris, Fisk University archivist, went to great lengths to help, making available previously unknown materials from the Julius Rosenwald Archive that illuminated the relationship between Rosenwald and Homer G. Phillips Hospital. Charles Brown and Alyssa Persson of the St. Louis Mercantile Library were also gracious in providing key photos, while Wendy Shook and Amy Frazier of the Middlebury College library and Alison Starkey of the Clifton Park-Halfmoon Public Library clarified endnotes. My great thanks to them all.

Bringing this project to production involved the advice of a friend, Dr. Kenneth Winn, and literary agent Gail Hochman. Thanks so much to them both. I am also grateful to my family, particularly my husband Robert Wiltenburg, who read every chapter, often several times, and who helped prepare the index.

Last but certainly not least, I'd like to express my enormous appreciation to the University of Missouri Press, most of all to

Andrew Davidson, editor in chief, who offered expert advice as well as unwavering support. Other Press staff were of key help, including the terrific associate acquisitions editor Mary Conley, marketing manager Robin Rennison, with her great expertise, and production manager Drew Griffith. I'd also like to thank the wonderful freelance copy editor Bonnie Spinola Perry.

# NOTES

### Introduction

1. Editorial, *Journal of the National Medical Association*, February 1934.

2. Vanessa Northington Gamble, *Making a Place for Ourselves: The Black Hospital Movement, 1920–1945* (New York: Oxford University Press, 1995), 28-193.

3. David McBride, *Integrating the City of Medicine: Blacks in Philadelphia Health Care, 1910–1965* (Philadelphia: Temple University Press, 1989).

4. Priscilla Anne Dowden, "'Over This Point We Are Determined to Fight': African-American Public Education and Health Care in St. Louis, Missouri, 1910–1949" (Ph.D. dissertation, Indiana University, 1997).

5. Frank Richards, "The St. Louis Story: The Training of Black Surgeons in St. Louis, Missouri," in *A Century of Black Surgeons: The USA Experience*, eds. Claude H. Organ Jr., and Margaret M. Kosiba (Norman, OK: Transcript Press, 1987), 197-264.

6. Isabel Wilkerson, *The Warmth of Other Suns: The Epic Story of America's Great Migration* (New York: Random House, 2011), viii, 10.

### Chapter One

1. Official Minutes, United Methodist Church (U.S.) Conference, 1889.

2. Official Minutes, 1889.

3. "For a Noble Cause," *Sedalia Democrat,* May 31, 1893.

4. "College Scandal," *Sedalia Democrat,* April 18, 1895.

5. "Republicans Meet," *Sedalia Democrat,* July 2, 1896.

6. "Too Free with His Opinion," *Ironton County Register*, January 19, 1899.

7. "Law School Graduates," *Evening Star*, Washington, D.C., May 26, 1903.

8. Untitled article, *Sedalia Weekly Conservator*, January 8, 1904.

9. Homer G. Phillips, *Sedalia Weekly Conservator*, January 28, 1907.

10. "Negro Club Incorporated," *Sedalia Democrat*, June 22, 1909.

11. "Plan Court Fight to Prevent Segregation of St. Louis Negroes," *Evansville Press*, March 15, 1916.

12. "The Initiative and Referendum Used in St. Louis to Pass Segregation Laws," *New York Times*, February 29, 1916.

13. "Segregation in St. Louis," *New York Times*, March 1, 1916.

14. "Republicans Fail to Elect Negro Delegate," *St. Louis Argus*, 1916.

15. "Negro Department Store Planned Here," *St. Louis Post-Dispatch*, August 6, 1919.

16. "The *Star's* Handling of the Ellis Murder," *St. Louis Star and Times*, November 12, 1920.

17. "One Negro Fights Site for Hospital Favored by City," *St. Louis Star and Times*, May 24, 1927.

18. *St. Louis Post-Dispatch*, December 6, 1930.

19. Ernest Calloway, untitled article, *St. Louis American*, June 7, 1973.

20. Editorial, *St. Louis Argus*, June 26, 1931.

21. "Throngs Attend Funeral of Slain Negro Attorney," *The St. Louis Star*, June 23, 1931.

22. "Crusader with a Legacy," *St. Louis Globe-Democrat*, February 20, 1979.

23. *Sedalia Democrat*, June 18, 1931.

24. Edward T. Clayton, "The Strange Murder of Homer G. Phillips," *Ebony*, September 1977, 160-64.

## Chapter Two

1. "Negro Nurses in City Hospital," *St. Louis Star and Times*, April 9, 1910.

2. City of St. Louis Health Department, Twenty-Fourth Annual Report of the Health Commissioner, Max C. Starkloff, Commissioner, St. Louis, Missouri, 1901.

3. "Minutes of Meeting of Committee for Social Service Among Colored People," February 7, 1911.

4. "St. Louis Hospital No. 2, What It Means to Us," *St. Louis Argus*, December 23, 1921.

5. "Dr. R.C. Haskell Appointed Supt. Of New Hospital," *St. Louis Argus*, December 13, 1918.

6. H. Phillip Venable, "The History of Homer G. Phillips Hospital," *Journal of the National Medical Association* 53, no.6 (November 1961): 541-55.

7. "St. Louis Hospital No. 2, What It Means to Us," *St. Louis Argus*, December 23, 1921.

8. Frank Richards, "The St. Louis Story: The Training of Black Surgeons in St. Louis, Missouri," in *A Century of Black Surgeons: The USA Experience*, eds. Claude H. Organ Jr. and Margaret M. Kosiba (Norman, OK: Transcript Press, 1987), 197-264.

9. "St. Louis Hospital No. 2, What It Means to Us," *St. Louis Argus*, December 23, 1921.

10. William H. Sinkler, "The History and Development of Homer G. Phillips Hospital," St. Louis, Missouri, 1945.

11. "Colored Nurses Resign Positions at City Hospital," *St. Louis Argus*, May 30, 1919.

12. "445 New Cases Set High Mark for Flu Here," *St. Louis Star and Times*, January 29, 1920.

13. "Jordan Would Abandon City Hospital No. 2," *St. Louis Star and Times*, May 9, 1922.

14. "St. Louis Must Care for its Own," *St. Louis Star and Times*, January 19, 1923.

15. W. Montague Cobb, "Medical Care and the Plight of the Negro," National Association for the Advancement of Colored People, New York, August 1947.

16. Frank Richards, "The St. Louis Story: The Training of Black Surgeons in St. Louis, Missouri," in *A Century of Black Surgeons: The USA Experience*, eds. Claude H. Organ Jr. and Margaret M. Kosiba (Norman, OK: Transcript Press, 1987), 197-264.

17. "Cunliff and Bunn Tell of Needs at Hospitals Here," *St. Louis Star and Times*, January 18, 1923.

18. "The Bond Issue," *St. Louis Argus*, February 2, 1923.

19. George Lipsitz, "Homer G. Phillips Hospital: Promises to Keep," in *The Sidewalks of St. Louis: Places, People, and Politics in an American City* (Columbia, MO: University of Missouri Press, 1991), 53.

20. Vanessa Northington Gamble, *Making a Place for Ourselves: The Black Hospital Movement, 1920–1945* (New York: Oxford University Press, 1995), 28.

21. "Race Medicos Hold 28th Annual Session at St. Louis with Splendid Attendance," *The New Age*, September 15, 1923.

22. "Propose Changing Site of New Hospital," *St. Louis Argus*, May 22, 1925.

23. "Site of New $1,250,000 Colored Hospital Set" and "More Resignations at City Hospital No, 2," *St. Louis Argus*, March 6, 1925.

24. "A Former Mayor of St. Louis Dies," *Chillicothe Constitution-Tribune*, January 6, 1955.

25. "Burns Fiery Cross After Miller Wins," *St. Louis Argus*, April 10, 1925.

26. "City Hospital No. 2," *St. Louis Argus*, November 20, 1925.

27. "Hospital No. 2 Discussed by Mayor Miller," *St. Louis Argus*, December 4, 1925.

28. "Ruling Against New Hospital," *St. Louis Argus*, March 26, 1926.

29. "The Hospital Again," *St. Louis Argus*, January 27, 1928.

30. "$250,000 Savings on Hospital Site," *St. Louis Argus*, February 17, 1928.

31. "Why Hold Up City Hospital No. 2?" *St. Louis Argus*, July 6, 1928.

32. "Judge Fitzsimmons' Hospital Decision," *St. Louis Argus*, February 21, 1930.

33. "Citizens Start Fight for a New Hospital Building," *St. Louis Argus*, September 27, 1929.

34. "Danger Seen in Delay of Selecting Site for New City Hospital No. Two," *St. Louis Argus*, October 4, 1929.

35. "New Hospital's Cornerstone Laid," *St. Louis Argus*, December 15, 1933.

### Chapter Three

1. George Lipsitz, "Homer G. Phillips Hospital: Promises to Keep," in *The Sidewalks of St. Louis: Places, People, and Politics in an American City* (Columbia, MO: University of Missouri Press, 1991), 53-54.

2. "World's Finest Negro Hospital Dedicated," *St. Louis Star-Times*, February 23, 1937.

3. "St. Mary's Infirmary to Reopen as Negro Hospital on Sunday," *St. Louis Globe-Democrat*, March 17, 1933.

4. "Drive for Hospital Bond Issue Planned," *St. Louis Post-Dispatch*, November 1, 1933.

5. "302 Patients Are Moved to New Hospital," *St. Louis Argus*, June 4, 1937.

6. William Sinkler, "The History and Development of Homer G. Phillips Hospital," 1963.

7. "Phillips Hospital Aids with Medical Lecture Events," *St. Louis Argus*, May 27, 1938.

8. "'Blood Bank' Successful at Phillips Hospital Here," *St. Louis Post-Dispatch*, January 11, 1939.

9. Frank Richards, "The St. Louis Story: The Training of Black Surgeons in St. Louis," in *A Century of Black Surgeons: The USA Experience*, eds. Claude H. Organ Jr. and Margaret M. Kosiba (Norman, OK: Transcript Press, 1987), 216.

10. "First Women Interns," *St. Louis Argus*, July 14, 1939.

11. Frank Richards, "The St. Louis Story: The Training of Black Surgeons in St. Louis," in *A Century of Black Surgeons: The USA Experience*, eds. Claude H. Organ Jr. and Margaret M. Kosiba (Norman, OK: Transcript Press, 1987), 218.

12. Mabel C. Northcross, "Our Staff Program," *The American Journal of Nursing* 39, no. 7 (July 1939): 738.

13. "Hospital Attachés Complain," *St. Louis Argus*, April 15, 1938.

14. "Nurses Changing at Phillips Hospital," *St. Louis Argus*, June 3, 1938.

15. "Adds to Teaching Staff at Homer Phillips," *Pittsburgh Courier*, August 24, 1940.

16. "Attorneys Given Data by Doctors at Negro Hospital," *St. Louis Star and Times*, June 2, 1939.

17. "Grand Jurors Score Viaduct Auto Hazard," *St. Louis Star and Times*, February 2, 1940.

## Chapter Four

1. Isabel Wilkerson, *The Warmth of Other Suns: The Epic Story of America's Great Migration* (New York: Random House, 2010),10.

2. Wilkerson, *Warmth of Other Suns*, vii.

## Chapter Five

1. Donald H. Ewalt Jr. and Gary R. Kremer, "The Historian as Preservationist: A Missouri Case Study," *The Public Historian* 3, no. 4 (Autumn 1981): 11.

2. Walter Johnson, *The Broken Heart of America: St. Louis and the Violent History of the United States* (New York: Basic Books, 2020), 254.

3. Johnson, *The Broken Heart of America*, 255.

4. Johnson, *The Broken Heart of America*, 255.

5. Colin Gordon, *Mapping Decline: St. Louis and the Fate of the American City* (Philadelphia: University of Pennsylvania Press, 2008), 4.

6. Gordon, *Mapping Decline*, 1.

7. "Restrictive Covenants are Dead," *St. Louis Argus*, St. Louis, Missouri, May 7, 1948.

8. Gordon, quoting a *St. Louis Star-Times* article, October 2, 1948.

## Chapter Six

1. "Negro Physician from Central Africa," *St. Louis Post-Dispatch*, August 17, 1940.

2. Daniel R. Berg, "A History of Health Care for the Indigent in St. Louis: 1904–2001," *Saint Louis University Law Journal* 48, no. 1 (2003): 191.

3. "Award Against City Upheld," *St. Louis Post-Dispatch*, April 8, 1943.

4. *St. Louis Argus*, 1954.

5. "The Homer G. Phillips Hospital to be Base Hospital in Defense Plans," *St. Louis Argus*, January 30, 1942.

6. L.S. Dean to Philip Shaffer, 1938, Becker Medical Archives, Washington University School of Medicine.

7. Letter to the Editor, *St. Louis Star-Times*, December 17, 1948.

8. "Report Suggests . . .," *St. Louis Post-Dispatch*, March 6, 1941.

9. Malcolm MacEachern to Dr. Frank Bradley, October 26, 1942, Becker Medical Archives, Washington University School of Medicine.

10. Frank O. Richards, "The St. Louis Story: The Training of Black Surgeons in St. Louis, Missouri," in *A Century of Black Surgeons: The USA Experience*, eds. Claude H. Organ Jr. and Margaret M. Kosiba (Norman, OK: Transcript Press, 1987), 218.

11. Richards, "The St. Louis Story," 218.

12. Dr. M.O. Bousfield to Mrs. Marion Blossom, December 26, 1939, Becker Medical Archives, Washington University School of Medicine.

13. Riddle and Bousfield letter exchange, 1940-42, Fisk University Archives.

14. "Nurses Win Their Fight," *St. Louis Argus*, September 4, 1942.

15. "High Tuberculosis Rates Here Cited," *St. Louis Post-Dispatch*, May 10, 1948.

16. Minutes, meeting of March 14, 1946, Becker Medical Archives.

17. W. Montague Cobb, *Medical Care and the Plight of the Negro* (New York, NY: Published by the National Association for the Advancement of Colored People, 1948).

18. Henry Pringle and Katharine Pringle, "The Color Line in Medicine," published by the Committee of 100, New York, NY, 1948.

19. Pringle and Pringle, "The Color Line in Medicine."

## Chapter Seven

1. Zenobia Thompson, interviewed in *A Jewel in History: The Story of the Homer G. Phillips Hospital for Colored*, directed by Chike C. Nwoffiah, Mukulla J. Godwin, and Florence Stroud (San Francisco, CA: Homer G. Phillips Project, 1999).

2. Nwoffiah et al., *A Jewel in History*.

3. Chart of "Total Operative Procedures Performed, 1938–1958," from Frank O. Richards, "The St. Louis Story: The Training of Black Surgeons in St. Louis, Missouri," in *A Century of Black Surgeons: The USA Experience*, eds. Claude H. Organ Jr. and Margaret M. Kosiba (Norman, OK: Transcript Press, 1987), 222.

4. T.K. Brown, "A History of Homer G. Phillips Hospital," *Medical Alumni Quarterly* 3, no. 3 (1940): 134-38.

5. Richards, "The St. Louis Story," 255.

6. Richards, "The St. Louis Story," 255.

7. William H. Sinkler, "The History and Development of Homer G. Phillips Hospital," St. Louis, Missouri, 1945.

8. Gloria Ross, "Pioneering Surgeon Passes," *St. Louis American*, Feb. 27–Mar. 5, 2014.

9. Ross, "Pioneering Surgeon Passes."

## Chapter Eight

1. William Sinkler and Sadye Coleman, "The History and Development of Homer G. Phillips Hospital," 1945, 36.

## Chapter Nine

1. *St. Louis American*, April 17, 1952.

2. *St. Louis American*, December 21, 1950.

3. Frank Richards, "The St. Louis Story: The Training of Black Surgeons in St. Louis, Missouri," in *A Century of Black Surgeons: The USA Experience*,

eds. Claude H. Organ Jr. and Margaret M. Kosiba (Norman, OK: Transcript Press, 1987), 263.

4. *St. Louis Post-Dispatch*, January 30, 1957.

5. Dr. Robert Elman to Dr. Charles O. Warren, The Commonwealth Fund, February 11, 1952, Becker Medical Library Archives.

6. H. Phillip Venable, "History of Homer G. Phillips Hospital," *Journal of the National Medical Association* (November 1961): 550.

7. Interview, Washington University School of Medicine, October 20, 2014.

8. *St. Louis American*, February 19, 1953.

9. *St. Louis American*, April 20, 1950.

10. *St. Louis American*, January 12, 1950.

11. *St. Louis Post-Dispatch*, April 4, 1952.

12. *St. Louis Globe-Democrat*, April 5, 1952.

13. *St. Louis Globe Democrat*, March 15, 1954.

14. *St. Louis Globe-Democrat*, September 8, 1954.

15. *St. Louis Post-Dispatch*, November 8, 1955.

16. *St. Louis American*, July 23, 1959.

17. Joseph Heathcott and Maire Agnes Murphy, "Corridors of Flight, Zones of Renewal," *Journal of Urban History* 31, no. 2 (January 2005): 155.

18. Heathcott and Murphy, "Corridors of Flight," 163.

19. Leo Bohannon, "Population Mobility: Its Effect on Agency Program," presented at an Urban League luncheon, April 26, 1957.

20. *St. Louis Post-Dispatch*, October 27, 1955.

21. *St. Louis Globe-Democrat*, October 19, 1956.

22. "Tax Increase," *St. Louis Post-Dispatch*, April 11, 1958.

### Chapter Eleven

1. "Aldermen Seek Explanation on Mental Care," *St. Louis Post-Dispatch*, January 31, 1957.

### Chapter Twelve

1. St. Louis Public Radio/NPR broadcast, interview with Dr. Whittico, November 9, 2009.

2. Vanessa Gamble, *Making a Place for Ourselves: The Black Hospital Movement (1920–1945)* (New York, NY: Oxford University Press, 1995), 193.

3. "St. Louis Opens 'War' on Negro Mortality Rates," *The Springfield News-Leader*, Springfield, Missouri, May 7, 1965, courtesy AP.

4. Dr. Seymour Monat to Dr. James Meade, September 21, 1960.

5. *St. Louis American*, May 4, 1961.

6. *St. Louis American*, April 19, 1962.

7. "Plan to Strengthen Homer Phillips Hospital Announced by Tucker," *St. Louis Post-Dispatch*, November 15, 1964.

8. *St. Louis American*, April 14, 1966.

9. "Nursing School," Letter to the Editor, *St. Louis Post-Dispatch*, June 24, 1975.

10. Dr. Park J. White, *Annual Report of the Department of Pediatrics, Homer G. Phillips Hospital, 1959.*

11. Daniel R. Berg, M.D., "A History of Health Care for the Indigent in St. Louis: 1904–2001," *Saint Louis University Law Journal* 48 (2003): 200.

12. Berg, "A History of Health Care," 200.

13. "City to Seek Bigger Phillips Obstetrics Unit," *St. Louis Post-Dispatch*, February 16, 1967.

14. *St. Louis American*, January 19, 1967.

15. H. Phillip Venable, M.S., and Julian C. Mosley, M.D., "The Black Physician in St. Louis," Part III, Sesquicentennial Series, *Metro Medicine*, May 1986.

16. *St. Louis American*, November 19, 1970.

17. *St. Louis Post-Dispatch*, November 18, 1973.

18. *St. Louis American*, October 5, 1972.

19. *St. Louis American*, June 3, 1976.

20. *St. Louis American*, April 21, 1977.

21. *St. Louis Post-Dispatch*, February 8, 1979.

22. *St. Louis Post-Dispatch*, August 5, 1979.

## Chapter Thirteen

1. "Policemen Shield Phillips Transfer," *St. Louis Post-Dispatch*, August 17, 1979.

2. "Two Leaders Arrested in Protest at Phillips," *St. Louis Post-Dispatch*, August 16, 1979.

3. Interview with Ella Brown, Washington University, July 27, 1990.

4. Chike C. Nwoffiah, Mukulla J. Godwin, and Florence Stroud, *A Jewel in History: The Story of Homer G. Phillips Hospital for Colored, St. Louis, Missouri*, film, 1999.

5. Letters to Mayor Conway, 1979, from his collection.

6. "Ready to Walk Off Job, Some City Doctors Say," *St. Louis Post-Dispatch*, April 3, 1980.

7. "Whatever His Party, Mayor Will Be Young," *St. Louis Post-Dispatch*, April 5, 1981.

# BIBLIOGRAPHY

IN WRITING THIS book, I relied on many sources, though two were most important. For background, I read hundreds of articles about Homer G. Phillips Hospital from the newspapers and journals listed below. For the personal side of the story, I was heavily dependent on the interviews I did with the hospital's former nurses, doctors, and other staff members, as well as people from the community.

Other resources—in the collections of various libraries, particularly the archives of the Becker Medical Library at the Washington University School of Medicine, the Missouri Historical Society Library and Research Center, Fisk University, and the Mercantile Library—were also important.

## Newspapers and Journals

*Evening Star*, Washington, D.C.
*Iron County Register*
*Journal of the American Medical Association*
*New York Times*
*St. Louis American*
*St. Louis Argus*
*St. Louis Globe-Democrat*
*St. Louis Post-Dispatch*
*The St. Louis Star and Times*
*Sedalia Democrat*
*The Sedalia Weekly Bazoo*
*Sedalia Weekly Conservator*

## Articles and Dissertations

Adams, Numa P.G. "An Interpretation of the Significance of the Homer G. Phillips Hospital." *Journal of the National Medical Association* 26, no. 1 (Feb. 1934): 13–17.

Bailey, Charles. "The Ville: A Study of a Symbolic Community in St. Louis." PhD diss., Washington University in St. Louis, 1978.

Berg, Daniel R., M.D. "A History of Health Care for the Indigent in St. Louis: 1904–2001." *Saint Louis University Law Journal* 48 (2003).

Brown, T.K. "A History of Homer G. Phillips Hospital." *Medical Alumni Quarterly* 3, no. 3 (April 1940): 134–38.

Buck, Debra L. "The Closing of Homer G. Phillips Hospital." M.A. thesis. Claremont Graduate School, 1984.

City of St. Louis Health Department. Twenty-Fourth Annual Report of the Health Commissioner. Max C. Starkloff, Commissioner, St. Louis, Missouri, 1901. Accessible at: https://www.google.com/books/edition/Annual_Report_of_the_Health_Commissioner/HeNIRzZ4XiEC?hl=en&gbpv=1&dq=St.%20Louis%20Health%20Department.%20Twenty-Fourth%20Annual%20Report%20of%20the%20Health%20Commissioner&pg=PA142&printsec=frontcover&bsq=St.%20Louis%20Health%20Department.%20Twenty-Fourth%20Annual%20Report%20of%20the%20Health%20Commissioner.

Clayton, Edward T. "The Strange Murder of Homer G. Phillips." *Ebony Magazine*. September 1977, 160–64.

Cobb, W. Montague. "Medical Care and the Plight of the Negro." National Association for the Advancement of Colored People, New York, August 1947.

Cornely, Paul B., M.D. "Negro Students in Medical Schools in the U.S., 1955–56." *Journal of the National Medical Association* 48, no. 4 (July 1956): 264–66.

"The Cost of Segregation in Lives." *The Southern Patriot*. New Orleans, Louisiana, March 1958.

Department of Health & Hospitals, City of St. Louis, newsletters. Missouri History Museum, St. Louis.

Dowden-White, Priscilla A. "'Over This Point We Are Determined to Fight': African-American Public Education and Health Care in St. Louis, Missouri, 1910–1949." PhD diss., Indiana University, 1997.

Elman, Robert, M.D. "News from the Medical School." Washington University School of Medicine, remarks made on August 11, 1954, annual convention of the National Medical Association. Missouri History Museum, St. Louis.

Ewalt, Donald H., Jr., and Gary R. Kremer. "The Historian as Preservationist: A Missouri Case Study." *The Public Historian* 3, no. 4 (Autumn 1981): 4–22.

Harris, William Jefferson. "The New Deal in Black St. Louis, 1932–1940." PhD diss., Saint Louis University, 1974.

Heathcott, Joseph, and Máire Agnes Murphy. "Corridors of Flight, Zones of Renewal: Industry, Planning, and Policy in the Making of Metropolitan St. Louis, 1940–1980." *Journal of Urban History* 31, no. 2 (January 2005): 151–89.

Homer G. Phillips Hospital *Bulletins*, beginning in 1954. Missouri History Museum, St. Louis.

Homer G. Phillips School of Nursing, Class of 1966, Fiftieth Anniversary, June 2016. Resolution No. 53, by St. Louis Board of Aldermen. Homer G. Phillips Nursing Alumni Association, Inc.

Homer G. Phillips Hospital brochures for patients and prospective patients, 1950s onward. Missouri History Museum, St. Louis.

Ihrig, B.B. "The History of Smithton," undated, privately printed booklet. Courtesy of the Pettis County Historical Society.

Kirouac-Fram, Jaclyn. "'To Serve the Community Best': Reconsidering Black Politics in the Struggle to Save Homer G. Phillips Hospital in St. Louis, 1976–1984." *Journal of Urban History* 36, no. 5 (Sept. 2010): 594–616.

Kolnick, Dean Lee. "Pride and Promise(s): The Closure of The Homer G. Phillips Hospital." B.A. thesis, Washington University in St. Louis, 2003.

Lawrence, Montague, M.D., Dorothy Stauffer, M.S.W., and William H. Sinkler, M.D. "An Experiment in Rehabilitation at the Homer G. Phillips Hospital." *Journal of the National Medical Association* 47, no. 5 (Sept. 1955): 325–26.

Medical Examiner's Report, "Death of Homer G. Phillips." Office of the Medical Examiner, City of St. Louis, Missouri.

National Register of Historic Places, National Park Service, Registration Form for Homer G. Phillips Hospital, September 23, 1982. Accessible at: https://mostateparks.com/sites/mostateparks/files/Phillips%2C%20Homer%20G.%2C%20Hospital.pdf.

Patient Care Committee newsletters, Homer G. Phillips Hospital, various years. Missouri History Museum, St. Louis.

Police Report, Death of Homer G. Phillips. St. Louis Police Department, City of St. Louis, Missouri.

Pringle, Henry, and Katharine Pringle. "The Color Line in Medicine." New York, NY: The Committee of 100, 1948.

Report of Health Service System Task Force to Mayor James F. Conway, December 16, 1977. Missouri History Museum, St. Louis.

Report on the Study on Hospital Needs Under the Jurisdiction of the City of Saint Louis, Missouri, for the Board of Estimate and Apportionment, September 28, 1976. Missouri History Museum, St. Louis.

Riddle, Estelle, and Josephine Nelson. "The Negro Nurse Looks Toward Tomorrow." *The American Journal of Nursing* 45, no. 8 (August 1945): 627–30.

Sinkler, William H., M.D. "The Challenge of Medicine in the Future." *Journal of the National Medical Association* 37, no. 6 (Nov. 1945): 198–200.

———. "The History and Development of Homer G. Phillips Hospital." January 1, 1945. Bernard Becker Medical Library, Washington University School of Medicine, St. Louis.

Toft, Carolyn Hewes, ed. "The Ville: The Ethnic Heritage of an Urban Neighborhood." Booklet. Distributed by ERIC Clearinghouse, 1975.

Venable, H. Phillip. "The History of the Homer G. Phillips Hospital." *Journal of the National Medical Association* 53, no. 6 (Nov. 1961): 541–55.

Venable, H. Phillip, and Julian C. Mosley. "The Black Physician in St. Louis." Part III, Sesquicentennial Series, *Metro Medicine*, May 1986.

Wesley, Doris. Oral History Interview with Dr. James M. Whittico Jr. March 13, 1997. Western Historical Manuscript Collection, University of Missouri–St. Louis.

————. Oral History Interview with Dr. John Wright, March 13, 1997. University of Missouri–St. Louis.

White, Park, M.D. "Annual Report on the Activities of the Division of Pediatrics." Homer G. Phillips Hospital, St. Louis, Missouri, 1958. State Historical Society of Missouri, St. Louis Research Center, University of Missouri–St. Louis.

### Collections

Conway, James F. Mayor Conway's letters from his personal files.

Conway, James F. Papers. Western Historical Manuscript Collection, St. Louis.

Homer G. Phillips collections (particularly the Dr. Park W. White Papers, the Department of Surgery files, and oral histories of such faculty as Dr. Helen E. Nash). Bernard Becker Medical Library, Archives and Rare Books Division. Washington University School of Medicine in St. Louis.

Julius Rosenwald Fund Archives (uncatalogued files, particularly in relation to Homer G. Phillips Hospital). Franklin Library Special Collections and Archives, Fisk University.

*St. Louis American* and *St. Louis Argus* (microfilm files) and numerous other files. Missouri Historical Society Library and Research Center, St. Louis.

Saint Louis Research Center, The State Historical Society of Missouri, Thomas Jefferson Library, University of Missouri–St. Louis.

Schoemehl, Vincent. Papers. Western Historical Manuscript Collection, St. Louis.

### Films

Fitzpatrick, Joyce Marie, and Brian Shackelford. *The Color of Medicine: The Story of Homer G. Phillips Hospital.* Los Angeles, CA: FlatCat Productions and Tunnel Vizion Films, Inc., 2018.

Nwoffiah, Chike C., Mukulla J. Godwin, and Florence Stroud. *A Jewel in History: The Story of Homer G. Phillips Hospital for Colored, St. Louis, Missouri.* San Francisco, CA: Homer G. Phillips Project, 1999.

### Books

Buckner, John D. *Negroes: Their Gift to St. Louis.* St. Louis: Employee's Loan Company, 1964.

Conner, Douglas. *A Black Physician's Story: Bringing Hope in Mississippi.* With John Marszalek. Jackson, MS: University Press of Mississippi, 1985.

Crighton, John C. *The History of Health Services in Missouri.* Omaha, NE: Barnhart Press, 1993.

Dowling, Harry F. *City Hospitals: The Undercare of the Underprivileged.* Cambridge, MA: Harvard University Press, 1982.

Early, Gerald, ed. *"Ain't But a Place": An Anthology of African American Writings about St. Louis.* St. Louis, MO: Missouri Historical Society Press, 1998.

Epps, Charles H., Jr., Davis G. Johnson, and Audrey L. Vaughan. *African-American Medical Pioneers.* Rockville, MD: Betz Pub. Co., 1994.

Gamble, Vanessa Northington. *The Black Community Hospital: Contemporary Dilemmas in Historical Perspective.* New York, NY: Garland Publishing, 1989.

————. *Making a Place for Ourselves: The Black Hospital Movement, 1920–1945.* New York, NY: Oxford University Press, 1995.

Gordon, Colin. *Mapping Decline: St. Louis and the Fate of the American City.* Philadelphia, PA: University of Pennsylvania Press, 2008.

Greene, Lorenzo J., Gary R. Kremer, and Antonio F. Holland. *Missouri's Black Heritage.* Columbia, MO: University of Missouri Press, 1993.

*The Guardian.* Homer G. Phillips Nursing School yearbooks, various years.

Johnson, Walter. *The Broken Heart of America: St. Louis and the Violent History of the United States.* New York, NY: Basic Books, 2020.

Lipsitz, George. *The Sidewalks of St. Louis: Places, People, and Politics in an American City.* Columbia, MO: University of Missouri Press, 1991.

McBride, David. *Integrating the City of Medicine: Blacks in Philadelphia Health Care, 1910–1965.* Philadelphia, PA: Temple University Press, 1989.

Morais, Herbert M. *The History of the Negro in Medicine.* New York, NY: Publishers Company, 1968.

Morris, Ann, ed. *Lift Every Voice and Sing: St. Louis African-Americans in the Twentieth Century.* Columbia, MO: University of Missouri Press, 1999.

O'Neal, Lawrence, M.D. *Vignettes of St. Louis Medicine.* North Charleston, SC: BookSurge Publishing, 2005.

Reed, Wornie L. *Health and Medical Care of African-Americans.* Westport, CT: Praeger, 1993.

Rice, Mitchell F., and Woodrow Jones Jr. *Health of Black Americans from Post-Reconstruction to Integration, 1871–1960.* Westport, CT: Greenwood Press, 1990.

————. *Public Policy and the Black Hospital: From Slavery to Segregation to Integration.* Westport, CT: Greenwood Press, 1994.

Richards, Frank O. "The St. Louis Story: The Training of Black Surgeons in St. Louis, Missouri." In *A Century of Black Surgeons: The U.S.A.*

*Experience*, Vol. 1, edited by Claude H. Organ Jr. and Margaret M. Kosiba, 197–264. Norman, OK: Transcript Press, 1987.

Rosenberg, Charles E. *Care of Strangers: The Rise of America's Hospital System*. New York, NY: Basic Books, 1987.

Smith, JoAnn Adams. *Selected Neighbors and Neighborhoods of North St. Louis and Selected Related Events*. St. Louis, MO: Friends of Vaughn Cultural Center, 1988.

Stevens, Rosemary. *In Sickness and in Wealth: American Hospitals in the Twentieth Century*. Baltimore, MD: Johns Hopkins University Press, 1989.

Wesley, Nathaniel Jr. *Black Hospitals in America: History, Contributions, and Demise*. Tallahassee, FL: NRW Associates Publications, 2010.

Wilkerson, Isabel. *The Warmth of Other Suns: The Epic Story of America's Great Migration*. New York, NY: Random House, 2011.

# INDEX

Page numbers in *italics* indicate illustrations